AF705331

WESTERN WATER RESOURCES

WESTERN WATER RESOURCES:
Coming Problems and the Policy Alternatives

A Symposium Sponsored by the Federal Reserve Bank of Kansas City
September 27–28, 1979

Routledge
Taylor & Francis Group
NEW YORK AND LONDON

First published 1990 by Westview Press, Inc.

Published 2021 by Routledge
605 Third Avenue, New York, NY 10017
2 Park Square, Milton Park, Abingdon, Oxon OX14 4RN

Routledge is an imprint of the Taylor & Francis Group, an informa business

Copyright © 1990 by Taylor & Francis

All rights reserved. No part of this book may be reprinted or reproduced or utilised in any form or by any electronic, mechanical, or other means, now known or hereafter invented, including photocopying and recording, or in any information storage or retrieval system, without permission in writing from the publishers.

Notice:
Product or corporate names may be trademarks or registered trademarks, and are used only for identification and explanation without intent to infringe.

Library of Congress Cataloging in Publication Data
Main entry under title:
Western water resources.
Papers, compiled by Marvin Duncan, from a symposium held in Denver, Colo., Sept. 27-28, 1979.
1. Water resources development—The West—Congresses. 2. Water—Law and legislation—The West—Congresses. 3. Water-supply—The West—Congresses. I. Duncan, Marvin R. II. Federal Reserve Bank of Kansas City.
TC423.6.W47 333.91'00978 80-14142

ISBN 13: 978-0-3672-1351-0 (hbk)
ISBN 13: 978-0-3672-1632-0 (pbk)

Contents

Foreword

Water, which for centuries has been regarded as a virtually limitless resource, has recently come to be seen as a vital commodity in increasingly short supply.

The western United States, with its uncertain sources of supply and its rapidly increasing industrial, personal, and agricultural water demands, is currently facing many of the problems of water supply and allocation that eventually will confront the nation.

The Federal Reserve Bank of Kansas City hosted a symposium entitled "Western Water Resources: Coming Problems and the Policy Alternatives" on September 27 and 28, 1979, in Denver, Colorado. I hope that the following proceedings of that symposium will provide an opportunity for those with an interest in water issues to learn more about the future of this critically important natural resource.

These proceedings were compiled by Marvin Duncan, assistant vice president and economist with the Federal Reserve Bank of Kansas City. Assistance was provided by Ann Laing and Kerry Webb, research associates with the bank.

Roger Guffey
President
Federal Reserve Bank of Kansas City

The Contributors

Charles W. Howe, presently a professor of economics at the University of Colorado, has extensive water resource experience. He has served as director of the Water Resources Program at Resources for the Future, Inc. and has been editor of *Water Resources Research,* a research journal of the American Geophysical Union. He has also served in water consulting roles to the United Nations Development Programme, the World Health Organization, OECD, and the governments of Ghana, Kenya, Botswana, and Mexico. Dr. Howe has written numerous articles on water resource development as well as four books on the subject.

Respected both nationally and internationally for his work with water and land development, **John F. Timmons** is one of the leading natural resources economists in the country. He is presently a Curtiss Distinguished Professor of Agriculture at Iowa State University and is a Fellow in the American Agricultural Economics Association. He has served in advisory and consulting positions for numerous organizations including USDA-AID, The World Food Institute at Iowa State University, and the National Committee on Land and Water Use of the National Academy of Science. Dr. Timmons has also been vice president of the American Agricultural Economics Association and has directed extensive graduate research on water development programs since 1947.

Theodore M. Schad is the deputy executive director of the Commission on Natural Resources for the National Research

Council. Since graduating with a civil engineering degree from The Johns Hopkins University, he has spent over thirty years with various federal agencies examining and directing numerous water resource development projects. He has worked with the Army Corps of Engineers, the Bureau of Reclamation, the Bureau of the Budget, and the Congressional Research Service. He has also served as staff director of the U.S. Senate Select Committee on National Water Resources and as executive director of the National Water Commission. Schad is a Fellow in the American Society of Civil Engineers and has authored numerous official federal agency reports and papers in professional journals on water resources research, development, and policy.

Since 1977, **Leo M. Eisel** has been the director of the U.S. Water Resources Council in Washington, D.C. As head of the council (consisting of the secretaries of the departments of Agriculture, Defense, Commerce, Energy, Interior, Transportation, and Housing and Urban Development), it is Eisel's job to insure that the federal water programs respond to the nation's water resources problems and needs. Eisel has also been director of the Illinois Environmental Protection Agency, a research associate with the Harvard University Development Advisory Service, and has worked on water resource problems in Pakistan, Denmark, and Brazil.

George E. Radosevich specializes in the economic and legal aspects of water resource development. A member of the American Bar Association's Committee on Environmental Quality and Committee on Water Resources, as well as the Colorado and Wyoming bar associations, Mr. Radosevich is a partner in a Denver law firm and an associate professor of water law and economics at Colorado State University. He is nationally and internationally known for his expertise in natural resource use and water law.

Frank J. Trelease is currently professor of law at the McGeorge School of Law at the University of the Pacific. He is also dean emeritus of the College of Law at the University of Wyoming, having been associated with the university since 1942. Mr. Trelease is the author of numerous articles and editor of three casebooks on water and natural resources law. He has been a consultant on the reform and revision of water laws to several states, countries and international organizations, including the United Nations. Professor Trelease has also advised the Missouri Basin Survey Commission, the Public Land Law Review Commission, the National Water Commission, and the National Commission on Water Quality.

Daniel W. Bromley is a professor in the Department of Agricultural Economics and director of the Center for Resource Policy Studies and Programs at the University of Wisconsin–Madison. He has done extensive consulting work with numerous federal and state agencies including the U.S. Water Resources Council, the National Commission on Water Quality, and the Texas Water Development Board. He has also worked with the Agency for International Development on natural resource and water development problems in several Caribbean countries. Dr. Bromley has authored two books and numerous articles on public decision-making in natural resources and is editor of the journal *Land Economics.*

Speakers

As president-designate for Resources for the Future, Inc., **Emery N. Castle** directs the leading natural resources research organization in the country. Dr. Castle is a Fellow in the American Academy of Arts and Sciences and the American Agricultural Economics Association. Associated with Oregon State University for most of his professional career, he served as professor and head of the Department of Agricultural Economics and dean of the Graduate School. Dr. Castle's work with the economic consequences of natural resource policies is well known and is published in many professional journals.

Kenneth E. Boulding is among the most respected and eminent economists in the nation. Presently a Distinguished Professor of Economics at the University of Colorado, Professor Boulding has served on the faculty of several major universities. He has been a visiting professor to ten universities worldwide and is a Fellow in the American Academy of Arts and Sciences and the American Philosophical Society. Professor Boulding is the 1979 president of the American Association for the Advancement of Science and has been president of the American Economics Association. He has authored over thirty books, hundreds of articles, and holds honorary degrees from twenty-eight colleges and universities.

Discussants

Harvey O. Banks is internationally recognized for his work in planning and management of water resources. He is president of the Water Resources Division of Camp Dresser and McKee, Inc., Environmental Engineers, Planners, and Scientists. He also serves as the project director for the Six-State High Plains–Ogallala Aquifer Area Study under contract with the U.S. Economic Development Administration. The California Department of Water Resources was organized under his direction, becoming one of the major multidisciplinary water agencies in the world. Banks is active in the American Society of Civil Engineers, the National Academy of Engineering, and is a Fellow in the American Consulting Engineers Council. He has advised numerous state and national governments as well as authoring several technical papers on water resource development.

Richard A. Simms is the General Counsel to the New Mexico State Engineer and Interstate Stream Commission. Since entering the legal profession, Mr. Simms has been in the forefront of litigation over the nature and extent of federal and Indian reserved water right claims. He was responsible for the U.S. Supreme Court's 1978 decision in *United States* v. *New Mexico,* which clarified and further defined the legal basis of Indian water rights.

A citizen of Canada, **Keith A. Henry** is president of CBA Engineering, Ltd. Mr. Henry directs extensive water resource development studies in various parts of the world. From 1972 to 1978, he served as the Canadian Commissioner of the International Joint Commission and worked with the appraisal and evaluation of land and water use programs as they had international implications for the United States and Canada. Henry is a member of the International Water Resource Association, a registered professional engineer in British Columbia, Alberta, Ontario, and Oregon, and a Fellow of the American Society of Civil Engineers.

B. Delworth Gardner is widely known for his work in water resource development. Dr. Gardner has been on the faculties of Colorado State, Brigham Young, and Utah State universities as well as serving as a visiting scholar at Resources for the Future, Inc. He has been a consultant for several foreign governments including Bolivia, Iran, India, and Ecuador. Presently Gardner is a professor of agricultural economics at the University of California–Davis and the director of the Giannini Foundation at the University of California–Berkeley.

A. Allan Schmid is a professor of agricultural economics and resource development at Michigan State University. He has also worked as a visiting scholar at Resources for the Future, Inc., and as a budget analyst for the U.S. Corps of Engineers. He is the author of various studies on the political economy of water resources including *Impact of Alternative Federal Decision-Making Structures for Water Resource Development* prepared for the National Water Commission.

As director of planning and development for the Texas Department of Water Resources, **Herbert W. Grubb** has in-depth experience in water resource development. Dr. Grubb directs the water use analyses and projections for the major water-using activities in Texas. His responsibilities also include the evaluation of alternative policies and programs—viewed from environmental, economic, and engineering standpoints—for developing water supplies to meet future needs throughout Texas.

As an author of many excellent articles on water development issues, **Maurice M. Kelso** is widely regarded for his expertise in water resource management. Kelso is a professor emeritus at the University of Arizona and has had extensive experience working with state and federal agencies as well as teaching at several major universities. Dr. Kelso has been president of the Western Farm Economic Association and is a Fellow in the American Agricultural Economics Association.

Allen V. Kneese is presently professor of economics at the University of New Mexico and a Senior Fellow at Resources for the Future, Inc. He has been associated with these two institutions over many years. Dr. Kneese is a prolific author on issues related to natural resources and the environment having authored or coauthored numerous books and articles in scientific journals. He is coauthor of *Environmental Improvement Through Economic Incentives,* published in 1978.

1

KEYNOTE ADDRESS
Western Water Resources: The Coming Problem and Policy Alternatives

Emery N. Castle

There is considerable nostalgia associated with keynoting this conference. It was just a quarter century ago that I was a member of the research department of the Federal Reserve Bank of Kansas City. Further, I was reared in Kansas and much of my professional work has been done in the West. No doubt Allen Kneese, also from Resources for the Future and who is on this morning's program, shares many of my emotions. Allen also once was employed by the research department of the Federal Reserve Bank of Kansas City but, I hasten to add, less than a quarter of a century ago. I am told that some of his writings on water and benefit-cost analysis, done while he was at the Bank, are still in print and are still being used. Thus, this is something of a homecoming for both of us.

But if homecomings are sentimental and heartwarming, they also can have their uncomfortable dimensions. And I have had some uncomfortable hours preparing these remarks. Your program is well planned to provide coverage of the major dimensions of water problems in the West, and it was difficult to imagine what I might say that would not be developed in greater depth by one or more of the other speakers. The problem was made even more formidable when I considered those who will follow me on the program. Much of what I know about economics and water has been taught to me by people such as Kenneth Boulding, Maurice Kelso, Frank Trelease, Del Gardner, Allen Kneese, and Charles Howe. One might think that I could take some comfort in the fact that one of my former students, Dan Bromley, is giving a major paper. After all, a common impression is that former graduate students are disciples who spend their professional lives extending the teachings and extolling the wisdom of their major professors. While I do not wish to comment about the students of others, I must say it probably would be more hazardous for me to try to build a framework for my former students than for those from whom I have learned so much.

It is not difficult to document the many existing and emerging water problems in the West. People in this region are acutely aware of declining ground water levels, which have triggered major adjustments by individual water users as well as by communities. There is widespread knowledge that the energy resources of the region require substantial water if they are to be developed. And, as water usage becomes more intensive as well as extensive, the characteristics of water have been changed and quality problems are commonplace. These conditions and others are so familiar to this audience that it is unnecessary for me to convince you they are real.

Nor do I believe you will disagree when I say that we are having real difficulty in addressing these problems. The historic western response to solving water problems has been to develop more water. Basically, this means putting to human use more of the water provided by nature and involves building more dams, drilling more wells, and importing water from other areas. But the best sites have been developed, the water near the surface has been pumped, and nearby water-surplus areas already have been tapped. Even though water is becoming more valuable, the cost of water development has increased significantly even as federal investment in it has declined. In addition, we have become aware that water development often has significant effects on the environment that need to be considered before such development is undertaken.

One might expect that our capacity to direct water to its best use would improve as water becomes more valuable and as water development declines. While there is a difference of opinion among informed people, probably few would say that our legal and administrative institutions are ideal for dealing with the water problems before us. Most of these institutions came into existence when people wished to use cheap and abundant water to develop an area. It was the function of one set of institutions to permit water to be developed, and it was the purpose of another set of institutions to keep the rights to water straight—to provide security in regard to the water that was developed. The re-allocation of water was not a major problem when water institutions came into existence, and perhaps it is not surprising that considerable variation now exists among the western states in the way this problem is addressed.

As water becomes more valuable in an economic sense, one would also expect the efficiency with which it is used to improve accordingly. Certainly this has been occurring in some instances. In the Ogallala aquifer region, for example, both an increase in the cost of energy and a greater lift have occurred with water pumped, and farmers have responded accordingly. But the increased economic value of water generally has not been reflected in user cost throughout the West, the amount of water required to provide a unit of goods, services, and satisfactions has changed but little, and the real value of water typically has not been reflected in individual decision making.

Thus, an outline of our existing and emerging water problem is easy to draw. Our economy is expanding and the need for water also is growing, probably not proportionately, but at least absolutely. Our capacity to respond to these new challenges seems to be less than we would like. Those who arranged this program recognized these conditions and obviously intended that in this conference we would attempt to identify ways of dealing with these difficulties. They have specifically requested that I give attention to efficiency and equity conflicts.

On the one hand, we know there are opportunities to make better use of water—it would be possible to produce just as much in many cases with less water, and it appears there are opportunities to shift water to higher-valued uses—but on the other hand, these adjustments often are not made. The conclusion usually is reached that equity and efficiency considerations are in conflict and are at the seat of the difficulty.

Economic efficiency is a reasonably well-understood concept. It has been defined rigorously by economists and we know a good bit about its measurement. But it is far more difficult to treat equity in a comparable fashion because there are some philosophic contradictions that arise when we begin to use the term. For example, few believe it is "equitable" to ignore the needs of those who are unable to contribute to the creation of goods and services that all find useful. Yet short of complete dependence, there is tremendous individual variation in ability to produce. Is everyone who is capable of some contribution to be compensated strictly in accordance with that production? And how is that contribution to be valued? Further, what account will be taken, if any, of those factors that may influence productivity over which an individual has no control and that arise from the natural and social environment? Those who have experienced the simultaneous occurrence of a drought and depression in the Great Plains know what I am talking about.

Thus, equity is too illusive a concept to deal with directly. Rather, I have chosen a different approach and will attempt to identify fundamental aspirations of people in our society and to see whether water policies cause these aspirations to be in conflict or in harmony. If they are in conflict, adjustments will be necessary in what we are trying to accomplish. But if these basic aspirations are not in conflict–if instead the means chosen to realize those aspirations have become obsolete–then the problem is of a very different kind. I have chosen to get at the equity-efficiency question in this way.

Many years ago a philosopher named John Brewster traced the role of the principal values in America. He identified these principal values as (1) the work ethic, (2) the enterprise creed, (3) the creed of self-integrity, and (4) the democratic creed. The *work ethic* holds that if people worked proficiently and well, they would close the gap between their present circumstances and their aspirations. The *enterprise creed* implies that proprietors have the right to prescribe the working rules for their production units: the individual family is responsible for its own economic security, and the role of government is to prevent interference with proprietors to run their businesses as they see fit. The *creed of self-integrity* provides for the right and obligation of the individual to dissent from generally held opinions, customs, and traditions. The *democratic creed* involves the judgment that all men are of equal worth and dignity, and that no man is wise enough or good enough to have dictatorial power over any other.

It was Brewster's thesis that at one time these values could be held simultaneously and in harmony. But he argued that the industrial revolution threw them into conflict, and he highlighted those conflicts in graphic terms by using agricultural problems in this country as an example. Brewster's analysis was based on a study of the writings of Thomas Jefferson, John Locke, and Adam Smith. Brewster and others have shown that the form of government and the type of economic organization adopted in this country were based on the philosophy of these writers.

It is no less useful to apply this kind of analysis to the resource development policies that have emerged in this country. Many of those policies were based on the thesis that the development of natural resources would create economic opportunity so that the values of the work ethic could be realized. Private rights in natural resources, until recently, have been quite consistent with the enterprise creed—that the private holder of rights should have considerable freedom in the way those rights would be exercised—and water law, as an example, has given the holder of water rights substantial security in their use. Such a system worked quite well so long as there was water to be developed, the federal government was investing in its development, and environmental effects could be ignored or easily internalized. These conditions have changed, but our policies and institutions have not changed accordingly. But enough of generalities. Let me now be specific with respect to the kinds of conflicts with which we must deal if we are to bring specific goals into harmony.

At the risk of oversimplification I would like to state what I believe to be the two fundamental problems pertaining to natural resource policy. First, a major problem in our society arises from a desire to provide for that combination of market and nonmarket activities that best serves our needs. This problem is often stated as the conflict between economic growth and environmental quality, and that is part—but only part—of a more basic conflict. On the one hand, the enterprise creed recognizes the power of private property and the profit motive in providing market goods and services. The "right" of the proprietor to run his business as he sees fit derives from the fundamental assumption that this will best serve a greater good. For many years we relied heavily upon relatively unregulated markets to serve this greater good. A rising standard of living over a long period of time was evidence that the policy worked. If this now sounds quaint and old fashioned, let me call your attention to the August 27, 1979, issue of *Time.* One finds here a discussion of declining productivity in the United States and what it means. We are discovering that many social tensions have been alleviated historically because we had an economy that each year produced more on a per capita basis than it did the previous year. Even though we are a rich nation, concern about market goods and services is not out of style.

But there are many things we value that are not well produced by the unregulated market. Environmental quality is a major policy consideration for every resource today—energy, water, air, land, and food. The market, left alone, will not do a very good job of protecting the air we breathe or the waters that many of us would like to use in common. We have also decided that the market alone will not always provide adequately for the health and safety of workers. Further, the democratic creed and the creed of self integrity have led us to stipulate that economic opportunity will not be denied on the basis of race, color, creed, sex, and, increasingly, age. In addition, we have been unwilling to trust the market completely to provide either for basic research or the education of the populace.

It is my hope that this conference would not assume that the market economy and the enterprise creed are obsolete. But I would also hope that there will be general recognition that the market does not provide automatically for all of those things that are important to our society. There is a need to agree as to how the desired combination of market and nonmarket goods and services will be determined.

As difficult as it is to determine an acceptable combination of market and nonmarket goods and services, the *way* in which such decisions are made is also of great importance and is the second fundamental problem area in national resource policy. Thus, harmonizing individual and group decision making must be considered simultaneously with the question of what will be produced. Kenneth Boulding has said:

> On the whole, political thought in the West has emphasized form: constitutions and procedures, who is to judge things rather than

> what is to be done. Socialist thought has emphasized substance to the neglect of form, at least in the light of a particular ideology, with the result that socialist societies have found themselves defenseless against tyranny. Both form—who does it—and substance—what is to be done—are important, and we must give increasing attention to both if the next hundred years is not to be a disaster.[1]

The development of modern technology has made very large systems both possible and, for the private sector, profitable. Individual proprietorship has not been nearly as effective for many in closing the gap between reality and aspirations as working within a larger enterprise owned by others. Government policies designed specifically to assist small farms and small businesses have been ineffective in curbing this trend toward bigness. Government has grown larger, sometimes to deal with big business or big labor, but sometimes also just because certain kinds of technology have made larger government possible. For example, it is hard to imagine our social security system functioning as it now does in the absence of modern electronic technology.

But largeness in one dimension may involve a sacrifice in another dimension. A municipality may be better able to deliver varying quantities of good quality water to a large number of users and collect payment for this service than it is in designing an incentive system that will result in efficient use of that water. Large systems may do very well in supplying great quantities of an item of uniform quality, but they may have limitations in serving the needs of people where variation in consuming units must be taken into account or where quality of product is an important consideration. One reason large public sector systems may be less than satisfactory is that the public may expect too much. It is not enough that the Bureau of Reclamation provides water to agriculture and municipalities. It also must try to create opportunity in agriculture by establishing many small units on irrigation projects even though farm consolidation has been the trend in agriculture. While the "work ethic" is still a valid aspiration, the 160-acre farm probably is not a very good way to provide for its accomplishment.

The second major problem area, then, is deciding how to harmonize individual and group decision making. But the matter does not end there. Once it is decided that group decision making is desired for the accomplishment of a particular goal, objective, or task, how is the group to be formed? How large will it be and how will it be made responsive to the needs of those who constitute the group?

In confronting the water problems of the West, I believe we must always keep in mind these two major dilemmas that confront all of resource policy. We will not be successful if we believe we must choose once and for all either between economic growth or environmental quality, on the one hand, or that we must choose, in a general sense, between individual prerogative and group need. But there must be procedures and guidelines for resolving conflicts in particular situations. In the time remaining I will identify four major guidelines for water policy in the West which will need to be observed if these two major problems are to be addressed.

1. Water policies of the future need to recognize the powerful role of *individual incentives.* Incentives affecting individual behavior are of many kinds, but many of the economic incentives imbedded in water policies are counterproductive to the objectives identified earlier. They enhance neither economic progress nor environmental quality. The underpricing of water may have made sense when the objective was to encourage the use of an abundant input to develop other resources—but that objective is long gone. There are many parallels between the pricing of water and energy, with the result of these policies generally being the same. There now seems to be a slowly growing recognition that the pricing of energy at less than its replacement cost will serve neither to provide an energy supply nor to protect environmental quality. Let us hope that a similar realism can be introduced into water policy.

Economic incentives, which grow out of the marketplace, also can be used to obtain those goods and services that typically are not produced by the market. Allen Kneese has done as much as anyone to call attention to the potential use of such economic incentives as effluent charges to bring about desired levels of environmental quality.

2. A second guideline is that future western water policies should focus attention on the critical importance of improve-

ments in *state water law.* Some water institutions may suffer from an advanced case of "institutional arthritis." Individuals knowledgeable about water law in the West differ as to whether the arthritis that afflicts state water law is crippling or only aggravating. My own belief is that the law in most states has the capacity to accommodate substantial change in water use but that there is much room for improvement.

Water law in the West can best serve those who now hold rights (as well as emerging water needs) if existing rights can be defined and quantified, if the extent of third-party interests can be specified, and if water rights can be transferred through the payment of compensation. This, of course, is a tall order, because water is a fugitive resource and third-party interests are very difficult to treat. But some states have done much better with these matters than others. One does not have to be an idealist to believe that a systematic comparison of what already exists might serve to bring about substantial improvements.

If the law permits rights to be identified and measured, and if rights can be transferred by the payment of compensation, many opportunities exist that would not otherwise be available. For example, the public could acquire, perhaps for in-stream purposes, rights that now divert water out of the stream. The transfer of rights would also permit new uses to be accommodated, such as energy development, but if a community wished to maintain, say, its agricultural base, rights might be acquired by a community or a group for that purpose. Communities acquire open space in urban areas and hold it free from commercial development. The acquisition of water rights would permit communities to control development in a comparable fashion.

3. A third area of emphasis for future western water policy is one that is already receiving considerable attention. This is the determination of the *appropriate role of government at various levels* in water programs and policy. No doubt subsequent speakers will refer to the declining role of the federal government in financing water development projects. This development has been stimulated in part by the recognition that not all of the benefits of such projects are national in

character and also by increased competition for the federal budget. But there are other reasons. I first became familiar with water policies in Oregon in the mid 1950s. The water policy of the state at that time consisted largely of efforts to make federal water investment in Oregon as large as possible. Just as I left Oregon in the mid 1970s the state had decided it did not want a dam built that had already been authorized and for which funds had been appropriated by the Congress. By that time the water policy of the state required that federal investment be examined from several points of view. Such an examination resulted in the state saying "thanks, but no, thanks," even when a dam would have been built with all federal money. This kind of examination and change can be expected to continue.

There are several reasons this is occurring. It is partly due to renewed interest in resource management in general at the local and state level. Communities have discovered that land-use control is one of the few techniques available to them for the management of growth. But land-use planning often forces a look at all resources. More than one state has discovered inconsistencies between its land use plans and its water policies.

There also is the fundamental question as to which unit of government is best suited for certain tasks. The construction of a Grand Coulee or a Hoover Dam obviously requires the involvement of a very large unit of government. But if massive investment is not required, certain facets of water policy might better reside at a lower unit of government. It may well be that the capacity of the federal government to address truly large problems adequately is diminished if it assumes functions for which it is not well suited. Of course, there are advantages and limitations at all levels of government, and the matching of problems with the appropriate jurisdiction promises to be a major element of water policy for some time to come. Small is not necessarily beautiful, but neither is bigger necessarily better.

4. Group decision making or government intervention is undertaken for the purpose of improving on individual decision making or affecting individual decision making in some beneficial way. It was noted earlier that the market alone may not do a very good job of providing for environmental quality. It was also noted that one of the most basic problems faced by

our society involves selecting the appropriate mix of market and nonmarket goods and services. The output of markets can be modified and supplemented in a number of ways, including direct regulation, effluent charges, subsidies, a redefinition of property rights, and government ownership. Yet private performance may be very different depending on the method of government intervention chosen. *An important part of the cost of modifying market performance may be the cost and uncertainty of the rule itself. Accordingly, the fourth guideline is that a special effort should be made to reduce the uncertainty associated with group action affecting water policy.* Studies that I have seen suggest that the economic cost of achieving significant improvement in environmental quality may not be large if the cost of rule making, enforcement, and the additional uncertainty created by the intervention is not considered. Environmental goals and objectives need to be made explicit, and the means for achieving them need to be stabilized. Private sector decision making will respond to incentives and it will adjust to regulations. But if the ground rules are constantly changing, if regulations are applied in what appears to be a capricious manner, or if public sector decisions as to what is permissible are slow in coming or uncertain as to when they will be made, private sector performance is much hampered and environmental quality objectives are not necessarily enhanced in the process.

In summary then, it is accurate to say that this conference is timely, and that it is about an important subject. Water policy decisions during the coming decade will force us to consider how we are going to achieve some of our most fundamental goals. But it is hoped we will not opt for policies that will result in more polarization and in stalemate. Rather, we need to use our genius to develop approaches that will permit the simultaneous accomplishment of our deeply held values. The general choice must not be between economic growth and environmental quality. Rather, the appropriate policy is one that will permit us to choose a combination of market and nonmarket goods that is to our liking and chosen by means that will not damage us in the process. The choice need not be between extreme individualism and collective paralysis. Rather, the appropriate policy is one that recognizes that certain problems require concerted action but that also tries to create an environment for individual decision making that will promote the common good.

Notes

1. Kenneth Boulding. *Daedalus,* Fall 1973, pp. 100–101.

Part 1

Dimensions of the Water Resources Problems

2
The Coming Conflicts over Water

Charles W. Howe

Introduction

The reader may note that the title of this paper has omitted the word "use" given in the program. Reflection on the problems and potential conflicts surrounding our water resources convinced the writer that water use is not the only problem area, even if "use" is broadly construed. Indeed, some of the major issues arise from environmental considerations, from impacts of water development on other systems such as transportation, and from the ways in which the benefits and costs of water development and use are distributed among the population.

The 1960s and 1970s have been active and exciting times for water resource policy and practice. Until 1974 or so, there seemed to be a very gradual but quite certain trend toward the rationalization of water policy. A sequence of important legislative and administrative steps had been taken at the federal level to improve planning and evaluation procedures, to coordinate the programs of the major water related agencies, and to assist the states in developing water management capabilities. The Water Resources Planning Act of 1965 established the Water Resources Council, allowed for the establishment of a national net of River Basin Commissions, provided aid to the states, mandated a reconsideration of benefit-cost practices, and required a periodic "national assessment" of the water situation. While appearances always greatly exceeded substance, these were the foundation stones for potential policy and procedural improvements of great significance.

The states, recognizing the increasing scarcity and importance of water, made very substantial strides in developing water planning and management capabilities. The exhaustion of good, large reservoir sites and other highly productive water development opportunities appropriate for federal construction indicated an increasing role for the states and a distinctly diminished role for the federal agencies. New large interbasin transfer projects and new irrigation seemed things of the past. Policy analysts like Professor Henry Caulfield noted the weakening of the old water interest coalitions that had lobbied successfully for federal projects for many decades. This weakening stemmed partly from public concern over sharply increasing costs of federal projects and partly from the more active role being played by the states.

The Carter Administration came in with a strong intention of further rationalizing water policy, especially in the directions of environmental concern and financial responsibility. An extensive policy review process was started that promised to reinforce the trends noted earlier. However, the brash manner in which the policy reform process was announced—and especially the publication of the celebrated "hit list" of cancelled projects without adequate consultation with the affected states—caused a violent reaction *against* the Administration's basically constructive efforts, seeming to preclude attempts to reopen rational discussions between the states and the Administration.

The Administration's falling popularity served to slow and moderate the water policy revision process to some extent, while the rising prices imposed by OPEC and the Iranian political crisis in 1978–79 served to submerge water policy under the growing concern about energy. The President's energy message of July 1979 has left the future of water policy very unclear but has opened the possibility that rational water policy will be seriously impaired or abandoned in a panicky rush to develop national energy resources.

Definition of Conflict

It is probably true that most U.S. residents think of the western water situation as rife with conflicts reminiscent of the gun battles over water that occurred in the California gold camps. Those very gun battles stimulated the development of our "doctrine of prior appropriation," a form of water law that has served reasonably well to resolve water conflicts over the long run (although not so well in the short run). In addition to the saleability of water rights and the court review provided under western water law, there are many other mechanisms that serve to reduce potential conflicts, such as the organization of efficient water distribution organizations like the Northern Colorado Water Conservancy District, interstate compacts on the division of river waters, regulations limiting groundwater use, and short-term agreements to share water during drought.

If a given action (such as a policy change or a new water project) made all affected parties better off, there would be no conflict. Such an action might be labelled "socially efficient" since we can judge it to be good without having to compare the welfare of different groups.[1] Thus "conflict" must refer to a situation in which the perceived improvement of one or more groups is accompanied by a perceived decrease in the well-being of other groups as a result of the proposed action.

Unfortunately, the markets and legal setting within which water-related changes take place frequently either fail to compensate some groups adequately or overcompensate others. Downstream irrigators are not compensated for damages from salinity stemming from new upstream projects—a case of under-compensation. A prospective seller of water rights to a new high-value user may be prevented by the water courts from doing so because of minor damage to other users—a case of too much weight being placed on the interests of third parties. Thus, in the absence of adequate compensatory channels, potentially "socially efficient" policies and projects remain situations of conflict.

A Classification of Potential Conflicts

Taxonomy is the perpetual game of biologists and the bane of most other professions, but it seems to be necessary to organizing any topic. I have chosen, not totally arbitrarily, to utilize three types of potential water-related conflicts:

1. Conflicts over the use of present water supplies
2. Conflicts over future water development

3. Conflicts arising over water policies and the institutional framework for policy execution

It is clear that these categories are not clean-cut nor independent of one another. Conflicts related to the mining of nonrenewable groundwater might be placed in any of these boxes, and it is clear that the extent to which the conflicts in (1) are resolved will have an important affect on (2) and perhaps (3). Nonetheless, we proceed to use these categories.

Conflicts over the Use of Present Water Supplies

Water use can refer to withdrawals from water sources, to the quantity of water actually consumed, or to instream uses. Some economic activities withdraw very large volumes but consume only a small fraction, e.g. thermal-electric power generation. Others withdraw very large quantities while consuming a major portion, especially agriculture, which consumes over 50 percent of its large withdrawals. Other valuable activities utilize water right in the stream, usually with little or no consumption over normal evaporation, e.g. hydro-electric power, fish and wildlife maintenance, and water quality improvement through flow augmentation. We will concentrate on consumptive uses and instream flows.

Measures of Potential Water Conflicts

The dominant uses of water in the western United States that will be competing for the available water are:

- irrigated agriculture;
- energy production (other than hydro-electric) and other minerals industries uses;
- water quality and instream flow maintenance for fish, wildlife, and recreation;
- domestic, commercial, and manufacturing uses; and
- claims for water use on federal and tribal lands.

Since federal and Indian claims will be discussed by other speakers, they will not be treated further here. Note should be taken, however, of the great uncertainty and possible sizes of these claims. The domestic, commercial, and manufacturing category is typically small relative to other uses. Further, the economic (and political) values of these uses is so high that we can reasonably assume they will take precedence over other uses. Thus we can concentrate on the potential trade-offs among the large volume uses: irrigation, energy-minerals production, and instream flow maintenance.

Water supplies in several southwestern river basins are already approaching a state of full utilization, especially in the Lower Colorado, the Great Basin, and the Rio Grande. In such basins, the expansion of new water-using activities will require either the development of new water supplies (probably through very costly additional storage or long-distance interbasin transfers) or the transfer of water from present uses to the newer, growing uses. Table 1 exhibits in very aggregate terms the water supply and demand picture in the river basins of the United States as given by the U.S. Water Resources Council in the recent Second National Water Assessment (1978).

The following points are quickly observed from Table 1:

- Irrigation is by far the largest consumptive use of water in the West.
- The combination of domestic, commercial, and manufacturing water consumption is small relative to irrigation.
- Energy-related consumptive uses (represented by thermal electric plus more than 60 percent of the minerals sector consumptive use) are projected to grow substantially but remain, on the average, less than 5 percent of the irrigation consumptive use.
- Instream flows will drop substantially below the levels that are deemed desirable from the fisheries and recreation point of view in at least the Rio Grande, Lower Colorado, and Great Basins.

The degree of geographical aggregation in the Table 1 data does, however, cover up some difficulties that can occur within smaller regions (especially states) and particular basins. The actual division of the water shown as available is constrained in the following ways:

TABLE 1
Summary of Present and Projected Western Fresh Water Supplies, Consumptive Uses, and Streamflows
(in thousands of acre-feet per year)

Water Resource Region	*Year*	*Inflow + Basin Runoff*[a]	*Irrigation Consump.*	*Domestic + Commer. Manfg. Consump.*
Missouri	1975	68908	15920	523
	1985	68908	19709	531
	2000	68908	19720	652
Arkansas[f]	1975	75817	7894	575
	1985	75817	8364	682
	2000	75817	7980	861
Texas-Gulf	1975	39901	10469	1207
	1985	39901	8509	1762
	2000	39901	6832	2885
Rio Grande	1975	5946	4352	194
	1985	5946	4390	220
	2000	5946	3998	245
Upper Colo.	1975	15631	2457	34
	1985	15631	2976	36
	2000	15631	3070	39
Lower Colo.	1975	10522	4509	324
	1985	9662	4437	383
	2000	9292	4166	524
Great Basin	1975	6693	3612	192
	1985	6693	3452	237
	2000	6693	3580	310
Pacific Northwest	1975	300746	12349	665
	1985	300746	14965	870
	2000	300746	14799	1319
California	1975	76216	27196	1894
	1985	76216	28150	2223
	2000	76216	29468	2695

[a] Figures for 1985 and 2000 assume no groundwater overdrafts.
[b] Including metals, nonmetals, and fuels.
[c] Including reservoir evaporation and exports.
[d] Negative values represent amount of groundwater overdraft needed to sustain projected uses.
[e] U.S. Fish and Wildlife Service estimates for "optimal" fish and wildlife habitat conditions.

Thermal Elec. Consump.	*Minerals*[b]	*Total Consump.*[c]	*Remaining Streamflow*[d]	*Desirable Streamflow*[e]
76	124	22840	49392	38033
268	156	27474	41919	38033
713	183	28722	40186	38033
100	194	11960	70112	51709
265	206	13080	62935	51709
512	244	13436	62604	51709
111	622	14520	31662	25667
302	659	13554	26380	25667
1110	708	14024	25911	25667
20	115	5566	1378	2561*
10	144	5694	475	2561*
6	168	5377	792	2561*
44	53	4431	11200	8901
119	81	5291	10340	8901
169	161	5662	9969	8901
71	169	11491	1736	7688*
150	243	11267	-1605	7688*
141	314	11021	-1729	7688*
3	31	4599	2869	3796*
47	49	4588	2304	3796*
58	72	4893	2081	3796*
15	20	15598	285902	239684
116	21	18665	282134	239684
385	30	19352	281446	239684
28	205	30587	53060	36520
113	252	32044	48729	36520
271	239	34031	46531	36520

[f] Including the White and Red River Basins.

*Indicates a shortfall from desirable level of instream flows.

Source: U.S. Water Resources Council, *The Nation's Water Resources, 1975-2000*, Volume 1, Summary, December 1978.

- by interstate compacts among basins,
- by interstate compacts within a basin,
- by topographic features and physical distribution systems at the micro-basin level,
- by legal difficulties in transferring water rights among users.

Thus with respect to the Upper Colorado Basin, Gray, Sparling, and Whittlesey (March 1979) state:

> However, the problem of the oil shale industry is one of water availability due to the fragmentation of the water market in the upper reaches of the Colorado River Basin. Three states hold rights to the water while the state with the greatest share of oil shale (Colorado) has the least undepleted surface water flows. While it seems likely that water rights can and are being bought from agriculture, the very localized nature of the oil shale industry seems to indicate that agricultural production in certain areas near the Piceance Basin may be drastically reduced as a result of sale of water rights to the oil shale industry.

We must, therefore, anticipate localized problems within sub-basins even where the aggregate data exhibit no problems.

The same problems can be anticipated with respect to instream flows. Table 1 shows only three regions having problems with undesirably low instream flows. There will, however, be many localized problems of instream flow deficiency and degraded water quality, especially as new pollution sources develop in connection with energy. These factors promise to interfere with recreational opportunities, too, both those activities based directly on water and those only indirectly linked to the resource. Table 2 gives an idea of the anticipated high rate of growth of water dependent and water-enhanced recreation activities.

An additional factor not exhibited in Table 1 is the uncertainty surrounding the quantities of water available. While this may not be important for some regions, it can be crucial in basins like the Colorado where surface waters are already fully used. The availability of 15.6 million acre-feet (maf) in the Upper Colorado Basin as shown in Table 1 is rather optimistic in comparison to other currently used figures. The Bureau of Reclamation has used a range of 13.0 to 13.5 maf. The average

TABLE 2
Water-Dependent and Water-Enhanced
Outdoor Recreation Activity Occasions, 1975–2000
(in millions of occasions[a])

Water Resource Region	*1975*	*1985*	*2000*
Missouri	94	103	118
Arkansas	63	68	78
Texas-Gulf	85	99	120
Rio Grande	16	18	20
Upper Colorado	4	4	4
Lower Colorado	25	31	42
Great Basin	13	16	20
Pacific Northwest	70	76	87
California	220	257	310
Totals	590	672	799

[a] An "activity occasion" is defined as participation by a person 12 years or older in an activity regardless of duration.

Source: U.S. Water Resources Council, *The Nation's Water Resources, 1975–2000*, Volume 1, Summary, December 1978, p. 45.

runoff from 1954 to 1963 was only 11.6 maf.

The implications of this range of uncertainty for water availability in the several Upper Colorado River Basin states is striking, for the Upper Basin is required by compact and Supreme Court interpretation to provide 8.25 maf annually to the Lower Basin (including one-half the Mexican Treaty obligation). Gray et al. (1979), by applying the rules of the Upper Basin Compact, exhibit the results shown in Table 3.

The actual availability within this range of uncertainty will clearly be extremely important to the future of the Upper Basin states and will, in part, determine the severity of the trade-off between growing energy uses and agriculture.

The Trade-Off Against Agriculture

The usual approach of "water for energy studies" (e.g. see Gray et al., 1979, or U.S. Department of Interior, July 1974) is to extrapolate the existing trends of change in present consump-

TABLE 3
Estimated Allocation of Colorado River Water
Based on Alternative Gross River Flows
(in millions of acre-feet per year)

Annual Flow	*Lower Basin*	*Colorado*	*Utah*	*Wyoming*
18.00	8.30	5.02	2.23	1.36
15.50	8.30	3.73	1.66	1.01
14.10	8.30	3.00	1.33	0.81
13.30	8.30	2.59	1.15	0.70
11.60	8.30	1.71	0.76	0.46

Source: S. Lee Gray, Edward W. Sparling, and Norman K. Whittlesey, "Water for Energy Development in the Northern Great Plains and Rocky Mountain Regions," draft paper, Department of Economics, Colorado State University, Fort Collins, Colorado, March 1979, Table 2, p. 69.

tive water uses in the future, then to compare those projected aggregate consumption figures with anticipated water availability, taking into account physical availability and compact and export obligations. Any remaining unused water is then identified as being "available" for energy development or other new uses.

Of course, this is not the way things will in fact happen for at least two reasons. The first was elaborated in the preceding section, namely that the excess water may not be available where it can be used by the new activities. The second reason is that water reallocation will start to take place from existing uses to the new uses long before all the excess water is used up. The reason is simply that some reallocation will be less costly, both privately and socially, than developing and transporting portions of the excess waters. The more efficiently this reallocation process works, the gentler the trade-offs of new against old activities will be.

For example, it would be desirable to transfer to the growing, high-valued use water from the lowest-valued uses in the basin, taking into account the direct and indirect values involved. If the legal setting and topography permit, this is likely to happen. Water rights owners who apply water to low-income-producing activities and who are located close to the new uses will find themselves better off by selling at least part of their water. The new activities would thereby acquire water at low private and social cost. However, insofar as physical and legal barriers impede such transfers, the reallocations likely will be from higher-valued uses and are more likely to be concentrated in a small area, as noted by Gray et al.

How serious are such trade-offs in terms of social benefits lost from the old activities (usually agriculture) that sell the water? The lost benefits of importance to the region would include: (1) regional income losses, both direct and indirect; (2) loss of jobs, both direct and indirect; and (3) loss of aesthetic amenities and the "economic balance" associated with agriculture. The last is hard to quantify but of definite weight in state water policy formulation.

A recent study by Gisser et al. (June 1979) has analyzed the direct and indirect losses of regional income and employment that are likely to occur in the Four Corners area as agricultural water is transferred to expanding thermal electric generation.[2] The analysis utilized detailed linear programming models of Four Corners agriculture, thus assuming that water generating the lowest on-farm income would be the first transferred. Both income and employment losses were then blown up by regional multipliers derived from regional input-output models. Table 4 presents the study results for both a 10 percent and 30 percent transfer of water out of Four Corners agriculture.

The results indicate a rather low cost per acre-foot at all levels of transfer up to 30 percent of the water currently used in agriculture in the Four Corners area, and the cost remains fairly steady over that range, rising from $29 per acre-foot to only $32 per acre-foot. There are certainly no possibilities of augmenting physical supplies in that area at such low costs. Naturally, if the pattern of water transfer differed from the computed least-cost pattern, then the costs would be higher.

From the national point of view, any impediments to the transfer of water out of agriculture into the new energy uses would cause higher costs to be incurred and would, therefore, be undesirable. The regional and state points of view might, however, be quite different. The income and employment losses are not insignificant relative to the low income and employment

TABLE 4
Regional Income and Employment Losses from Transferring Water out of Agriculture in the Four Corners Area

	10% of Water Transferred	*30% of Water Transferred*
Total water transferred	88,750 a.f.	266,250 a.f.
Total regional employment lost	142 man-yrs/yr	416 man-yrs/yr
Regional employment lost/acre-foot	.0016 man-yr/a.f.	.0016 man-yr/a.f.
Total regional income lost/year	$2,565,900/year	$8,532,494/year
Regional income lost/acre-foot	$29/acre-foot	$32/acre-foot

Source: Gisser, Micha et al., "Water Trade-off Between Electric Energy and Agriculture in the Four Corners Area," *Water Resources Research*, Vol. 15, No. 3, June 1979.

levels of the area. If new energy activities could be provided with water from sources other than agriculture, it might be highly desirable from the region's viewpoint, especially if the usual federal project financing with its huge subsidies were available.

Additional information on the income consequences of transferring water out of agriculture was generated by a recent study by Howe and Young (June 1978). A salinity control alternative for the Upper Colorado Basin would be to phase out irrigated agriculture in some of the less productive areas that are known to contribute large volumes of salt to the river system (through return flows). For a phase-out of 8,800 acres in the Grand Valley and 10,200 acres in the Uncompahgre Valley, the direct and indirect income losses were estimated in Table 5.

While the regional cost per acre-foot of water transferred out of agriculture appears to be substantially higher than in the Four Corners area, additional benefits are gained in the form of reduced salt loadings. Howe and Young (1978) found that a reduction of one ton of salt loading in the Upper Colorado River would result in increased agricultural yields in the Lower Colorado Basin worth at least $8 per ton (in terms of increased regional incomes). Thus, from a national point of view, any

TABLE 5
Direct and Indirect Income Losses from Acreage Phase-Out in the Grand and Uncompahgre Valleys

Direct loss in farm output ($/yr)	1,926,000
Direct + indirect regional income loss ($/yr)	2,058,000
Reduction in consumptive water use (a.f./yr)	30,800
Regional income loss per acre-foot saved ($/a.f.)	67
Reduction in salt loading (tons/year)	76,000 +

Source: Charles W. Howe and Jeffrey T. Young, "Indirect Economic Impacts from Salinity Damages in the Colorado River Basin," Table 7-4, Appendix 7 in Jay C. Anderson and Alan C. Kleinman, *Salinity Management Options for the Colorado River,* Report P-78-003, Utah Water Research Laboratory, Utah State University, Logan, Utah, June 1978.

permanent income losses to the Upper Basin would be partly offset by income gains to the Lower Basin (70,000 tons x $8).

Again, the state and national viewpoints are likely to differ. The loss of farm output and income is likely to be picked up elsewhere in the nation (especially since we still have an acreage reduction program), and thus correctly not counted as a national loss. The water saved and salt loading reduced will permit savings in the Lower Basin, even in the face of production control programs. The state is likely to be quite concerned about the income and employment losses from this acreage reduction unless it appears that the re-investment of the payments made for the phased-out land (or its water rights) will provide sufficient added income. Thus the state is likely to oppose any program of acreage phase-out and opt for salinity control measures that will be paid for largely by the federal government, such as point source controls and (horror of horrors!) desalting plants, even if those projects are much more costly in real terms.

In summary, what we have found is that the trade-offs between agriculture and newly emerging water uses (such as energy) are not likely to be at all severe from a national point of view and that little conflict is likely to be involved. The state or region, however, will see the conflict as much more severe. As a consequence, there will also be severe conflicts between state and regional interests and the federal government over the most appropriate ways of dealing with emerging problems.

Conflicts over Future Water Supply Development

Out of the many possible dimensions of future water supply development, we have chosen to discuss three: the high costs of all future additions to supply, interbasin transfers of water and interregional conflict, and groundwater exploitation as conflict between present and future.

Future Supply Developments to Be Costly

The most widely used form of supply development in the United States has been the impoundment of seasonally and annually varying surface flows. As the best reservoir sites have been used and the most regularly flowing rivers have been tapped, the marginal costs of additional reliable water supplies from surface sources have risen rapidly. Detailed analyses of these marginal costs for the major water resource regions were carried out by Wollman and Bonem (1971). The cost figures are for storage only and do not reflect distribution or treatment costs. Table 6 gives the Wollman-Bonem figures, raised by a factor of three, which is the approximate increase in the industrial construction price index since the Wollman-Bonem figures were compiled.

Marginal storage costs appear to increase quite rapidly with the state of development within each region. Agricultural distribution costs could double or treble these costs at the farm headgate. Most noticeable, however, is the absence of data from six major western water regions. In these regions, surface flows are already so highly regulated that further development is either impossible or prohibitively costly. This doesn't mean that additional supplies couldn't be developed on particular streams within each region, but the overall river system yield would not be significantly increased and might well decrease because of additional reservoir evaporation.

A second proposed source of additional water supplies for western regions is the large scale interbasin transfer. Such projects only redistribute water geographically but they can increase the locational utility of water. Howe and Easter (1971) collected data on the costs of various Columbia-to-Colorado transfer schemes and found a 1970 range of $36 to $130 per

TABLE 6
Marginal Storage Costs for Western Surface Water Development

Region	*Cumulative Developed Supply (maf/yr.)*	*Marginal Storage Costs*[a] *($/a.f.)*
Lower Missouri	6 (1970 level)	-
	10	3.3
	12	6.9
Lower Arkansas	27 (1970 level)	-
	30	4.2
	45	5.4
Western Gulf	17 (1970 level)	-
	20	7.8
	22	11.7
	25	20.4
Central Pacific	29 (1970 level)	-
	42	8.7
	46	25.5
Pacific Northwest	70 (1970 level)	-
	120	4.2
	145	15.6
Upper Missouri	see text	
Upper Arkansas	see text	
Colorado	see text	
Great Basin	see text	
Rio Grande	see text	
Southern Pacific	see text	

[a]The interest rate used in computing these costs was only 3.5 percent so the costs are probably understated.

Source: Charles W. Howe and K. William Easter, ***Interbasin Transfers of Water: Economic Issues and Impacts*** (Baltimore: Johns Hopkins University Press, 1971). Original data from Wollman and Bonem.

acre-foot, a range that by now would probably be approximately three times as high. Aside from the range of costs, the main features of interbasin transfers are that: (1) there are substantial economies of scale, (2) the cost of power for pumping is a critical element in total cost, and (3) the extent to which power recovery is possible (from downhill water movement) is extremely important in determining cost.

Desalination of brackish or ocean waters received great attention in the 1960s. Costs in the U.S. never fell below $1 per thousand gallons ($326 per acre-foot) even with low energy costs. Present costs would be prohibitive for any but domestic and high-value manufacturing uses.

Groundwater has provided a valuable supplement to western water supplies, but in many important regions there has been severe mining with resultant falling water tables and problems of surface subsidence. Energy costs for pumping have risen to nearly 10 cents/ac.ft./ft., so that a 100-foot lift costs $10 per acre-foot. Many western areas are pumping from 300 feet or more, so that costs severely restrict the crops that can be profitably irrigated.

If the sharply increasing costs of water development are borne by the water users, few conflicts would be generated. However, under existing federal financial policies, huge subsidies are provided for federal water projects. These subsidies must be covered by the federal budget and eventually by the general taxpayer. Current pressures to balance the federal budget and taxpayer resistance to increasing tax burdens thus bring future water development into direct conflict with the general taxpayer and nonwater programs vying for federal financing.

The form and extent of federal water project subsidies have been analyzed extensively. North and Neely (1977), using data on 5,000 federal water projects and programs, have shown agricultural water supply projects repay only 19 percent of real project costs, M&I projects repay 64 percent, harbor projects 16 percent, waterways 6 percent, other navigational programs 7 percent, and hydro-electric power generation 64 percent. Some of these subsidies "feed" on each other, as when an irrigation project is allowed to buy underpriced electric power from a federal hydro-electric project. Many huge subsidies are hidden from public view by ignoring the time costs of money (e.g. allowing "repayment" of capital costs over fifty years without interest or allowance for inflation) and by such gimmicks as the "basin account" that permits power profits to repay irrigation costs.

Conflicts over Interbasin Transfers

Large-scale interbasin transfers may, at some point in time, comprise an important part of rational regional or national water plans. Naturally, all costs (economic, ecological, and social) as well as all benefits must be taken into account. To date, interbasin transfers have been a source of great interregional conflict. Potential exporting basins jealously guard their supplies, and perhaps rightfully so, for the importers of water generally provide no compensation to the exporting region. Opportunity costs of the exported water may be substantial, even for exporting regions having plentiful water supplies. These opportunity costs can take the forms of ecological damage due to reduced streamflow, water quality problems because of decreased dilution, foregone hydro-electric power, and foregone future economic development.

The U.S. Congress has been unwilling to have interbasin transfer conflicts faced or resolved openly. The Water Resources Planning Act of 1965 precludes the River Basin Commissions established under its authority from considering the development or movement of waters outside its jurisdictional area. The National Water Commission that was established from 1967 to 1974 to study the national water situation was expressly forbidden to study interbasin transfers. It has been speculated that the former prohibition explains the absence of River Basin Commissions across the southern half of the United States.

Future proposals are likely to include Columbia-to-Colorado transfers as energy development mounts in the Colorado Basin, and Arkansas or Mississippi River-to-High Plains transfers to alleviate the problems of exhausting the waters of the Ogallala aquifer. These transfers will surely be resisted by the proposed exporting regions because of lack of compensation or guaranteed future water supplies.

The state-regional versus federal conflict that was noted in connection with proposed transfers of water out of agriculture will recur in two forms in connection with interbasin transfers: (1) some transfers that are not desirable from a national standpoint will be strongly promoted by the importing regions and resisted by the exporting regions, and (2) transfers that are desirable from the national viewpoint will still be resisted by the exporting region.

Groundwater Use as a Present Versus Future Generations Conflict

Groundwater can be either a renewable resource (if recharge possibilities exist) or a nonrenewable resource (e.g. the Ogallala aquifer). In either case, the issue of determining an appropriate pattern of use over time is important and fascinating. Present use of groundwater can have three major effects on the future:

1. It can lower the water table, increasing future pumping costs.
2. It can deny the future the use of water now in the aquifer.
3. It can destroy the aquifer itself by allowing compaction or allowing the possibly irreversible intrusion of salt water.

In a situation of rapid recharge, none of these effects may be significant (but the recharge may be at the expense of surface water uses). In the pure mining case, all may be highly significant.

In the mining case, there is a subtle problem of balancing present generation and future generation interests. If the present generation uses up all the water, all future water-dependent activity will stop. If the present generation conserves water so severely that it becomes impoverished, then it can leave little in the way of capital and technology to future generations. Without them, the untouched water resource may be worth very little. This is the general dilemma of nonrenewable resources.

The way we manage groundwater is a measure of our concern for future generations. Recognizing the fugitive, common property nature of the resource, we know that unregulated use will result in an irresponsibly rapid depletion. Thus we must devise control strategies that will restrict the tendency toward "beggar thy neighbor and children" behavior. Indeed, most states are now developing extensive groundwater regulations to avoid extensive current and future conflicts.

Conflicts Arising from Water-Related Policies and Institutions

The closing section of this paper identifies three policy issues not specifically identified in earlier sections: (1) fairness or equity in water management and development, (2) inconsistencies between water policies and policies in agriculture, transportation, and inflation control, and (3) the form and control over the institutional framework within which federal water policy and practices are established.

Fairness or Equity in Water Policy

Fairness and equity refer to an explicit identification and evaluation of who receives the benefits and who pays the costs of water programs. The major water development programs of this country were conceived as subsidized programs for opening up and managing our western natural resources: the Corps of Engineers navigation program, the Reclamation Program, and the Soil Conservation Program. The relevant fairness or equity questions to be asked about these programs are:

- Are the programs still required, or have their objectives largely been realized?
- Insofar as the continuation of the programs *is* justified, are the distributions of benefits and costs consistent with the aims of public policy?

An earlier section of this paper noted that only a small part of project cost is repaid to the federal government by the beneficiaries of many water projects. Is this still intended and, if so, are the net benefits being distributed in an acceptable way?

This distribution of net benefits is an increasingly important issue in a period of budget stringency because of the huge subsidies paid by the general taxpayer. It is the essence of the famous 160-acre limitation—one of our hottest current conflicts. Seckler and Young (1978) have shown for the 527,000-acre

Westlands Project in California that the returns to land ownership of about $135 per acre per year are totally attributable to the irrigation water subsidy. With such a subsidy being paid by the general federal taxpayer, it is interesting to note that the Southern Pacific Land Company holds 80,000 acres, the Boston Ranch Company 26,000 acres, and Westhaven Farms 11,000 acres. Seckler and Young conclude (p. 580):

> In sum, it is reasonable to say that . . . the amounts of money being made and the distribution of public funds through the water subsidy are little short of the grotesque. The agitation against the present situation is well founded.

The question of whether or not there are significant economies of scale in irrigated agriculture has not been settled. Carter and Dean (1961) concluded that there were economies of up to 640 acres for California cash crop farms, and Martin (1978) seems to accept that economies may extend above 1,000 acres. Until this issue is settled, it is difficult to analyze the efficiency implications of enforcing the 160-acre limit, but the equity implications seem clear. It is interesting to note that neither those favoring enforcement of the limitation nor those against enforcement have advocated dropping the large water subsidies.

Discouragingly, water agency practices ignore most of the equity issues involved in project analysis, in spite of being directed by the U.S. Water Resources Council (1973) to analyze and present them as part of project evaluation.

Inconsistencies Between Water Policies and Other Policies

Federal water development has frequently been at odds with other policies being pursued by other agencies. The post-war period until 1970 saw the expansion of irrigated acreage at a time when the Department of Agriculture was trying to reduce national output and acreage. The effects of this inconsistency have been analyzed by Howe and Easter (1971). The issue remains alive since new irrigation capacity is being planned while acreage reduction programs for the same crops remain active.

The second major form of inconsistency is with transportation policy. The expansion of the inland waterways system long ago reached the point of sharply increasing marginal costs. Figure 1, taken from a very old source (1959), shows the steeply increasing investment per mile then being encountered as the inland system was extended into smaller reaches of the river system. The then-proposed Tennessee-Tombigbee Canal is currently under construction and will be by far the most costly navigation project in U.S. history, should the courts permit the project to proceed.

Of course, high costs themselves do not imply that water transport facilities should not be built. It is clear, however, that current project evaluation procedures grossly overstate the benefits from having waterway transportation, largely by ignoring the availability of and impacts on the rail system. The expansion of subsidized waterway capacity (bargelines pay nothing for the use of the channels and locks on the inland system and pay only a very nominal fuel tax) in regions where railroads have excess capacity and are failing financially indicates, at best, the absence of a coordinated transportation policy!

The Institutional Framework for Federal Water Policy Formulation and Execution

The introductory section of this paper mentioned the post-war attempts toward a more rational national water policy as manifested in the recommendations of the Hoover Commissions, the work on benefit-cost practices in the federal agencies, the Water Resources Planning Act, and the studies and recommendations of the National Water Commission. These efforts had to fight the political clout of established water interests and, even to get as far as they did, had to compromise with those interests. Two major policy thrusts were, in effect, still-born: the Water Resources Council and the River Basin Commissions authorized under the same act. The Council (comprised of the secretaries of Agriculture, Army, Commerce, Energy, HUD, Transportation, and Interior) brought together all of the traditional water programs of the country that might be changed by the effective execution of the Council's charge to coordinate and rationalize the national water program. The River Basin

Figure 1

Distribution of original navigation investment expenditures on the Mississippi River System and adjacent waterways.

Source: U.S. Department of Commerce, *User Charges on Inland Waterways* (January 1959).

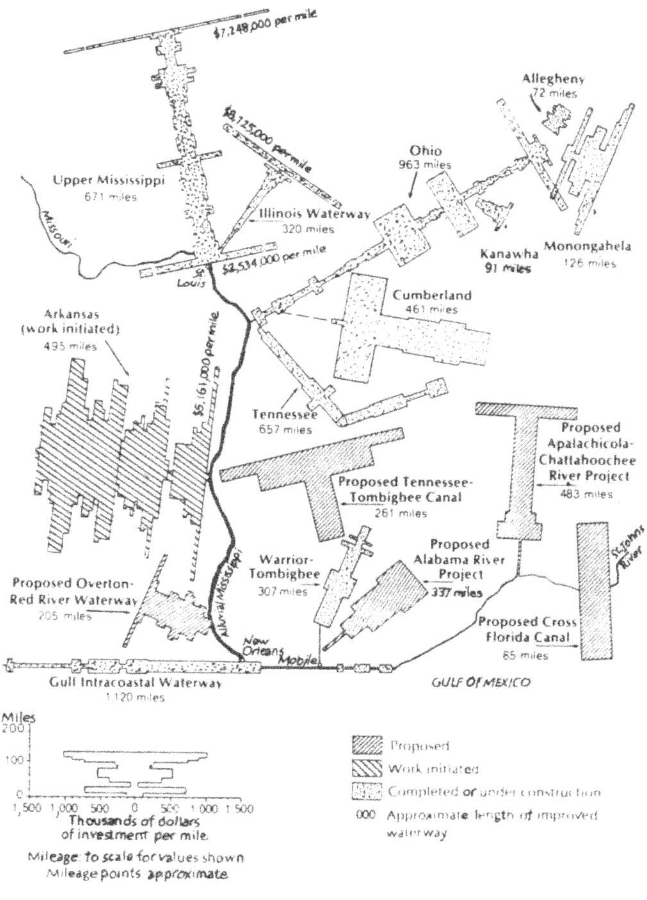

Commissions, in similar fashion, have their membership so defined that regional representation is dominated by the federal agency members.[3] As long as the traditional programs dominate the "coordination" process at both the federal and regional levels, there will be little coordination—as experience has indeed borne out.

Opportunities for redressing these particular imbalances have been created by two bills, one passed by Congress in 1978 and the other pending in the Senate. PL 95-502, authorizing the replacement of Locks and Dam 26 on the Mississippi and establishing a fuel tax for the inland waterways, directed the Upper Mississippi River Basin Commission to develop a "comprehensive master plan" for the management of the Upper Mississippi system, to identify the economic, recreational, and environmental objectives of the system, and to propose methods to assure achievement of such objectives. It is hoped that such proposals could include a more rationally representative composition of the Commission itself. Senate Bill 1241, introduced by Senators Domenici and Moynihan, proposes to reconstruct the Water Resources Council in such a way that it can more objectively pursue its coordination function. Such important institutional changes are by no means assured. One can reasonably expect substantial conflict over institutional reform.

Notes

1. Economists would call this a Pareto optimal change.
2. The same analysis of the cost side would apply independent of the nature of the new use.
3. For example, the membership of the Upper Mississippi River Basin Commission consists of six state commissioners and ten federal agency members.

References

Carter, H. O. and Dean, G. W. "Cost-Size Relationships for Cash Crop Farms in a Highly Commercialized Agriculture," *Journal of Farm Economics*, vol. 43, 1961.

Gisser, Micha et al. "Water Trade-off Between Electric Energy and Agriculture in the Four Corners Area," *Water Resources Research*, vol. 15, no. 3, June 1979.

Gray, S. Lee; Sparling, Edward W.; and Whittlesey, Norman K. "Water for Energy Development in the Northern Great Plains and Rocky Mountain Regions," draft paper, Department of Economics, Colorado State University, March 1979.

Howe, Charles W. and Easter, K. William. *Interbasin Transfers of Water: Economic Issues and Impacts* (Baltimore: Johns Hopkins University Press, 1971).

Howe, Charles W. and Young, Jeffry T. "Indirect Economic Impacts from Salinity Damages in the Colorado River Basin." Appendix 7 in Jay C. Andersen and Alan P. Kleinman, *Salinity Management Options for the Colorado River*, Report P-78-003, Utah Water Research Laboratory, Utah State University, Logan, Utah, June 1978.

Martin, William E. "Economies of Size and the 160-Acre Limitation: Fact and Fancy," *American Journal of Agricultural Economics*, vol. 60, no. 5, December 1978.

North, Ronald M. and Neely, Walter P. "A Model for Achieving Consistency for Cost-Sharing in Water Resource Programs," *Water Resources Bulletin*, vol. 13, no. 5, October 1977.

Seckler, David and Young, Robert A. "Economic and Policy Implications of the 160-Acre Limitation in Federal Reclamation Law," *American Journal of Agricultural Economics*, vol. 60, no. 4, November 1978.

U.S. Department of the Interior. *Report on Water for Energy in the Upper Colorado River Basin*, Water for Energy Team, July 1974.

U.S. Water Resources Council. *The Nation's Water Resources 1975-2000: Second National Assessment*, vol. 1, Summary, December 1978.

U.S. Water Resources Council. "Principles, Standards, and Procedures for Water and Related Land Resources Planning," *Federal Register*, vol. 38, no. 174, September 10, 1973, Part III, pp. 24778-24869.

Wollman, Nathaniel and Bonem, Gilbert W. *The Outlook for Water: Quality, Quantity, and National Growth* (Baltimore: Johns Hopkins University Press, 1971).

Commentary

Harvey O. Banks

Introduction

Dr. Howe's excellent paper sets forth clearly the present and future conflicts over water. He correctly points out that these encompass far more than conflicts over uses. Basic policies and institutions are in conflict as well.

For this presentation, only the following points of conflict and inconsistency will be discussed:

- federal policies, including inconsistencies;
- trade-offs against agriculture;
- funding for water development; and
- interbasin transfers.

All of these—and many more—are involved in the $6 million Six-State High Plains-Ogallala Aquifer Area Regional Study now in progress. This comprehensive study of resources and economic development alternatives will be briefly discussed in a separate paper.

Federal Policies

On June 6, 1978, President Carter sent to Congress a series of water policy initiatives designed to:

> . . . improve planning and efficient management of Federal water resource programs to prevent waste and to permit necessary water projects which are cost-effective, safe and environmentally sound to move forward expeditiously,

. . . provide a new, national emphasis on water conservation,

. . . enhance Federal-State cooperation and improved State water resources planning, and

. . . increase attention to environmental quality.[1]

On July 12, 1978, the president issued thirteen directives to the heads of executive departments and agencies to implement the water policy initiatives. Nineteen federal interagency task forces, with minor state participation, were established to prepare reports on implementation. Some final task reports have already been submitted.

The president's water policy initiatives cover a wide range of water and water-related proposals. All are of vital concern to the water industry, public and private. The financial community, with its large investments in activities dependent on adequate water supplies of proper quality, has much at stake. Several of the initiatives can be implemented by the issuance of regulations; some regulations have already been published. Others, such as increased cost-sharing by nonfederal interests, would require congressional action; bills are now pending before the Congress.

Space does not permit examination of all of the initiatives and their implications here. Discussion will be limited to:

- water conservation as a principal thrust in federal water resource planning and development,
- emphasis on instream flows,
- emphasis on enforcement of the environmental statutes,
- groundwater,
- nonstructural measures, and
- federal non-Indian reserved water rights.

None of the water policy proposals, except possibly in the long run those dealing with reserved water rights, would resolve any of the conflicts so ably discussed by Dr. Howe. In fact, some of the existing conflicts would be exacerbated. None present rational bases for achieving an equitable balance among the economic, environmental, and social values that should be considered in the allocation of scarce water resources and the funding necessary for water resource developments to meet the manifold demands.

Conservation

The administration places great emphasis on conservation, i.e. reduction in the use of or demand for water. All federal and federally assisted programs are to incorporate a water conservation element.[2] Conservation in use of water for irrigation is given special attention; it is alleged that 20–30 percent of the amount of water presently used for irrigation could be saved through various conservation measures.

There seems to be a feeling, particularly among the nonprofessionals who have involved themselves in the water resource field, that many of the current water problems and conflicts could be resolved through conservation and that, therefore, new water development projects are not necessary now nor for at least some time in the future.

There is no question that some water could be saved through conservation. However, it is not generally recognized that there are costs involved with implementation of any conservation measure that, in some cases, could exceed the resultant benefits. On a hydrologic unit basis, there are situations (the Central Valley of California, for example) where a significant reduction in irrigation usage would achieve little overall conservation on a basin-wide basis. It would, in fact, be detrimental to certain other uses and needs—downstream salinity control and important wildlife habitats, to cite but two examples. These realities are not widely understood. Some new conflicts may develop as the conservation measures are implemented.

Instream Flows

Much greater emphasis in federal water resource planning and development, including operation of existing federal projects, is to be given to instream flow needs, particularly as related to recreation, water quality control, aesthetics, and fish and wildlife habitat.[3] There is little question that these needs have been accorded inadequate attention in the past and that greater consideration in future water allocations is justified.

However, serious conflicts are almost certain to develop—particularly on the many streams already over-committed and in states where laws do not consider such needs as beneficial or where a relatively low priority is accorded to such uses.

Enforcement of Environmental Statutes

Some twenty-six environmental statutes are listed in the Task Force report.[4] These are to be carried out more vigorously by the federal agencies involved. New rules and regulations have been issued under the National Historic Preservation Act,[5,6] and implementing procedures are being prepared. Proposed rules and regulations under the Fish and Wildlife Coordination Act[7] have been published in the Federal Register.[8]

Of the twenty-six statutes, twenty-one impact directly on the planning, development, and utilization of fresh water resources, particularly surface waters. While full attention to protection and, where feasible, enhancement of the environment is certainly warranted, enforcement of several of these statutes will add to current controversies over allocation and use of scarce water resources for multiple purposes.

Groundwater

Increased attention to groundwater resources and problems is to be given in federal and federally assisted planning and programs that impact on groundwater resources. The ultimate objective is comprehensive water management.[9] The federal water resource agencies are to be much more involved with groundwater, both internally within the federal establishment and in cooperation with the states. Appointment by the president of a broadly-based National Groundwater Advisory Commission, with a three-year life, is recommended in the Task Force report to ". . . guide and assist the individuals and cooperative efforts of Federal, State, and local governments in the alleviation or prevention of major public problems associated with the conservation, utilization and management of the groundwater resource."

There is increasing recognition on the part of many groundwater users of the necessity of some degree of groundwater management, especially in critical groundwater overdraft areas.

There is, however, rather widespread antipathy on the part of groundwater users in Texas and other states toward having the responsibility of designing and implementing management programs vested in either the state or the federal government.[10] Local control is considered best.

Groundwater management for overdraft areas is interpreted by many as requiring reduction in extractions to the degree necessary to bring the basin or aquifer into balance. This would entail severe economic dislocations where other sources of water supply are not available. However, proper management even under such continuing overdraft conditions would be beneficial.

Nonstructural Measures

The president has directed that at least one nonstructural alternative be formulated and evaluated in all federal water resource planning efforts. This implies that there must be a nonstructural solution to each water resource problem. This is by no means necessarily correct nor would nonstructural measures necessarily minimize conflicts. Flood plain management may engender serious land use conflicts.

Federal Non-Indian Reserved Water Rights

Federal non-Indian reserved rights are to be quantified.[11] Negotiation rather than litigation is to be the method of settling disputes wherever possible. Close cooperation with the states is to be maintained. Assuming that quantification will be accomplished within the limitations on reserved rights established by the U.S. Supreme Court in *United States* v. *New Mexico*,[12] this could lay to rest some of the long-standing uncertainties and conflicts concerning federal water rights versus water rights acquired under state water laws.

Inconsistencies

Dr. Howe has pointed out the ". . . inconsistencies between water policies and policies in agriculture, transportation, and inflation control." The writer would go further and say that not only are there inconsistencies but that there is not now, there never has been, and there is not likely to be in the near future a consistent, comprehensive federal water policy pursuant to which rational decision as to water resource allocations, authorizations of projects, and appropriations of funds could be made. Much of what is termed water policy in fact concerns procedural matters. Nor are there defined policies in other resource fields that water supports. Water resources are developed and used in support of other resource developments and uses–irrigated agriculture, for example. In the absence of a defined policy with regard to the future of irrigated agriculture–and there is none–it is impossible to do rational water resource planning and make rational decisions as to the proper allocation of water resources to that purpose. The same is true with regard to other resources for which water is used–fish and wildlife, for example.

Decisions as to authorizations of projects, the allocations of yield therefrom, and the appropriations of funds continue to be made each year on an ad hoc basis.

Trade-Offs

As Dr. Howe states, in considering trade-offs between the use or the reallocation of water for high value uses (such as energy production) and its use for irrigation, there are costs in addition to the direct loss in farm output that must be evaluated–possible direct and indirect regional income losses, possible reduction in employment (both direct and indirect), social costs due to reduction in farm income and employment, and loss of the amenities and "economic balance" associated with agriculture. These are important values economically, environmentally, and socially and should be fully considered in federal planning as well as by the states and local governments.

Funding

Perhaps the most critical conflict at the present time is the competition for appropriations among the many programs financed from limited public revenues. The proportion of federal funds allocated for investment in water resources—apart from appropriations under the Clean Water Act—has been declining for several years past. There appears to be little prospect of halting this trend, at least under the present administration with its emphasis on the solution of problems primarily through conservation and nonstructural measures.

Appropriations each year are made largely on an expedient basis. There has been no comprehensive national planning or even thoughtful consideration as to the future demands, broken down by regions and subregions, for water and the needs for new projects over time. Thus, there exists no logical basis for decision-making with regard to project authorizations and appropriations.

Interbasin Transfers

As Dr. Howe correctly states, "Large-scale interbasin transfer may, at some point in time, comprise an important part of rational regional or national water plans." Interbasin transfers, both intrastate and interstate, will be necessary if the overdraft and eventual exhaustion of the groundwater resources of the Ogallala Aquifer (extending from western Texas and eastern New Mexico northward to South Dakota) is to be halted. The same is true of the east side of the San Joaquin Valley, California, with a current overdraft exceeding 1.5 million acre-feet per year, where this could be accomplished by an intrastate, interbasin transfer. Without imported water supplies, the flourishing irrigated agricultural economies of national importance will shortly begin to decline with resultant severe economic dislocations, and significant environmental and social costs.

As Dr. Howe aptly points out, the costs of future interbasin projects would be very high and would be subject to a high degree of political dissension. The political, financial, economic, environmental, and social problems inherent in any interbasin transfer must be fully recognized. These may be an order of magnitude greater for an interstate transfer scheme than for an intrastate transfer.

The writer has had considerable experience with the planning and implementation of one of the largest interbasin transfer projects in the United States—the $3 billion California State Water Project. It is his conclusion that for any such scheme to be implementable, the needs of the basins from which water would be exported must be recognized and fully provided for on a first-priority basis. This is an extremely complicated matter outside the limits of discussion here.

The basic questions are: Would the totality of national, state, and local benefits—economic, environmental, and social—resulting from an interbasin transfer scheme justify the large costs involved? What degree of federal investment would be justified, since federal participation would be required in most instances? What would be necessary to fully protect and satisfy the basins and states of origin? These are fundamental considerations in the $6 million Six-State High Plains–Ogallala Aquifer regional planning study discussed in the accompanying paper.

Conclusion

Little if anything has been actually accomplished toward resolution of the conflicts in water that have been with us for many years. In fact, some may have been exacerbated under the president's water policy, even though the objectives of certain of his initiatives may be worthwhile.

Notes

1. *Press Release,* The White House, Office of the White House Press Secretary, June 6, 1978.

2. *Water Conservation: Preliminary Proposals for Federal Agency Program Changes,* Water Conservation Task Force 6a, U.S. Department of the Interior, Office of Water Research and Technology, November 9, 1978.

3. *Guidelines for Determining Instream Flow Needs,* Interagency Task Force—Instream Flows, Water Policy Implementation, May 1979.

4. *Water Policy Implementation Task Force on Environmental Statutes,* Report, U.S. Department of the Interior, Office of the Assistant Secretary for Fish and Wildlife and Parks, August 1979.

5. 16 U.S.C. 470.

6. *Federal Register,* January 30, 1979.

7. 16 U.S.C. 661-667e.

8. *Federal Register,* May 18, 1979.

9. *Ground Water Supply—Federal State Cooperation, Report of Task Force 2b,* June 4, 1979.

10. *District Groundwater Planning and Management Policies on the Texas High Plains: The Views of the People,* Frank L. Baird, Associate Professor, Department of Political Science, Texas Tech University, Lubbock, Texas, July 1976.

11. *Draft Report of Federal Task Force on Non-Indian Reserved Rights,* Task Force 5a—President's Water Policy Implementation, June 1979.

12. 438 U.S. 696, 698-700 (1978).

3
Six-State High Plains–Ogallala Aquifer Area Regional Study

Harvey O. Banks

Introduction

This comprehensive resource and economic development study was authorized by Congress October 26, 1976, in Section 193 of Public Law 94-587, with authorization for a $6 million appropriation. The moneys were appropriated in fiscal years 1977–78 and 1978–79. Responsibility for the study was assigned to the Secretary of Commerce. The Economic Development Administration (EDA) of the U.S. Department of Commerce is conducting the study on behalf of the secretary.

At the insistence of the six states involved—Colorado, Kansas, Nebraska, New Mexico, Oklahoma, and Texas—the High Plains Study Council was formed, consisting of the governors of the six states, three representatives of each state appointed by the governor, and a federal member from EDA. The council is responsible for directing the study, for preparing final recommendations, and for submittal of the final report to the secretary of commerce. In February 1977, the council adopted a plan of study that is the basis for the comprehensive study now in progress.

On September 22, 1978, EDA awarded a contract to Camp Dresser & McKee Inc. (CDM) as prime contractor and leader of the general contractor team for the study, under the author's direction as officer-in-charge and project director. Ms. Jean O. Williams, CDM vice-president, is project manager. Associated with CDM on the general contractor team are Arthur D. Little, Inc. (ADL) of Cambridge, Massachusetts, and Black & Veatch (B & V), Consulting Engineers, of Kansas City, Missouri. ADL is responsible for the agricultural-economic-social aspects of the study, and B & V for the energy aspects. Each of the six states, as subcontractors to CDM, will conduct certain portions of the study as outlined below. The U.S. Corps of Engineers, under separate contract with EDA, is conducting studies of sources, yields, and costs of potential interbasin transfers.

The study is being coordinated with other relevant studies and programs by federal, state, and local agencies, including among many others those by:

- United States Geological Survey–Ogallala Modelling Study
- United States Bureau of Reclamation–Llano Estacado Study of Playa Lakes
- U.S. Department of the Interior, U.S. Bureau of Reclamation and U.S. Fish and Wildlife Service–Platte River Habitat Study
- U.S. Department of Agriculture
- U.S. Corps of Engineers

A draft final report is to be submitted by the general contractor to the High Plains Study Council on or before March 31, 1982, and a final report on or before June 30, 1982.

The Study Area

The Ogallala Aquifer and the study area are shown in Figure 1. The study area includes some 180 counties in the six states lying wholly or partly over the Ogallala and encompasses 225,000 square miles. The area is one of the largest and most important agricultural areas in the United States as shown by Charts 1-7 appended to this paper. It includes some 20 percent of the total national irrigated acreage. There are about 90 million acres of irrigable land. The soils are deep and fertile. The climate is conducive to high agricultural production. Over 40 percent of the beef cattle supplying the tables of U.S. citizens are fed on the High Plains. The Ogallala Aquifer is now the principal source of water for irrigation. Recharge to the aquifer is very small.

Figure 1

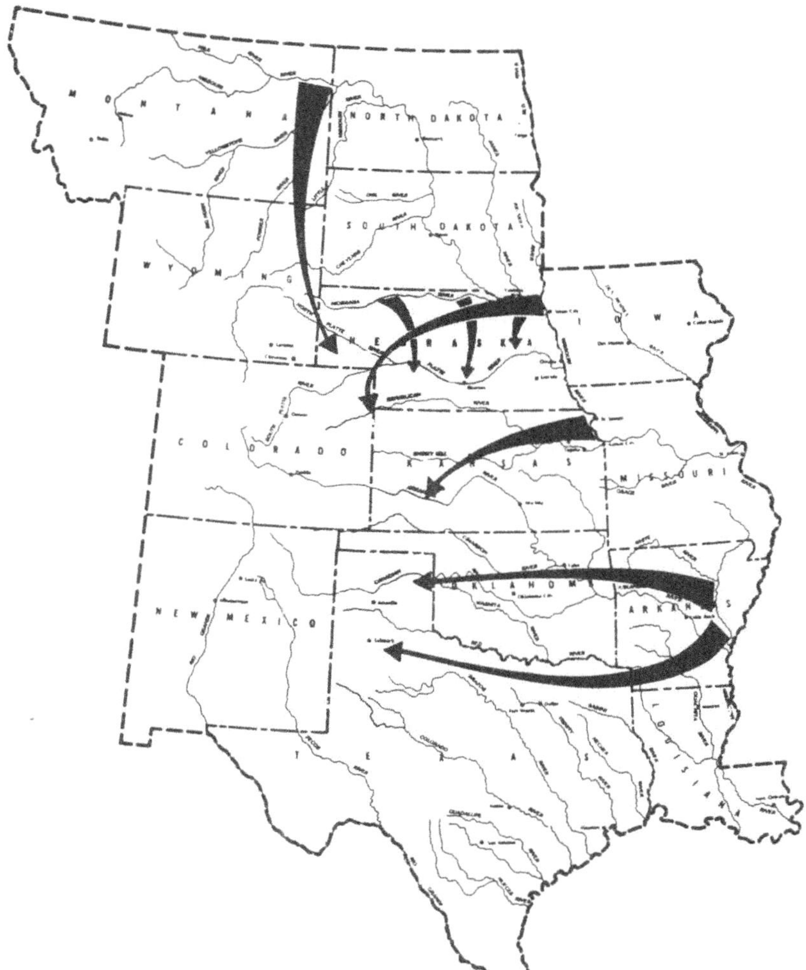

INTERBASIN TRANSFER STUDIES

The Problem

The region is faced with ultimate exhaustion of the groundwater resources unless additional water can be made available although the timing of final depletion would vary widely since the Ogallala is not uniform in thickness or in hydrologic-hydraulic characteristics. Groundwater levels are declining rapidly in most of the area, with consequent increases in pumping costs. Production of oil and gas, which has been an important aspect of the total economy of much of the area, is also declining. The price of energy for pumping irrigation water has increased rapidly. Much of the area could be forced to revert to dryland farming or be abandoned in the near future. Some farms, particularly in the south High Plains of west Texas have already reverted. Deterioration of the agricultural economy of the High Plains–Ogallala Aquifer Region would have grave consequences for the business and financial communities outside as well as those located within the region.

The Objectives

In authorizing the study, the Congress and the states recognized the problems associated with the decline and, over the long term, possible exhaustion of the Ogallala Aquifer and the economic effects of declining oil and gas reserves. The study is based on the recognition that the problems are regional in nature with potentially severe adverse national implications and that new institutions might be necessary.

The congressional objectives, as excerpted from Public Law 94-587, Section 193, are:

- to assure adequate water supplies to the area
- to assure an adequate supply of food to the nation
- to promote economic vitality of the High Plains region
- to develop plans to increase water supplies in the area
- to assure continued growth and vitality of the region

In its adopted plan of study, which is the basis for studies by the general contractor and the states, the High Plains Study Council stated the objectives as follows:

- to determine potential development alternatives for the High Plains Region
- to identify and describe the policies and actions required to carry out promising development strategies
- to evaluate the local, state, and national implications of these alternative development strategies or the absence of these strategies

The objective of the studies by the general contractor, including those by the states, is to develop factual evaluations of the several potential alternative futures or alternative development strategies for the High Plains–Ogallala Aquifer Region. This array of the region's potential and alternatives for achieving that potential will provide the High Plains Study Council, the Congress, the state legislatures, and other decision-makers a meaningful opportunity to make knowledgeable decisions as to the course this region may elect to follow and the role this region is to play in the nation's future.

As noted above, the general contractor will report its evaluations of the potential alternative futures to the High Plains Study Council, which in turn will report to the secretary of commerce with such recommendations for further action as it deems advisable. The secretary will report to the Congress.

The Study Organization

The Technical Advisory Group is composed of representatives of the principal federal agencies with interests in or involved with the study, appointed at the request of EDA. The Consulting Advisory Panel, appointed by the general contractor, comprises twelve nationally and internationally recognized experts in resource management, agriculture, economics, engineering, social analysis, and laws and institutions.

As previously indicated, CDM is responsible, as prime contractor, for management of the entire study, for the water resource, environmental, legal, and institutional studies, and for the final report. Arthur D. Little, Inc., is handling the agricultural, economic, and social aspects. Black and Veatch is conducting the energy studies. There is continuing interaction among the three firms.

Alternative Development Strategies

The following alternative development strategies, or alternative futures, have been formulated by the general contractor and approved by the High Plains Study Council for analysis and evaluation in the study.

Baseline. Continuation of current local, state, federal policies, and trends. No new state or federal programs.

Water Resources Alternatives. Alternatives are listed in order of increasing costs and increasing potential availability:

- Water Demand Management—encourage users to practice conservation through application of proven technology; provide incentives for the farmer to conserve.
- Water Demand Management—apply all advanced water and agricultural management technology on a broad scale, identifying any necessary constraints.
- Local Water Supply Management—augment water supplies at the local level with techniques such as artificial recharge, weather modification, land management, snow pack management, vegetation management, desalting, evaporation management, and others.
- Subregional Intrastate Importation Supply Management—augment local water supplies with interbasin transfers of surface water as available.
- Regional Interstate Importation Supply Management—augment local water supplies with major interbasin transfers of water, possibly providing for expansion of irrigated acreages.

Nonagricultural Development Alternatives. Nonagricultural Alternatives–development and use of available resources for purposes other than agricultural production. These alternatives are not mutually exclusive. For a particular subregion, or combination of subregions, a mix of alternatives may be found to be the best solution to meet objectives. The results of analyses and evaluations of the water resource and nonagricultural development alternatives will be compared to the adverse effects of the baseline or "no action" alternative.

It is important to note that this concept of analysis of alternative development strategies for the High Plains–Ogallala Aquifer Region was very clear in the thinking of the Congress, EDA, and the states as this study was formulated and authorized. The thrust of the regional approach embodied in the study is identification of these things:

- What choices for the region are available?
- Who must make those choices?
- What does each alternative mean in terms of possible beneficial and/or adverse economic, environmental, and social impacts?
- Are those impacts local, regional, national, or some combination?
- How, by whom, and at what costs could selected alternatives be implemented?
- To what degree would there be a federal interest and justification for federal investment?

State Research

State agencies and universities for each of the six states are now engaged in the following studies as specified by the High Plains Study Council:

A-1 State Agriculture and Farm Level Research

Project cropping patterns, agricultural output and output value, inputs and input costs, and agricultural employment and income for each alternative development strategy.

A-2 Energy Industry Impacts

Project energy production, energy requirements for irrigation, employment, royalties, and other income from energy, industry, and water requirements.

A-3 State Water Resources Evaluation and Impacts Research

A-3.a. Evaluate intrastate water resource situation; project intrastate water supplies and demands under each alternative development strategy.

A-3.b. Project economic adjustments and socioeconomic and environmental impacts at the subregional and state level resulting from changes in land use and changes in supply and uses of water, energy, and other sources under each alternative development strategy.

Results of the state research will be used by the general contractor in the regional and national analyses.

Research by General Contractor

The regional and subregional research studies by the general contractor will analyze:

B-1 Interbasin transfers–in cooperation with Corps of Engineers.

B-2 National and regional changes in commodity prices, shifts in agricultural production, changes in consumer prices and shifts in consumer expenditures.

B-3 Effects and costs of applying advanced agricultural and water management technologies to achieve more efficient use of water.

B-4 Environmental impacts.

B-5 Technologies for augmenting locally available water supplies and costs.

B-6 Legal and institutional frameworks for implementing alternative development strategies.

B-7 Crop price projections; analyses of total revenue and costs for wide range of commodity and livestock enterprise situations.

B-8 Energy prices and technology.

B-9 Impacts of transition to dryland farming.

B-10 Regional and subregional potentials for nonagricultural development.

B-11 Evaluation of alternative development strategies.

Evaluations of the alternative development strategies will be reported to the High Plains Study Council for consideration and recommendations to the secretary of commerce.

All of these studies, which were directed by the High Plains Study Council plan of study, are presently under way. The research is being fully coordinated with federal, state, and local plans and programs.

Interbasin Transfer Studies by U.S. Corps of Engineers

The Corps is studying potential sources of water that might be imported to the High Plains-Ogallala Aquifer Region, potential yields, costs of diversion, possible routings and costs for conveyance, amounts and costs of necessary terminal storage reservoirs, and environmental impacts. Possible sources and conveyance routings are shown in generalized fashion by Figure 2. The Corps studies are being carried out in close coordination with the studies of interbasin transfers being conducted by the general contractor.

Final Products of the Study

For the states involved, the region, and the nation, this study

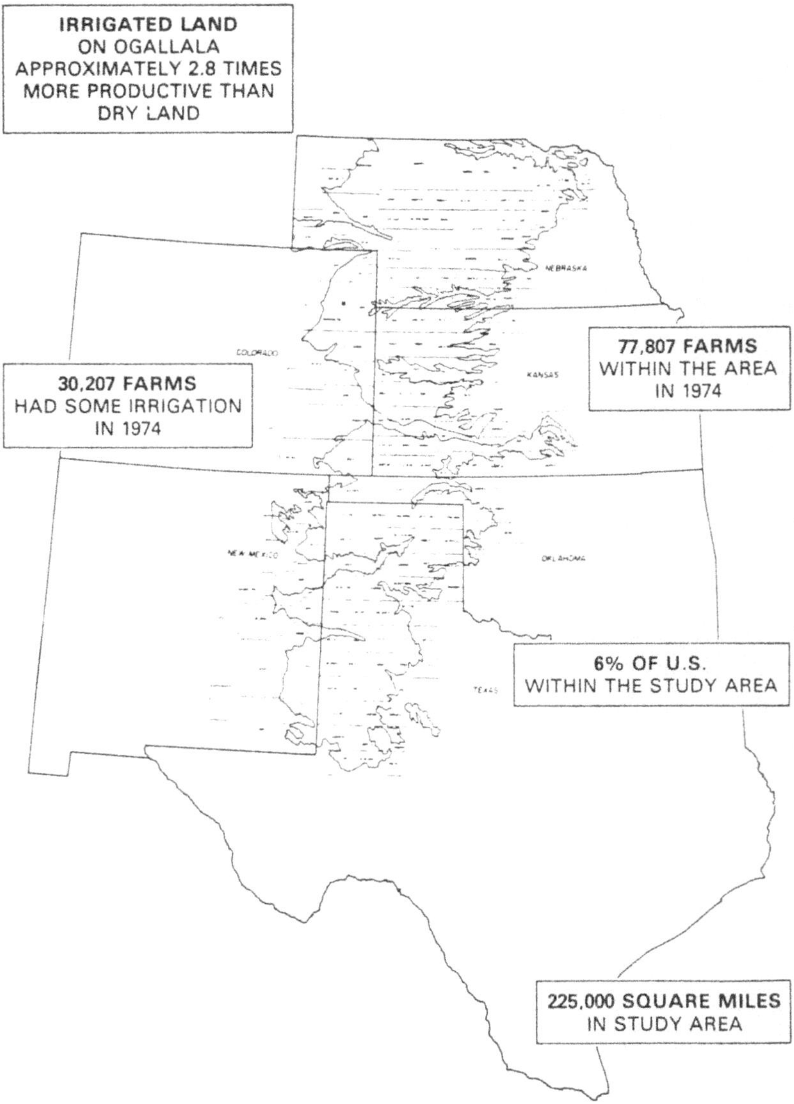

Figure 2
The Ogallala Aquifer and Study Area

will evaluate the effects of continuing existing trends and policies ("no action") and the effects of implementing each of the positive alternative development strategies on:

- the economy
- the environment
- the quality of life

The study will also determine:

- the costs of implementing each of the alternative development strategies
- the legal, institutional, financial, and organizational changes necessary to implement each of the positive alternative strategies
- the consequences of the "no action" option compared with the results of implementing positive action alternative development strategies

These study results will provide the High Plains Study Council, secretary of commerce, the Congress, state legislatures, and others an informed basis for reaching decisions as to the future of the High Plains-Ogallala Aquifer Region. Work by the general contractor must be essentially complete early in 1982.

It is planned to issue interim reports on the means, effects, and costs of applying advanced agricultural and water management technologies to achieve a more efficient use of water, and technologies for augmenting locally available water supplies and costs, during the first quarter of 1980. There are some measures that could be implemented early that would allow some degree of alleviation of the overdraft on the Ogallala Aquifer. A major interstate, interbasin project could not be completed and operational in less than twenty years.

Chart 1

HIGH PLAINS IRRIGATED CROPLAND

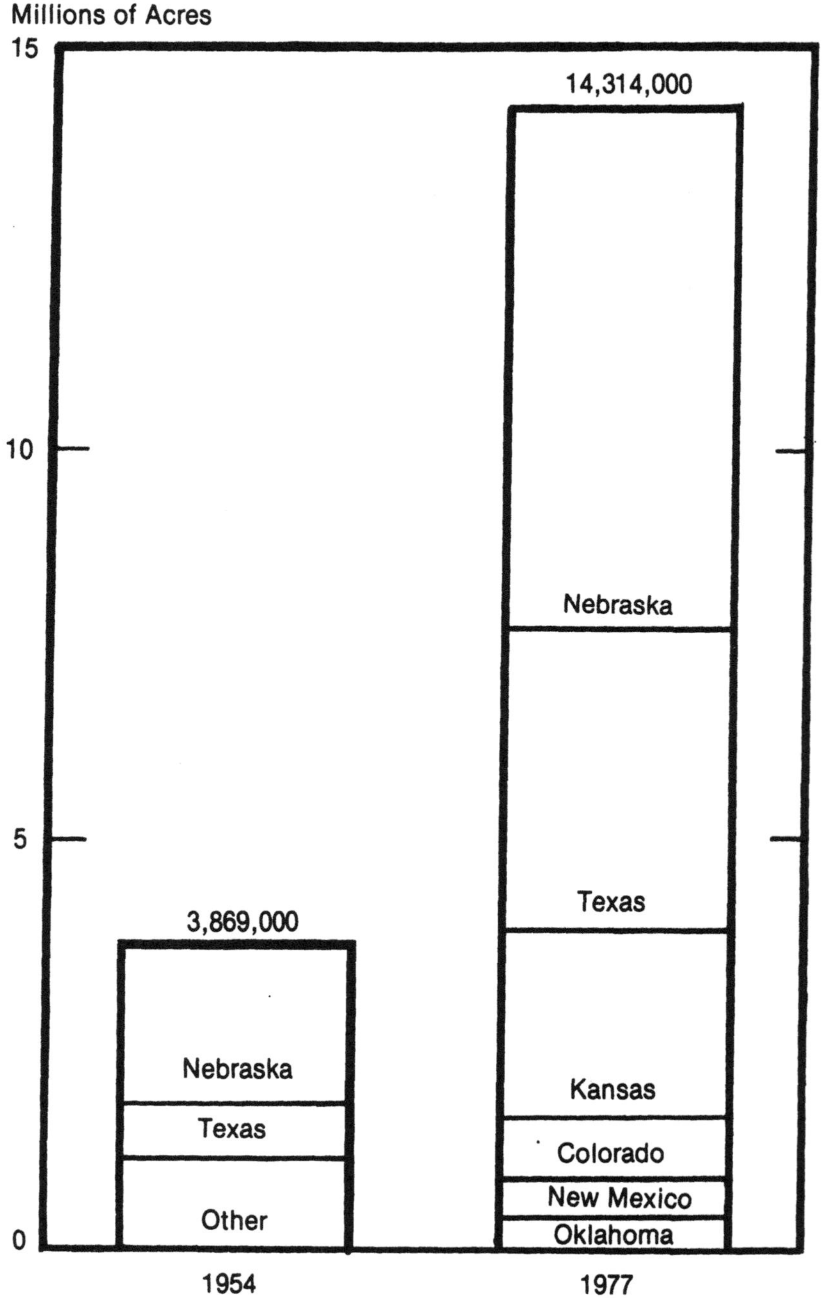

Chart 2

MAJOR HIGH PLAINS IRRIGATED CROPS

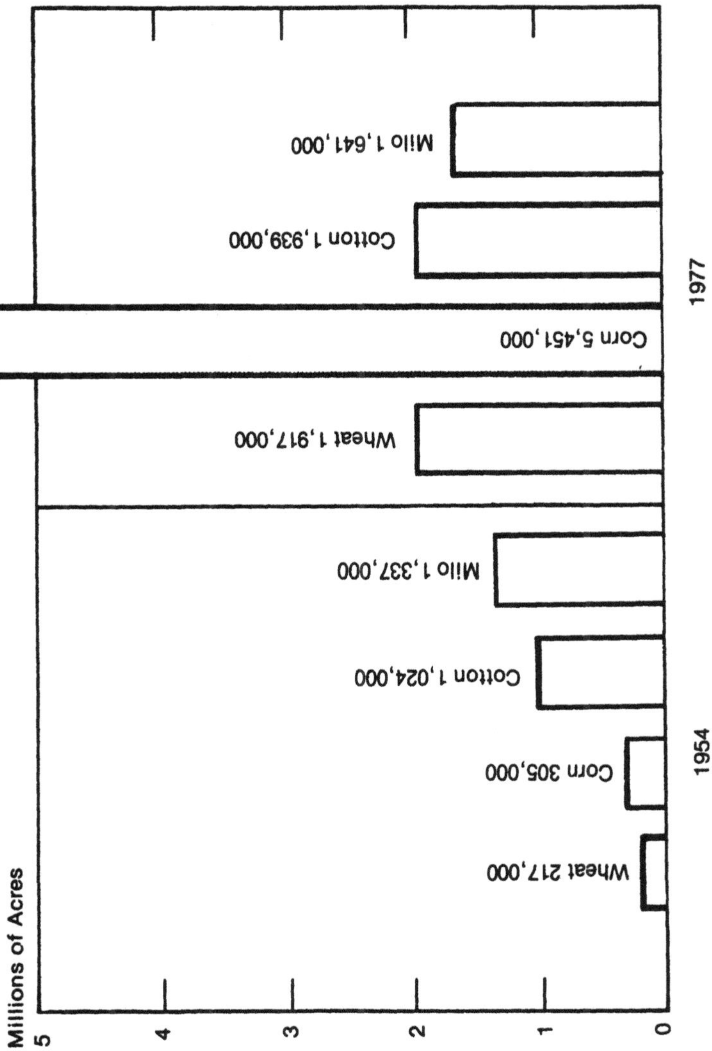

Chart 3

TYPICAL HIGH PLAINS CROP YIELDS 1977

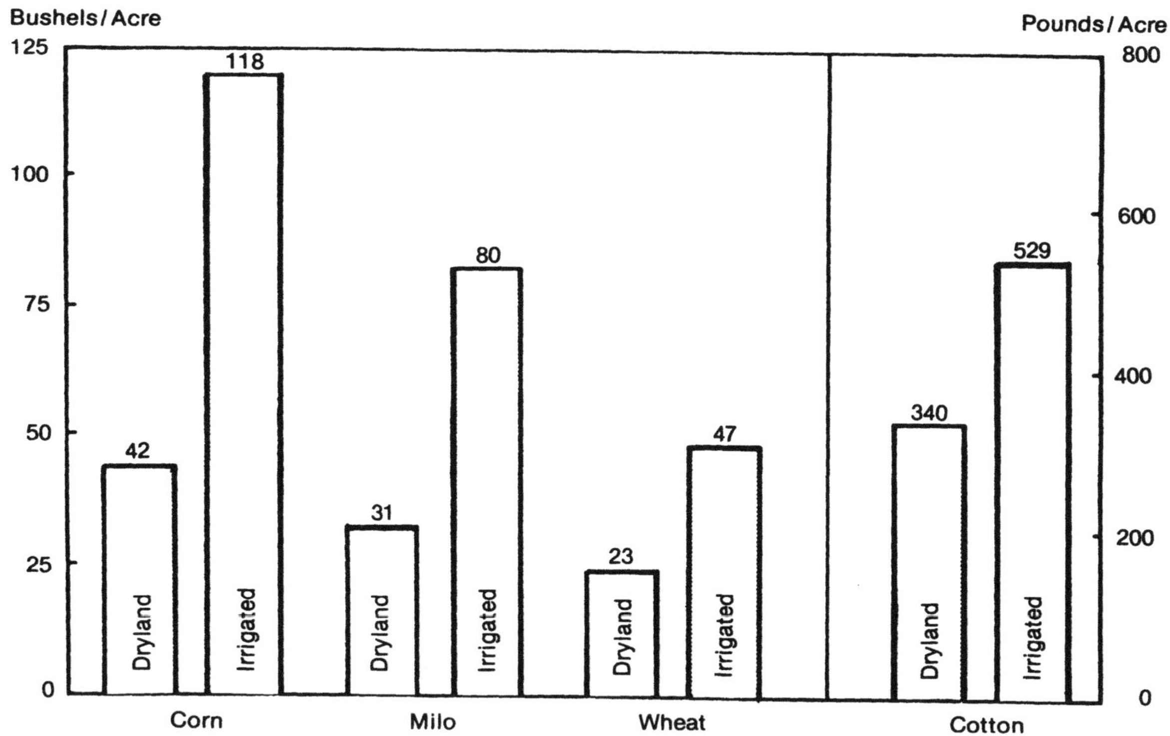

Chart 4

VALUE OF EXPORT SHARE OF TOTAL FEED GRAINS

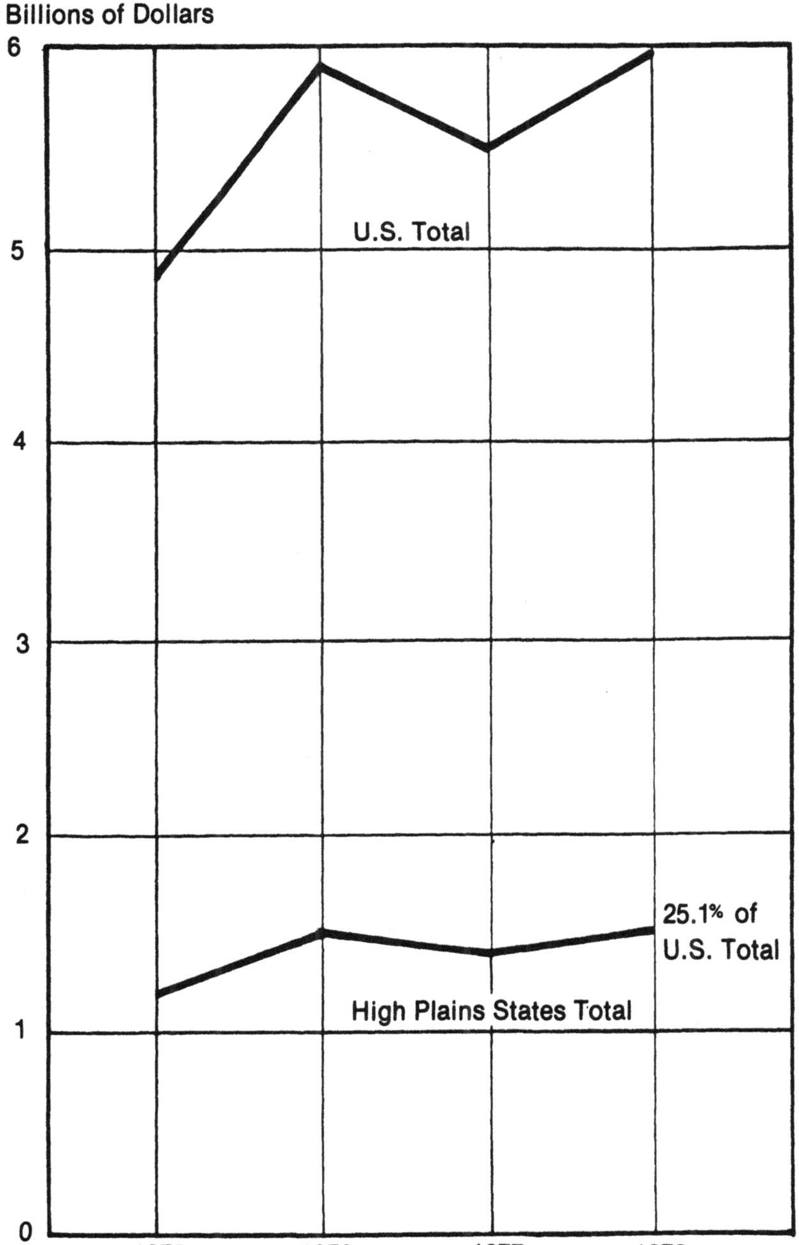

Chart 5

VALUE OF EXPORT SHARES OF WHEAT AND FLOUR

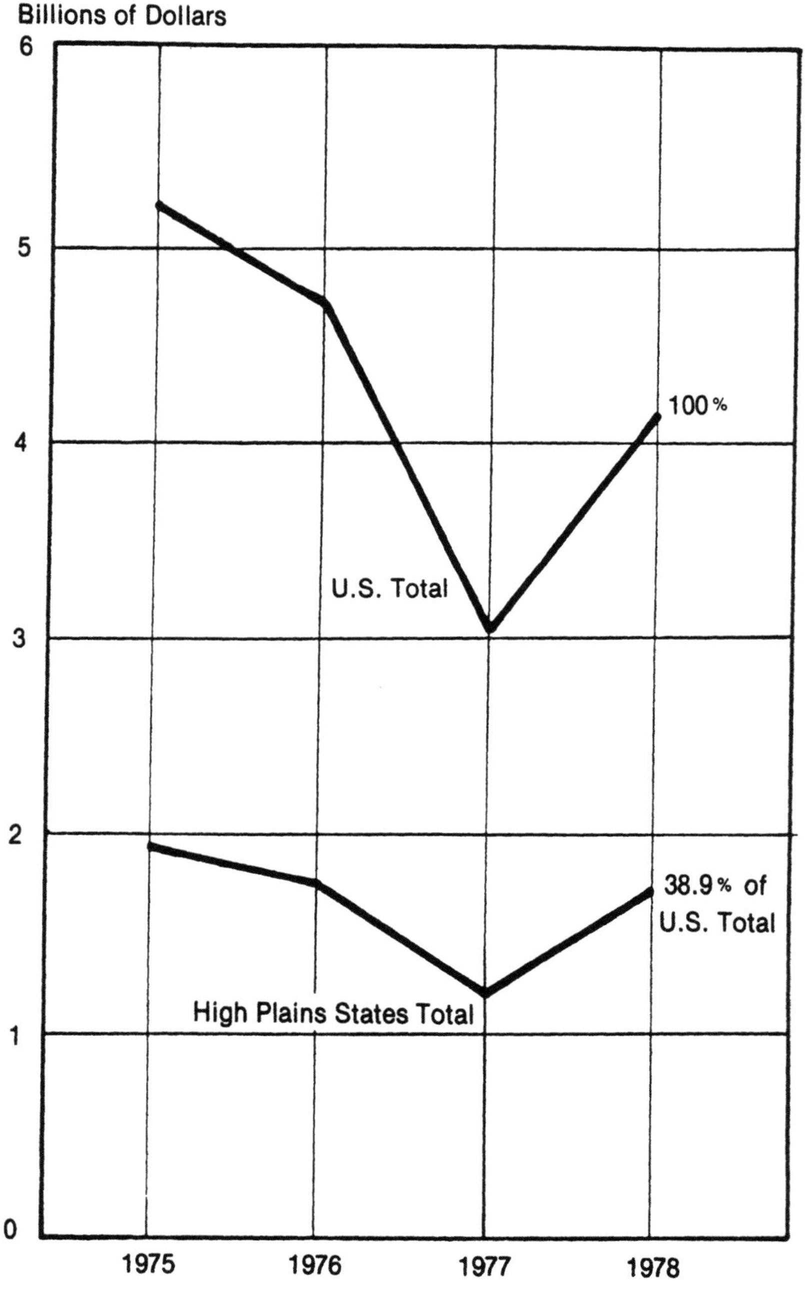

Chart 6

VALUE OF EXPORT SHARES OF COTTON, INCLUDING LINTERS

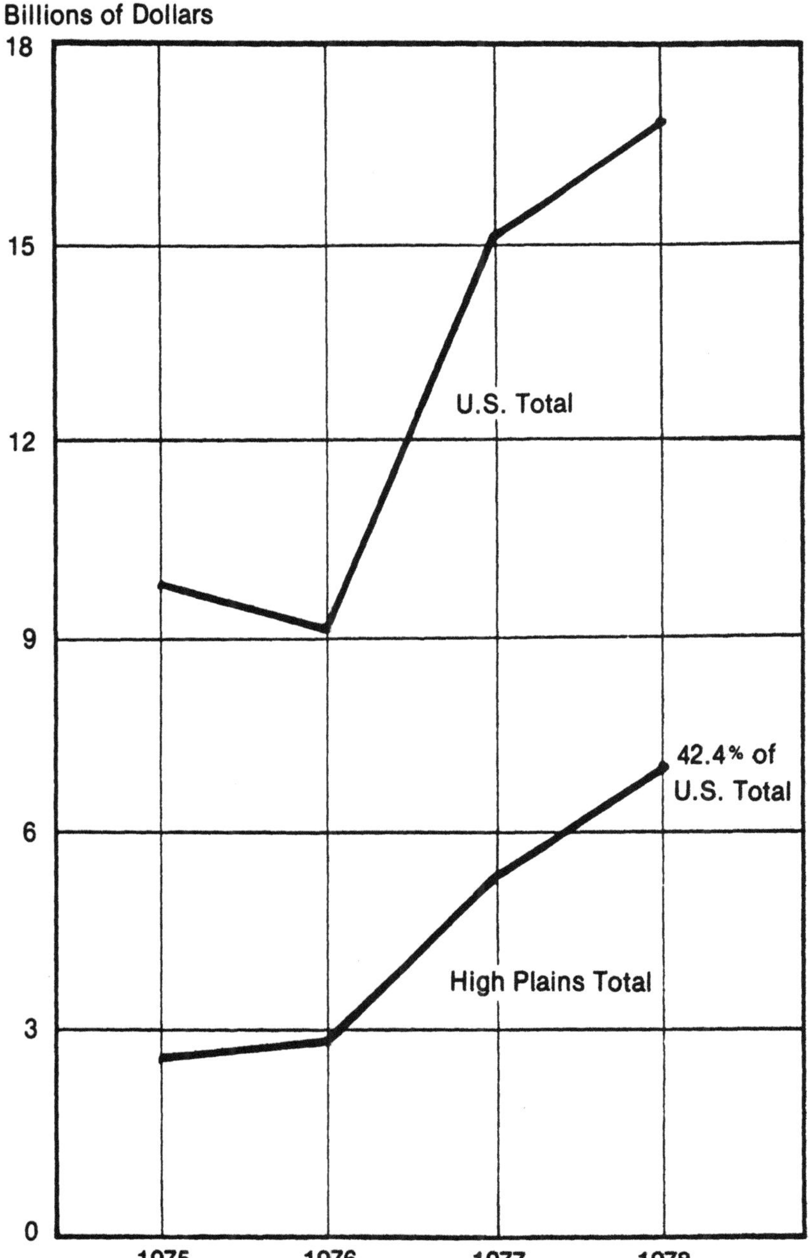

Chart 7

VALUE OF EXPORT SHARES OF ALL AGRICULTURAL COMMODITIES

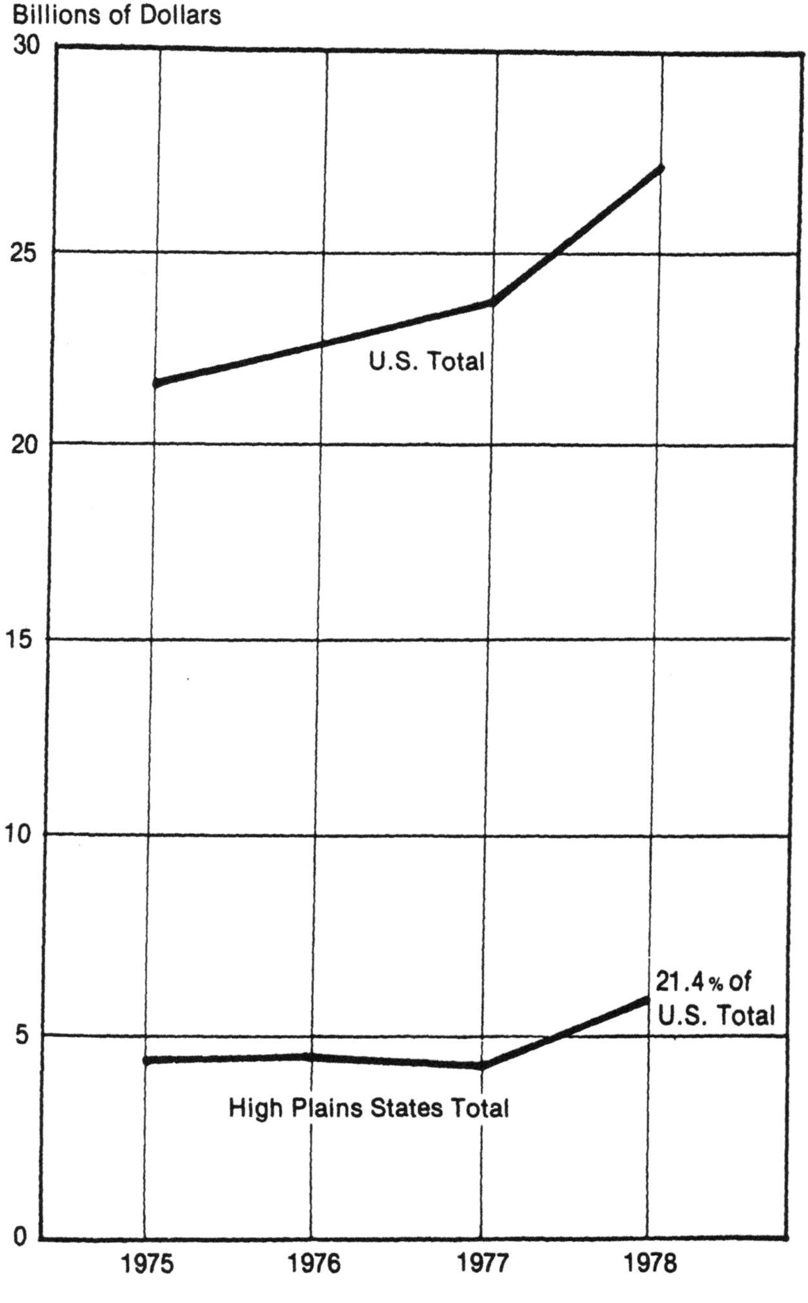

4
Issues in Determining Indian Water Rights

Richard A. Simms

Charles W. Howe and Harvey O. Banks have discussed the growing conflicts over the use of present water supplies, over future water development, and over water policy and the institutional framework for policy execution. Perhaps the area of greatest potential conflict over water in the West is the area of Indian water claims, virtually all of which remain unadjudicated. In a recent decision of the U.S. Supreme Court, Justice Brennan described Indian claims as "ubiquitous." I will attempt to explain the nature of their ubiquity and to discuss briefly the fundamental issues involved in the determination of Indian water rights.

In order to understand why there is so much antagonism between Indian claims of water rights and non-Indian water rights, the history of water-rights law in the West is important.

During the middle 1800s, title to most of the land in the western United States had been ceded to the country by various foreign powers, and until the latter part of the century, it remained in the public domain. That is, it was unencumbered, federally owned property, subject to sale or other disposition and not reserved or held back for any special governmental or public purpose. There were no private rights in the federally owned land—miners and others drawn to the West simply took up residence where they saw fit, acquiring at best incomplete, possessory interests. While water was being diverted for mining, agricultural, and domestic uses, there was no federal law governing its use. The United States simply acquiesced in the incipient development of local water law. The territories and fledgling states created their own water laws.

During the twenty-five-year period following the Gold Rush—1850 to 1875—the doctrine of prior appropriation was recognized by state or territorial statute or court decision in Arizona, California, Colorado, Montana, Nevada, New Mexico, and Wyoming. The doctrine was practiced in Utah, but not officially sanctioned. Between 1875 and 1900 the doctrine was officially expressed in the present areas of Idaho, Kansas, Nebraska, North Dakota, Oklahoma, Oregon, South Dakota, Texas, Utah, and Washington.

The doctrine itself was the natural legal consequence of water utilization in the arid and semi-arid part of the country where it was understood that there would not be enough to go around. Based upon the fact that the water supply could not meet the rapidly growing demands of industry and agriculture with the water storage facilities then available, the first appropriator of water for some beneficial purpose was recognized as having the better right to the extent of actual use. Accordingly, under state law many rivers and streams in the West became fully appropriated by the end of the nineteenth century. In times of shortage, the more recent appropriators suffered. Economically, the doctrine made good sense.

The only federal activity in western water law was manifested in the federal government's acquiescence in local state law. The Act of 1866 gave formal sanction to appropriations of water on public land, whether made before or after the act, provided they conformed to state or territorial laws. The Act of 1870 provided that all federal land patents, as well as preemption or homestead rights, would be granted subject to water rights accrued and vested under state law. Finally, the Desert Land Act of 1877 made all nonnavigable waters of the public domain public in nature, subject to the plenary control of the states, with the right in each state to fashion for itself the system of law under which water rights might be perfected. In combination, the Acts of 1866, 1870, and 1877 effected a complete cessation of the government's control over all of the nonnavigable waters arising on the public domain to the western states.

While this arrangement seemed sensible to everyone involved, the hidden implication was that there was no water left for the government with which to operate its various enclaves, which had been or might be carved out of the public domain. In 1908 the U.S. Supreme Court confronted the problem in the case of *Winters* v. *United States.* In that case the United States had reserved lands from the public domain to establish the Fort Belknap Indian Reservation. U.S. Indian policy at the time was one of assimilation–Indians were to be placed on reservations in order to be schooled in the ways of the Europeans, and ultimately when they became competitive (usually in farming) their trust lands were to have been individually allotted. In creating the Fort Belknap Reservation, however, with the planned Indian irrigation of nearly 5,000 acres, nothing was said about water, and the Indians had no right under Montana law. As a consequence, the Supreme Court held that when the United States withdrew the lands from the public domain to establish the Fort Belknap Indian Reservation, it also implied withdrawal from the then unappropriated waters of the Milk River sufficient waters to satisfy the purposes of the Indian reservation.

Because the federal government was recognized to have retained rights in "unappropriated" western waters, there appeared to be no conflict between non-Indian rights vested under state law and Indian rights under the Winters Doctrine. However, the doctrine stands for the proposition that the implied water right, with a priority as of the date of the reservation, is sufficient to satisfy the future as well as the contemporary needs of the Indians. In other words, if in 1980 an Indian tribe were to erect a paper mill, which consumes large amounts of public water, the tribe would arguably have a right to all the water needed with a priority of 1867 or whenever their reservation was created. To give you a concrete example of the present-day conflict, the Mescalero Apache tribe is located on a mountaintop reservation at the headwaters of the Ruidoso River in New Mexico, a tributary to the Pecos River. Along the Ruidoso–from the reservation at the top to Robert O. Anderson's ranch in the foothills west of Roswell–there are 2,164 acres of irrigation predicated upon water rights vested under New Mexico water law, with priorities ranging from 1867 to 1886. The average annual flow of the Ruidoso in its upper reaches is 9,640 acre-feet. This is not enough to satisfy the agricultural, industrial, and municipal needs of the non-Indians who settled there, which, as you'll recall, is why the doctrine of prior appropriation was developed. Now, however, in pending litigation to determine the nature and extent of the Mescalero Indian rights, the Indians are claiming a Winters right to over 17,000 acre-feet annually with a priority no later than 1873. If the Indian claims are sanctioned by the court, the non-Indian economy could be obliterated, at worst, and, at best, substantially affected.

The undecided issues in the determination of Indian claims tells you how large the conflict looms. They relate to priority of right, quantity of right, and the use and administration of water vis-à-vis non-Indian rights.

With the popularism and recent growth in Indian legal representation, Indian rights are being championed with considerable zeal and vigor. The Indians urge, for instance, that at least with respect to treaty reservations as opposed to executive order reservations, Winters rights are not federal water rights, but Indian water rights—that is, rights whose legal origins are aboriginal in nature. This is important in determining priority. If the Mescaleros, for instance, were determined to have an aboriginal priority instead of the date of their reservation, the doctrinal restriction to a right in unappropriated water would become meaningless. In other words, all non-Indian water rights on the Ruidoso would be subject to defeasance; to the extent Indian rights were needed beyond the annual supply, non-Indians would have to shut down.

Quantity is a major issue. *Winters* provides water sufficient to satisfy the purposes of the reservation. Non-Indian lawyers maintain that you must conceptualize the purposes contemporaneously, i.e., to satisfy comparatively modest needs. Historically, Indian reservations were to have been temporary. Today, however, the Indians uniformly assert that *Winters* provides them with enough water to maintain "a permanent tribal homeland," a concept that recently emerged from the Office of the Solicitor of the Interior and is being asserted by Justice Department lawyers in western water rights litigation. The Indians maintain that modern development objectives should form part of the basis of the determination—recreational lakes are as much within the right as traditional domestic requirements. The rights, according to the Indians, are not limited to agricultural needs, assuming the reservation was created to teach farming, but include claims for "fish and aquatic life, irrigation, recreation, domestic, municipal, and industrial uses," as the Jicarilla Apache tribe put it in another lawsuit in New Mexico. If the land was expressly reserved for sheep grazing, which requires no appreciable water, it would make no difference according to the Indians. In the words of the Jicarillas, they have a right "to impound and/or divert the use . . . the entire virgin flow run-off" of the Navajo River, "from both surface and underground sources."

The remaining issues derive from conflicts of position regarding use and administration. In *Arizona* v. *California,* in order to get around the problem of indeterminable population growth, the Supreme Court adjudicated to the Colorado River Indians the water needed to irrigate all of the practicably irrigable acreage on the reservations. The non-Indian lawyers urge that, if rights are to be quantified in such large quantities, the Indians should not be able to avail themselves of their rights until they actually need them. The Indians, on the other hand, wish to lease their rights to their non-Indian competitors in the interim—or forever, for that matter. On the Ruidoso, for example, the water conflict would be solved by the Indians leasing to the non-Indian settlers the same rights that were undone by the assertion of the Indian claims. In other words, the non-Indian economy could continue as long as the water users were considered licensees of the Indians. Similarly, it has been suggested by the Colorado River Indians that the City of Los Angeles and the other major users of Colorado River water will someday have to pay the Indians for the water that is really theirs.

While it is apparent that the potential conflicts between Indian claims and non-Indian water rights may have profound local effects, they may also have profound regional effects. Just as the federal government was negligently silent respecting water for Indian reservations, most interstate water compacts expressly disclaim any effect on the water right obligations of the United States to its Indian wards. In the Colorado River Basin there are about thirty Indian reservations consisting of about 26,000,000 acres, and yet it is apparent from the negotiating minutes of the Colorado River Commission that Indian water needs were thought to have been negligible. Modern claims mock that view. New Mexico's entitlement under the Upper Colorado River Basin Compact, for instance, is 11.25 percent of the Upper Basin's share after the deduction of 50,000 acre-feet for Arizona; assuming a full supply, New Mexico is entitled to deplete 838,125 acre-feet annually. Pursuant to the compact, any rights ultimately adjudicated to New Mexico Indians will be accounted against New Mexico's share. The combined claims of the Navajos, the Ute Mountain Utes, and the Jicarilla Apaches, however, will likely total in the millions of acre-feet. The absurd result is that the Indians would own many times New Mexico's share of San Juan River water. The non-Indians would go begging.

In conclusion, there are probably few more patent examples of the failure of government to deal with a major problem in the 200-year history of the United States. The basis of Indian water right claims derives from governmental indifference and is rooted in legal fiction—the tacit and implicit reservation of public waters. To top it off, however, the government does not appear to be changing its role. In the early phases of President Carter's formulation of a new national water policy, federal reserved water rights for all federal enclaves, including Indian reservations, were to have been treated in the same way, the primary objective being quantification at the earliest possible date to end the current uncertainty over federal claims. At the urging of Indian interests, however, Indian water rights are receiving separate treatment, which helps to perpetuate the ubiquity of Indian claims by disassociating those claims from the limitations placed on the Winters Doctrine in numerous non-Indian federal reserved right cases. The water policy concentrates on Indian water resource development instead of legislative treatment of the emerging conflicts. Historically, Congress *forgot* to address the issue. Today, the potato's gotten so hot Congress wouldn't touch it with a ten-foot pole.

5

The Quality of Water: Problems, Identification, and Improvement

John F. Timmons

Within the next two or three decades, water problems in the United States, particularly in the western region, may well constitute a greater crisis than does energy today.[1] The major difference between the water and energy crises is that there are no known physical substitutes for water in satisfying direct demands by people, but there are many known substitutes for petroleum in producing energy. This probably means we must learn how to live with our current water supply endowments through managing water in terms of its use, development and conservation.

Similarities between the present energy crisis and the expected water crisis emphasize increasing scarcities and increasing costs. Water is a necessity of life and constitutes an essential resource in most economic activities. Thus, increasing costs and scarcities of water are likely to bring profound effects upon economic progress affecting production, employment, income distribution, investment, and debt retirement in affected regions. Since approximately three-fourths of the world's area is covered with water, augmented by moisture fall and aquifers on and under the remaining one-fourth of the earth's surface, what is the basis for future concerns about water?

One answer was implied in the words of Coleridge's ancient mariner who, while dying from thirst, lamented "Water, water everywhere but not a drop to drink." This answer concerns water quality. The ancient mariner was served well by the transportation service of the ocean water that carried his ship, but the same water did not possess the quality to quench his thirst.

Irving Fox reminds us that "In the minds of many people, the existing and potential degradation of water quality is our foremost water problem" (4, p. 32). This problem is magnified by the many and increasing uses for water and their vastly different water quality requirements. The solution to water quality problems rests with water quality management. This solution provides opportunity for avoiding the expected water crisis in the future.

Limited to discussion of water quality, this paper strives (1) to describe the nature of water quality problems, (2) to investigate possible means for identifying water quality requirements for uses of water, and (3) to consider how water supplies may be managed in meeting future water quality demand requirements.

Origins and Nature of Water Quality Problems

Traditionally, water (as well as air and soil) has been used to assimilate, dilute, and recycle the residual wastes of human activity. But there are limits to the capacity of water to assimilate, dilute, and recycle all of our garbage. Currently, these limits are being violated through uses of technologies and practices associated with production, fabrication, distribution, and consumption of materials.

Presently, our use of technology affecting water quality is exceeding our ability to manage the quality of water. As an example, an estimated 30,000 chemical compounds are in use today with an estimated 1,000 new chemical substances created each year (10, p. 9). Most of these substances have been developed and put into use without adequate provision for their effects upon water quality. These are only examples of some of the substances and materials that may affect water quality.

Historically, natural resource scarcity has been interpreted in measures of quantities or resources, i.e., gallons of water, depth of soil, barrels of oil, etc. Increasingly, however, we are realizing that scarcity of water and other resources is largely a function of quality. This realization is part of a much larger syndrome developing in our culture that holds qualities are, within limits, more important than mere quantities. This syndrome is rejecting largeness and quantities in favor of qualities. For example, the longest river, the largest reservoir, the largest university, and the largest corporation, which Americans have bragged about in the past because of largesse or efficiency, are under serious indictment.

The total quantity of water, for example, may be abundant or even superfluous, but we may not have available sufficient water of a particular quality to satisfy a particular use-demand. The water may be too salty—as was the case with the ancient mariner—too hot, too toxic, etc. for a particular use. As a consequence, a use process may be made more costly, a use may be diminished, or a use may be precluded entirely because requisite quality is lacking, even though there is an abundant quantity of water in the aggregate.

As state and national governments proceed to take action in water quality management, costs of quality improvement are likely to meet resistance from many of the same people who previously supported quality enhancement efforts. As costs of pollution control press on producers, as prices of products reflecting pollution control costs press on consumers, as pollution control taxes press on taxpayers, and as pollution control measures restrict individual freedom in resource use, voluntary support and enthusiasm for water quality improvement may well diminish.

Such resistances may thwart quality improvement unless facts are ascertained and made available to people regarding (1) proposed water quality standards, (2) costs of achieving these standards, (3) benefits from quality improvements, (4) incidences of costs and benefits in terms of who pays them and who receives them in both short and long terms, and (5) nature and effects of antipollution regulations and controls upon individual freedom and choice (15).

These issues will be and are being decided in legislative, executive, and judicial processes of government. However, under our form of government, support for and enforcement of these decisions rest with the general citizenry. Their support and compliance in turn depend upon how well citizens are informed regarding these very important yet very complicated issues. How well people are informed, in turn, depends upon availability of relevant information and upon how well this knowledge is made available to citizens. As I understand it, this is an important purpose of this conference.

As a citizen, I am deeply concerned about the deterioration of our water quality. At the same time, I am optimistic concerning our ability to produce the facts and analyses needed in developing remedial policies and programs. Such policies and programs should seek (1) to improve the quality of our water and (2) to engender widespread understanding and acceptance by diversely affected groups of people, concommitantly. This is not an easy task.

In our attempt to comprehend and interpret water quality as a major public policy goal and in its relationship with other public goals, three difficult but strategic questions arise and demand answers. First, what are the measures of water quality that can serve as policy and program goals and at the same time engender widespread and continuing public understanding and support? Here I am thinking about the general nature of standards and targets for water similar to those needed in defining and achieving such goals as economic growth, full employment, income distribution, and inflation control. Second, what are the costs, both monetized and nonmonetized, of achieving and failing to achieve specified standards of water quality? Third, who pays the costs, with and without achievement of standards of water quality, and who gets the benefits?

Answers to these questions are difficult, but I believe they are essential in developing policy and programs in water quality management. In pursuing answers to these questions, it becomes apparent that the nature and level of standards are directly related to the nature and magnitude of costs. The nature of costs, in turn, determines their incidences, that is, on whom the costs will fall. The nature, magnitude, and incidence of costs affect the determination of quality standards and their achievement. In answering these questions, possible trade-offs and side effects with respect to other national goals, including production, full employment, inflation control, and income distribution will be revealed (3).

Water Quality Variability

The quantity theory of water emphasized in and perpetuated through the various doctrines of water rights, with few exceptions,[2] has tended to ignore variations in water quality and to treat all water alike. However, instead of being homogeneous, water is extremely heterogeneous in terms of its properties, its technologically permitted uses, and its economically demanded uses.

It becomes helpful, at least from an economic viewpoint, to regard water as differentiated in kinds and grades determined by its quality (1). Thus, supply and demand functions of water are each regarded as consisting of numerous quality oriented segments, each segment characterized by relatively homogeneous quality. This concept is further examined in the following two topics concerned with quality variations in supplies and in demands.

Quality Variations in Water Supplies

Water's chemical formula, H_2O, has tended to impute a homogeneity to each unit of water that does not exist. Actually, water is a very complex resource with large variations in its nature from one unit of supply to another unit that affect its use (14). Water occurs in three distinct forms: solid, liquid, and gas. Most substances contract when frozen, but water expands. Water possesses a very high heat capacity and surface tension. It dissolves many compounds that thereafter remain in solution. Thus, water has been called the "universal solvent." The character of water has been further complicated by the discovery of three isotopes for both hydrogen and oxygen that form thirty-three different substances.

In addition to its indigenous characteristics, water serves as a vehicle of transport for many exogeneous materials that become introduced into water through natural as well as human actions. Suspended silt from soil erosion is one of these materials that through adsorption and absorption serves as a transport agent for numerous residuals from fertilizers, pesticides, and other compounds. Thus, various water sources and supply segments possess different properties that must be analyzed in terms of the uses to be made from the water.

Quality Variations in Water Demands

Various demands for water require different water properties and vary in their toleration of particular properties (13). For example, living cells may require the presence of certain minerals in water, whereas battery cells may not tolerate the same minerals. Even organisms vary in their mineral requirements and toleration of minerals. Quality of water must necessarily be viewed in terms of a particular use if quality is to be manageable. Different qualities are required (or tolerated) for animal consumption, navigation, power, irrigation, food processing, air conditioning, recreation, manufacturing, and other uses of water. Even within each of these major categories, demands are specialized. Within manufacturing, for example, beer, aluminum, paper, and synthetic fiber production each possess important quality differentiations.

Water quality suited for one use may be absolutely unsuited for another use. Thus, it appears there is little, if any, relevance for a universal water quality standard. Instead, quality standards should be developed in relation to specific uses to be made of particular water supplies at particular points or periods of time in the process of satisfying specific human wants. Such differentiations will likely extend to segments of the same water source, be it a stream, a lake, or an aquifer. In other words, the quality mix of a particular water supply must be analyzed in terms of uses to which it is put (12).

Projections for water demand are basic and necessary in providing essential elements of a normative and predictive framework for planning and carrying out water policy. However, these projections should not be considered as aggregates. On the contrary, they must be disaggregated into segmented quality differentiations derived from relevant use demand requirements (1).

Included as demand by uses are qualities by amounts of water demanded. Also included are the spatial and temporal occurrences of quality-linked supplies available for serving quality-linked amounts to the estimated demands. Finally, the cost dimension is involved in terms of least cost alternatives for gearing (bringing or keeping) supply qualities to demand qualities.

Regarding demands, one further point should be considered. This involves a more refined differentiation into direct demand and derived demand components. Such a differentiation becomes important in systems analysis involving regional accounts as well as in those allocations which must be made through ordinal rather than cardinal criteria. Thus, not only must we undertake to solve the complex problem of determining technical coefficients for water used as an input but also the even more difficult one of specifying the demand for water as a "final product," with all of the difficulties inherent in nonquantifiable parameters which must be ordered by ordinal criteria.

Identification of Water Quality Demand Requirements

Qualities of water may be affected by human use or they may be produced in the natural state. One set of qualities within a natural supply of water may satisfy a particular use but may preclude another use. Furthermore, one use of water may leave a residue or an effluent within the water it has used that diminishes or precludes another use and that increases the cost of subsequent use of the same water.

This would constitute water pollution, which is a supply related concept. In economic terms, water pollution means a change in a characteristic(s) of a particular water supply such that additional costs, either monetized or nonmonetized, must be borne by the next use and the next user either through diminishing or precluding the next use or through forcing the next use (1) to absorb more costs in cleaning up the residue left by the initial use or (2) to develop a new source of water supply.

Externalities and Water Quality

One user of water may be in a position to retain the benefits from use while shifting costs to other users by lowering water quality. If that user had to bear the shifted costs, the motivation would be to use the water in a manner consistent with quality demanded by other users.

On the other hand, a user of water may be in such a position that if an outlay is made to maintain or improve water quality, the benefits from the outlay which shift to other users could not be captured by the user. If such benefits could be captured, the user would be motivated to make outlays which would maintain or improve the quality of the water after it leaves that use. Such terms as "side effects," "spillovers," "fallout," or "free-rider" have been applied to such shifts of costs and benefits.

These conditions are termed externalities by economists. The rationale for this term is that the consequences of the actions are external to the firm or industry responsible for the actions. Externalities are classified as economies and diseconomies. Beneficial effects are called external economies and harmful effects are called external diseconomies. Both have in common the phenomenon that the incidences of the effects are shifted beyond the user that causes them. The reason for this shift may be of either spatial, structural, or temporal origins, or a combination of reasons.

For example, a nuclear reactor in power generation uses water to disperse heat. If the increase in temperature adversely affects another use, say fish reproduction and growth, this effect is an externality of the power plant—in this case, an external diseconomy. We call it thermal pollution. On the other hand, if the effect of heat dispersion by the power plant is to warm up the water so that the water is more useful for swimming, an externality would be created; this instance would constitute an external economy since the next use would be favorably affected.

Although the problem of external economies is important, external diseconomies appear far more important in water quality management. For example, wastes from manufacturing or from chemical fertilizers, pesticides, and livestock moving into streams, lakes, or aquifers may foreclose other uses entirely or make other uses more expensive to undertake. Or they may endanger life and health of human beings.

Kneese concludes that "a society that allows waste dischargers to neglect the offsite costs of waste disposal will not only devote too few resources to the treatment of waste but will also produce too much waste in view of the damage it causes" (9, p. 43).

Externalities are powerful concepts developed by economists as a body of theory within welfare economics, with tools of analysis having application to water quality. Starting with the work of Pareto, published in 1909, to the work of A. C. Pigou, published in 1920, many economists have devoted attention to development of theory and tools that may now be transferred to water quality analysis. Pigou's work was motivated in part by the apparent adverse effect of smoke from English factories upon the English laborers and their families, an external diseconomy.

Water Quality Criteria

What does this reasoning have to do with developing quality standards for water? It suggests two necessary criteria, which are (1) the next use test and (2) the test of reversibility.

The first criterion, the next use test, holds that undesirable quality changes (or pollution) occur when the effluent or effect of an initial use adversely affects the next use to which the water may be put in meeting needs of people (i.e., quenching thirst, swimming, fabricating aluminum, etc.). If there are no adverse effects on any next use(s), then there is no cause for concern and no particular need for setting a quality standard. There are no costs shifted to another use. On the other hand, if the initial use creates adverse effects (external diseconomies), monetized or nonmonetized, on the next use(s), then the quality standard should reflect the costs, monetized or nonmonetized, to the next use as well as benefits gained in the initial use. This approach constitutes the basis for the "next use" model for deriving and testing environmental quality standards and has been applied in several of our recent Iowa studies on water quality (6, 7, 11, 16).

The second criterion, that of reversibility, means that a use of water should not result in an irreversible state of quality.[3] This criterion appears desirable in the formulation of quality standards in order to retain options for water use that may not be apparent at the moment but that may become viable through future technological developments and increases in demand. If irreversibility of water quality is permitted, certain future use options may become foreclosed.

Through application of these two criteria, two deductions may be made that possess important implications for policy and programs. First, only the irreversible criterion may be used as the basis for universal water quality standards. Second, the next use criterion means that quality standards will vary from area to area, from time to time, and from use to use, depending upon the actual and potential existences and requirements of other next uses. The latter deduction appears most likely to constitute a major concern for developing water quality standards for policy and programs.

Now, let us turn our attention to possible answers to the second question posed earlier, namely, "What are the costs, monetized and nonmonetized, associated with achieving or failing to achieve specified standards of quality?" The next use approach described earlier in developing quality standards also has a role to play in identifying, measuring, and assigning costs associated with water quality.

Water pollution, as defined earlier, results in additional costs to the next use(s) in the form of a reduction of quality of water for the next use, if there is a next use. If there is not a next use, there is no need for a quality standard and therefore no costs of pollution control arise, as stated previously.

Application of Water Quality Criteria

To illustrate application of the next use model to developing and costing environmental quality standards, let us take an example from a study in the Nishnabotna River Basin of western Iowa (11). Present use of resources for agriculture production in this basin delivers an estimated 10,600 milligrams of suspended sediment per liter of water annually to the river channel.[4]

Let us first assume that the two previously stated criteria, when applied in this basin, reveal that (1) soil and water resources used by agriculture are kept within reversible limits and (2) no other next use of the water is adversely affected by agricultural use. It would follow, then, that the optimum use of the basin resources for agricultural purposes is also optimum for the area, the state, and the nation insofar as the suspended sediment load of the watercourse is concerned. In other words, there are no external diseconomies generated by agricultural use.

Next, let us introduce additional uses of water in the stream in the form of (1) municipal demands for potable water, (2) warm water fish habitat, and (3) contact recreation (i.e., skiing and swimming), which would tolerate only an estimated 150, 75 and 37.5 mg/l of suspended sediment, respectively.

Through application of parametric linear programming to the quality constraint of suspended sediment per liter, the annual direct costs to agriculture within the basin in meeting the quality standards for the three specified next uses were estimated (in 1970 dollars) at $9.59, $9.66, and $9.74 million, respectively. This would translate into an average annual cost of around $2,400 per farm operating unit in the watershed.

In another study, effects on net farm income caused by direct outlays and reduced income (opportunity costs) from complying with these specific water quality standards ranged from estimates of $1,200 to $14,000 (in 1977 dollars) per farm per year, depending upon factor costs including energy costs, product prices, technologies applied, delivery ratios, and other variables (16).

Since the watercourse also serves as a possible transport agent for residues from pesticides, fertilizers, and feedlots that are found in the basin, the above method could be used to generate quality standards with their associated costs for each type or combinations of types of pollutants found in the water and in or on suspended silt in relation to quality demands for next uses.

Similarly, this method of analysis could be extended to analyze air quality standards within an airshed where silt by itself, or other pollutants for which silt serves as a transport agent, are found. If additional quality standards were established for these other pollutants in air and water other than the suspended silt actually used in the above studies, the pollution control costs to farm operating units would be increased proportionately.

This method demonstrates a procedure for developing quality standards along with the costs of achieving the standards. Furthermore, the analysis helps test water quality standards for next uses as to whether or not pollution control measures are worth the costs. In the process, trade-offs between uses and levels of pollution control could be developed.

Let us now turn our attention to possible answers to the third question stated earlier, namely, "Who pays the costs and who receives the benefits, with and without achievement of standards of environmental quality?" Continuing with our river basin analysis, let us examine who might be expected to pay the costs if the next use were contact recreation carrying the most stringent quality requirement (i.e., 37.5 mg/l sediment), which would cost the watershed's agriculture an estimated $9.74 million annually (in 1970 dollars) and which would average about $2,400 per farm operating unit annually (11).

There are several possible groups on whom these costs might fall, including (1) initial use (farm operating units), (2) next uses (contact recreation, fishing propagation, municipal water supply), (3) consumers of products and/or services produced by initial use and/or next uses, (4) taxpayers, and (5) combinations of groups.

Frequently, the assertion is made that the polluter, in this case the initial use, agriculture, should bear all the costs of farm operations, including any externally imposed costs on other uses. However, if there were no other next uses and if the soil and water resources remained within the reversible range, there would be no costs assignable against the initial use (or any other use) since no water quality standards would be violated. In this instance, the watercourse with its 10,500 mg/l suspended silt load might be performing a beneficial use in diluting, disintegrating, and recycling residues of the initial use.

Also, it is usually assumed that increased costs to a firm resulting from pollution abatement would be passed to consumers in the form of higher prices for the products.[5] However, for the agricultural entrepreneur, this option is not available since farm firms tend to be price takers, not price makers, operating as they do in the most nearly perfectly competitive of all real world markets.

Ultimately, however, higher costs of production caused by pollution control measures, unaccompanied by product price increases, would tend to force farmers, presumably marginal farmers, out of farming. Eventually, production would tend to decrease, which would in turn tend to be accompanied by increases in product prices which would indirectly reflect pollution control costs.

If pollution control measures result in reductions in the use of pesticides, fertilizers, and other production-increasing technologies, yields per acre and yields per labor hour would presumably decrease, causing increasing per unit output costs which would most likely be reflected in reduced production followed by increased prices to consumers.

Such consequences of setting and enforcing pollution control measures could be expected to result in reverberations beyond agriculture and the consumer. For example, industries providing technological inputs in the form of fertilizers and pesticides would be affected. Also, agricultural exports from the U.S. could be reduced, with effects on the terms of trade between the U.S. and other nations.

It should be noted that if one state legislated pollution control costs on its producers of a product that was also produced in other states wherein producers were not encumbered with such costs, the state with the legislation would discriminate against its own producers and tend to benefit producers in other states in terms of their net income.

Quality Measurement Problems

Along with externalities, the problem of measurement is crucial in water quality management. Traditionally, water has not been allocated through the market system as have most other factors, products and services. Certainly, water quality is not reflected in market values to an appreciable extent. Judging from the changing size of national, state, municipal, and other governmental budgets, an increasing share of the nation's resources is allocated through institutional rather than through pricing processes. This creates problems in resource management but these problems are not unfamiliar to the resource economist and are not outside the science of economics.

Professor Gaffney has expressed relevant views on this problem as follows:

> Economics, contrary to common usage, begins with the postulate that man is the measure of all things. Direct damage to human health

> and happiness is more directly "economic," therefore, than damage to property, which is simply an intermediate means to health and happiness . . . money is but one of many means to ends, as well as a useful measure of value. . . . "Economic damage" therefore includes damage to human functions and pleasures. The economist tries to weigh these direct effects of people in the same balance with other costs and benefits (5, p. 38).

There exist four major alternatives for dealing with the measurement problems in water quality management: (1) expand and create market mechanisms for differential water pricing by qualities or grades, (2) develop institutional pricing through synthesized market prices and costs as weights assignable to water grades or qualities, (3) take legal action through legislation and/or executive order with a public welfare basis, and (4) combinations of the three.

Achieving Water Quality Supplies to Satisfy Demand Quality Requirements

According to Irving Fox, "The institutional structure bearing upon water quality preservation and enhancement, although varying somewhat from state to state, may be briefly characterized as follows" (4, p. 32), and I paraphrase his characterizations. First, persons damaged by water pollution may seek redress in the courts under common-law procedures. Second, states may enact waste discharge regulations through either effluent standards or stream standards with federal government approval of standards for interstate waterways. (In addition, I would add actions by state departments of environmental quality and the federal Environment Protection Agency and other governmental pollution control agencies, to set and enforce water quality standards.) Third, tax incentives could be provided by state and federal governments to encourage reduction in waste discharges. Fourth, grants and loans from federal and state agencies could aid in construction of waste treatment facilities. Fifth, organized groups representing a wide array of interests may influence formal decision-makers.

A decade ago, Fox concluded from his examination of the institutional structure for water quality management:

> It would appear that a basic deficiency in the institutional structure for water quality management is that it fails to illuminate (a) the technical opportunities for improving quality in the most economical fashion and (b) the alternative arrangements for distributing costs and returns so that a basis for agreeing upon an appropriate pattern will be available for consideration. In addition it seems questionable, at least, that the decision-making machinery operates with dispatch and efficiency; the implementing arrangements, for the most part, are incapable of operating integrated regional plans, and feedback mechanisms are of limited effectiveness (4, p. 34).

More recently, Anderson et al. have attacked regulatory forms of quality determination and enforcement:

> Direct regulation, relying heavily upon centralized standard setting and enforcement, is vulnerable to inefficiency, enforcement difficulties, and unpenalized delay. As Ward Elliott has remarked, "direct regulation is geared to the pace of the slowest and the strength of the weakest." The shortsightedness of current programs suggests beginning a search for programs which emphasize more than end-of-pipe controls, capital-intensive solutions brought about by massive subsidies, and technical standard-setting for a variety of sources of environmental harm by large federal and state bureaucracies (2, p. 9).

Looking to the future, there exist several approaches to managing water quality supplies in satisfying water demand quality requirements. Returning to the reasoning developed earlier in the next use concept, there are five options implicit in the concept as follows:

1. The polluter (first user) assumes full cost of external diseconomies generated, thus motivating the polluter to reduce pollution.
2. The polluter (first user) shifts water use to other sources (or other technologies) from which external diseconomies causing pollution do not arise.
3. The next user assumes costs of the polluter's external diseconomies and proceeds to clean up the water quality to the level required by the next user's use demand.
4. The next user shifts water use to another source that remains unpolluted (or to other technologies) in terms

of the next user's quality demand requirement.

5. The polluter (first user) and the next user(s) join efforts and share costs in improving the water quality to the level required by the next user's demand quality.

Traditionally, the third option has been followed, that is, the next user of water assumes the costs of the polluter's external diseconomies and proceeds to clean up the water to the quality level that satisfies the next user's quality demand. This has meant that the polluter (first user) has used water uneconomically, all users considered, since the polluter did not pay the full cost for water pollution. It has also meant that the next user had to pay an additional cost increment which was probably passed to consumers of the product, depending upon market conditions.

From an economic viewpoint, the first option possesses certain advantages. The first user, the polluter, might bear full cost for use of the water in maintaining a level of quality which meets the needs of the next user. Economists have been giving this option attention for many years. For more than a decade, Kneese and others have been concerned with effluent charges geared to the achievement of water quality goals (9).

Recently, economists have teamed up with lawyers to develop means for environmental quality management relying heavily upon economic incentives. According to Anderson et al.:

> In this strategy, a legislature authorizes a money charge on environmentally harmful conduct; by raising the costs of continuing that conduct, the charge helps persuade the entity causing the harm to adopt less costly, more environmentally acceptable means of achieving its goals. Charges could be used in this way to combat a great variety of environmental problems (2, p. 1).

These charges provide economic disincentives to pollute. The authors point out that charges in pollution control have long been associated with water quality enhancement proposals and action in European countries and the United States. Applied specifically to water, these charges fall into the following categories: (1) "effluent charges intended to cause sources to reduce their discharges enough so that legislatively set water quality goals would be achieved," (2) "use of charge revenues to finance quality standards or other goals," and (3) "charges in conjunction with effluent standards" (2, p. 1).

Although the charges approach to water quality achievement has been used in Czechoslovakia, the Ruhr Valley in West Germany, East Germany, Hungary and other countries throughout the past decade, the United States remains in the proposal stage. Under two recent proposals, known as Meta System and Bower-Kneese, the Federal Water Pollution Control Act's 1983 standards would be replaced with effluent charges (2, p. 66). The Meta System is designed to achieve the same level of ambient quality as would the 1983 standards, but using a charge mechanism. The latter system (Bower-Kneese) is intended to establish the principle of polluters paying for their use of public resources and to provide incentives to enhance abatement levels after achievement of the 1977 standards (2, pp. 66–67).

Summary

Increasing degradation of water quality is rapidly becoming our foremost water problem and threatens to succeed energy as a national crisis in the future. Water quality degradation is exacerbated by increasing demands for quality water and by the proliferation of technologies and substances polluting water supplies. Traditionally, water has been used to absorb, dilute, and recycle residuals and wastes of civilizations. Currently, capacity of water to perform these garbage functions is being exceeded.

The quantity theories of water contained in our water rights systems have not focused attention on water quality. However, aggregate supply functions of water are becoming meaningless and superseded by capacity of particular water supplies to meet quality-oriented demands within particular regions.

In managing quality-linked supplies of water, three important questions arise. These pertain to (1) measures of water quality consistent with water quality demands and with other goals of the economy, (2) costs of achieving and failing to achieve specified levels of water quality, and (3) who pays the costs and who gets the benefits of water quality enhancement.

Historically, polluters have been able to shift the cost of pollution to other subsequent users of water. This behavior has resulted in serious deterioration of water quality and misallocation of resources. Current water quality enhancement policies and programs have concentrated on the establishment and enforcement of quality standards. These procedures have brought only limited success.

Current proposals would create economic incentives to improve water quality and economic disincentives to pollute water through a system of charges levied on polluters commensurate with the costs of water quality enhancement. These approaches have been used successfully in several European countries and warrant testing in the United States.

Notes

1. As the senior federal administrator charged with responsibility in the area of resource management, Secretary of the Interior Cecil Andrus expects this water crisis to occur (10, p. 4).

2. Under the riparian doctrine of water rights, the flow of water past the premises of the riparian continues unchanged in quality as well as undiminished or unaugmented in quantity.

3. Irreversible state of quality refers to the economic and not necessarily to the physical conditions of water.

4. Of course, the annual amount and density of suspended sediment does not represent the amount and density at any particular time. The actual amount at any particular time may be more or less than the level tolerated by environmental standards. However, in the absence of available data refined to time application, the annual estimate was used throughout the study as a proxy for more refined data. As more refined data become available, they may be substituted for these proxies.

5. This assumption depends upon supply and demand conditions for particular products in terms of price elasticity of product demand.

References

1. Ackerman, Edward, and Löf, George. *Technology in American Water Development.* The Johns Hopkins Press. Baltimore, 1959.
2. Anderson, F. R.; Kneese, A. U.; Reed, P. D.; Taylor, S.; and Stevenson, R. B. *Environmental Improvement Through Economic Incentives.*

Resources for the Future by the Johns Hopkins University Press. Baltimore, 1977.

3. Committee on Science and Technology and Committee on Agriculture. "Agricultural Environmental Relationships: Issues and Priorities." House of Representatives, Ninety-sixth Congress, First Session. U.S. Government Printing Office. Washington, D.C., 1979.
4. Fox, Irving K. "Promising Areas for Research on Institutional Design for Water Resources Management." Implementation of Regional Research in Water-Related Problems. Dean T. Massey, Editor. Department of Law, University Extension. University of Wisconsin, 1970.
5. Gaffney, Mason. "Comparison of Market Pricing and Other Means of Allocating Water Resources." *Water Law and Policy in the Southeast.* Institute of Law and Government. University of Georgia, 1962.
6. Jacobs, James J. "Economics of Water Quality Management: Exemplified by Specific Pollutants in Agricultural Runoff." Unpublished Ph.D. Thesis. Iowa State University, 1972.
7. Jacobs, James J. and Timmons, John F. "An Economic Analysis of Land Use Practices to Control Water Quality." *American Journal of Agricultural Economics,* vol. 56. November 1974, pp. 791–798.
8. Kneese, Allen V. and Bower, Blair T. *Managing Water Quality: Economics, Technology and Institutions.* Johns Hopkins Press for Resources for the Future. Baltimore, 1968.
9. Kneese, Allen V. *The Economics of Regional Water Quality Management.* The Johns Hopkins Press. Baltimore, 1964.
10. *Minnesota Volunteer,* "Water Awareness 1979." Department of Natural Resources, State of Minnesota. St. Paul, Minnesota, July–August 1979.
11. Seay, Edmund E., Jr. "Minimizing Abatement Costs of Water Pollutants: A Parametric Linear Programming Approach." Unpublished Ph.D. Dissertation. Iowa State University, 1970.
12. Timmons, John F. "Identification and Achievement of Environmental Quality Levels in Managing the Use of Natural Resources." Chapter 10 in *Economics and Decision Making for Environmental Quality.* Richard Conner and Edna Loehman, Editors. Florida State University Press. Gainesville, Florida, 1974.
13. Timmons, John F. and Dougal, Mervin D. "Economics of Water Quality Management," Proceedings of International Conference on Water for Peace, vol. 6. U.S. Government Printing Office. Washington, D.C., 1968.
14. Timmons, John F.; Kirkham, Don; and Committee. "Soil Science in Relation to Water Resources Development. V. Economic Evaluation of Water Resource Data." Soil Science Society of America Proceed-

ings, vol. 36, no. 1. January-February 1972.

15. U.S. Environmental Protection Agency. "Alternative Policies for Controlling Nonpoint Agricultural Sources of Water Pollution." Socioeconomic Environmental Studies Series, Environmental Research Laboratory. Athens, Georgia, April 1978.
16. Webb, David Kerry. "Energy, Environment and Agricultural Production Interrelationships: A Parametric Linear Programming Case Study in the Nishnabotna River Basin." Unpublished M.S. Thesis. Iowa State University, 1977.

6
Better Use of Water Management Tools

Allen V. Kneese

Emery did a very good job this morning expressing the nostalgia that's felt by those of us who worked with the Bank so long ago. I was thinking more about that when Harvey Banks was speaking. A story occurred to me that was making the rounds of the Research Division of the Bank when I was working there. Emery and I both worked in the Research Division and there were sometimes somewhat delicate relationships with other divisions. I'm sure that doesn't happen any more. At the time, the Bank used to have tours. They would take people around to view the money and such. I don't know if that happens anymore or not. Anyway, the tour was being made in the Bank one day (this was during the era of Joseph McCarthy). Somebody on the tour asked the tour director, "Do you have any economists at the Bank?" (Harvey reminded me of that story because he briefly misspoke "economist.") The tour director thought that the person had asked if there were any "Communists" in the Bank. A really strange notion! But anyway, "No," he replied. "No, there are none." And the person on the tour said, "Well, I heard there were some in Research." "No." The director thought a minute and added, "But if there were any, that's where they'd be."

John Timmons has done a good job of reviewing what economists and others have been doing in the area of environmental quality as applied to water resources. He's sort of focused where we are and how we got there and discussed some economic aspects of the problem. I would like not particularly to disagree with anything that he says—because I basically don't—

but rather to take the opportunity to supplement some of what he did say and possibly also to place it a bit more into the national policy context and the context of the current kinds of problems that we have to face. Most of the effort that has been given to water quality improvement, at least at the national level, has focused heavily on point sources of pollution and on a particular set of pollutants—primarily the massive amounts of organics that are associated with municipal sewage and several kinds of industry.

In the course of time, there has been a tendency to centralize the policy more and more at the central government level and to try to get more and more uniform standards right across the nation, regardless of the diversity of conditions that Dr. Timmons referred to. That's a very simplified, quick statement of where I think policy has come à la the 1972 Water Quality Act Amendment, which is the law that still governs.

But we are now facing what I would like to refer to as the "new generation of water quality problems." And, in my opinion, they are much knottier, and much more difficult, than anything that we've faced so far. They're knottier, and more difficult, both from the technical point of view and from the policy angle. John Timmons has referred to some of them. Let me speak briefly about one of this new generation, and that is toxic substances. They are, so far, essentially unregulated. But, in response to a law suit by the Natural Resources Defense Council, the EPA has now started to try to implement the toxic substances provision of the Clean Air Act. And it has identified sixty-five classes of toxic pollutants for regulation. This is going to be an extremely difficult task. Very little is known, and it is going to involve an enormous amount of data collection. Under the Act there is a requirement, for example, that the economic impacts of each regulation are to be assessed, and they are supposed to do all this by the early 1980s. This is going to be a far more difficult task than was confronted in the effort to regulate the more conventional kind of pollutants.

But, we may be facing some situations that are even more difficult than that—again, from a technical point of view and also from a policy point of view. And I'd like to make reference to one or two situations that have particular bearing on this part of the world.

Over the last few years, I've been directing a research project called the "Southwest Region Under Stress Project," which has involved research groups from around the country and chiefly the southwest region. One of the parts of that project has dealt with the question of air pollution control. I won't try to even sketch the whole range of things to be considered, but one part has been an effort to provide better models of dispersion pollutants from sources. Two results of that have been (1) that pollutants are transported much farther than was long believed and (2) that the deposition of materials in them takes place selectively at high altitudes. Both are what you would pretty much expect. But that leads to the suspicion that these materials might get into upper watersheds–specifically, into the snowpacks. There is presently no monitoring of that possible effect. Now, we say it is a possible effect. We know it happens some, but we don't know how much it happens, and we don't know, if it happens, whether it is necessarily that important. But one can be suspicious that this might be another kind of toxic pollution of our water courses. And we do have a contract with the Department of Energy to try to at least get some scope of how important this effect might be.

Another tough problem area is the possible development of energy resources. Some people believe that the main possibility for developing the shale resources of the region, for example, is an in situ process because of the cost of the processes and the difficulties that are involved with doing retorting above ground. With the in situ procedure that's now proposed, we'd mine part of the shale and then blast the rest of it, break it up, and have underground combustion. Now the shale, as with coal, contains many things other than hydrocarbons, including a good many heavy metals. Combustion itself could produce dangerous hydrocarbons, which would stay behind. The shale formations are water-bearing structures. They have to be pumped in order for such a process to take place. And the question is, What will happen when those water-bearing structures refill with water? What are their connections to surface hydrology? They are things I think are not at all well understood, and we may be playing Russian roulette in not understanding them better before we proceed with programs, for example, such as those the president proposed.

Another area I'd like to look at on the matter of this new generation of water quality problems is the nonpoint sources. Dr. Timmons spoke some about them. He gave some estimates from a very interesting study they had done in Iowa. But looking at it a little more broadly, the recognition is occurring that nonpoint sources are an extremely important part of the overall water pollution problem. As a matter of fact, some people have begun to wonder whether we can get much further at all in improving water quality with further work on the point sources that are our policy and regulation focus at the present time. I wouldn't want to bet my life on the following numbers, but they are from the Council on Environmental Quality. What they report is that sediment flows from nonpoint sources is 360 times the load that comes from municipal and industrial sources. We are not going to make much progress on that problem by further looking at the point sources. That may not be so surprising with respect to sediment, but they further say that BOD and nutrients from nonpoint sources are probably five to six times as large as from point sources. This is, of course, one of the chief pollutants that we have been trying to attack. They also report, and you see it to some extent in this region, that runoff from old mining operations is a major contributor of heavy metals to water courses.

Now, these are the members of the new generation of problems that we are just now coming to grips with. As I mentioned before, they are technically very difficult. There are very few data. It's hard to know what kind of policy would be effective with respect to them. But there are some characteristics they have in common. One is that to try to deal directly with them, we must understand better the natural systems that are involved. This may extend to systems other than the water system itself. We must understand the hydrology of the river basins better than we do. We must understand the chemistry of the river basins better than we do at the present time. But we may also have to look at how things get into them more carefully than we have in the past.

I've already mentioned the possible problem of heavy metals and other toxic materials getting into the watershed from the atmosphere. It is now becoming apparent that quite a lot of different things have polluted the water resources from the atmosphere. The most notable example, in the sense of having received most of the discussion, is acid rain, which is afflicting large areas of our northeast, much of the Laurentian shield in Canada, and great parts of northern Europe. This is a deleterious input to water courses from the atmosphere, having been generated largely by the combustion of coal—sometimes at very remote locations. One of the characteristics, then, is that there are systems involved that we don't understand as well as we need to if we are going to be able to manage these more subtle problems effectively. And those systems are more often than not of a regional character.

A second aspect, as is obvious, is that they cannot be controlled fully by conventional water pollution control measures. Dr. Timmons mentioned the sediment question. Here we are talking to a large extent about changes in agricultural practices on a relatively large scale. We are not equipped to handle such problems at the present time. Furthermore, it is sometimes possible to change the quality of a water course by doing things to the water course itself. A very often cited example is low flow regulation, which catches water during high flow periods and releases it during low flow periods when usually the quality of water in the stream is most degraded. There is, furthermore, the possibility of such a thing as a sediment-catching structure. There is even a possibility—and this is practiced to some extent in Germany, for example—of introducing air into the rivers at critical points where otherwise it would drop too low. Along this line there is considerable literature that has tried to look at pollution problems as a problem of regional water quality management upon which a wide range of policies and priorities can be brought to bear. And that literature has concluded that, even with respect to point sources, it is possible to achieve the water quality goals or standards that Dr. Timmons mentioned at much lower cost if a regional approach is used so that a wide variety of actions can be taken.

Now when we look at this new generation problem, which is even more inherently regional in character in a way, it seems to me we really have to think hard about the approach to water quality that has evolved at the national level. There has been more and more centralization and more and more of an effort at uniform rules across the country. A brief effort was made in the 1965 Water Act Amendments to begin to understand the water courses and to relate water quality policy to that understanding. That was completely wiped out later on. An effort was made to do everything with effluent standards, which were based on technology and had no relationship whatsoever to what happened in the rivers. I think we can't afford to do that anymore. I think we have to rethink that policy and begin to try to nurture regional institutions that are intended to come to grips with these problems and manage them. The tendency of our federal policy has been to destroy or weaken such regional institutions.

Part 2

Policies to Cope with the Problems

7
A Western Governor Looks at Water Policy

Scott M. Matheson

I am honored to be invited to participate in this symposium on western water resources. The Federal Reserve Bank of Kansas City is to be congratulated for its initiative and sensitivity in organizing and sponsoring this symposium, for no issue excites western sensibilities more than the topic of water. Without water, the arid lands of our region will never realize their promise nor their potential, and the capacity they have to produce food, fiber, or fossil fuel resources will remain forever beyond our grasp.

The western character has been shaped by the relentless struggle to put water to land. This is especially true in Utah. The Mormon pioneers who arrived in Salt Lake Valley in the summer of 1847 quickly built canals and dams to harvest what remained of the run-off from the mountain streams in order to grow a crop before winter. They were unconsciously reenacting a ritual that was five thousand years old and first employed by the Sumerians in the Middle East, where civilization as we know it came into being with the practice of irrigation. As W. H. McNeil notes in his classic study, *The Rise of the West,* "man's first civilized communities differed fundamentally from the Neolithic Village Communities, for the simple reason that the water engineering vital to survival required organized community effort." The parallel between the Sumerians and the Mormons is striking and instructive because both knew that the future in an arid region belonged not to the hunter, the trapper, the nomadic herdsman, or the seeker of precious metals, but to those who had the ingenuity and the discipline to make the desert bloom by putting water to beneficial use.

I was raised in a small community in one of the drier parts of a state that is the second most arid in the nation. Every rain storm in Parowan, Utah, was an event almost as big as the Fourth of July. You learned to reckon time by the intervals between rains. January 3, 1977, is memorable to me, not so much because it was the day I was inaugurated as the twelfth governor of Utah, but because it snowed that day. It was the first moisture we had received in three months and it was the last we were to see for another three months. The drought the west endured during the winter of 1976-1977 cost the region an estimated $15 billion. It may have been a harbinger of things to come.

The Water Resources Council has found that water shortages already exist in 21 of the 116 subregions of the country. These subregions lie in the central plains and the U.S. southwest. By the year 2,000, 39 of these subregions are likely to suffer severe water shortages, including areas of the northern plains, the Rockies, and California. This means that at the beginning of the twenty-first century, most of the nation west of the Mississippi will be in the grip of severe water shortages. This does not assume a prolonged drought, but only the extrapolation of the trend of overutilization of present supply combined with the underdevelopment of potential reserves. We can expect that periodic droughts, like oil embargos, will exacerbate a deteriorating situation. That is why a national water policy, like a national energy policy, is required if we are to complete what has been called the "American century" with anything resembling the optimism and confidence we had as a nation when we began it.

The Carter Administration's initiative to develop a national water policy got off to a very bad start, not only from a policy but also from a procedural perspective. The announcement of the infamous "hit list" was in the morning papers the day that western governors convened in Denver to discuss the deepening western drought with Interior Secretary Andrus, who had been in office less than a month. He, like the rest of us, read about it in the newspapers. That act did incalculable harm to the new administration insofar as its relations with the West was concerned. It was the cause of the skepticism that persists today over the true intentions of the administration in water policy.

In this regard, the decision of the president to sign the Public Works Bill even though it contained an appropriation to complete the Tellico Dam will go a long way toward dispelling this feeling. I salute the president for his decision. I know how much he disliked signing the bill with the Tellico Dam included among the water projects, but it was the prudent course to take. His objection to the dam was not based upon the threat to the snail darter, but because it was, in his opinion, a bad water project. Needless to say I am happy that the president signed the bill, and I hope that it is a prelude to a new relationship with the West in our continuing effort to shape a national water policy.

If the states are to be full partners in this process (and I have always maintained that there is an important distinction between a national water policy and a federal water policy) then the states must be in a position to seize the initiative and shape the outcome. My experience as chairman of the National Governors' Association Subcommittee on Water Management has convinced me that the key to an effective water resource policy for the states is in the institutions we build to manage the use of this resource.

The NGA Water Subcommittee is a coalition that merges the technical expertise of interstate water organizations, such as the Association of State and Interstate Water Pollution Control Administrators and the Interstate Conference on Water Problems. Together with regional organizations (such as the Great Lakes Commission and the Western States Water Council), we have been able to participate in and influence the national debate on water policy. It is an effective marriage of the political resources of the nation's governors and the technical skills of water quality and water quantity professionals. We have been able to protect state interests in the congressional debate on the Federal Water Pollution Control Act amendments of 1977 and the Safe Drinking Water reauthorization legislation that same year. More recently we have been involved in the fight to hold waste water construction funding in the FY 1980 Budget, and we look to be involved in the upcoming effort to secure adequate funding for controls over non-point-source pollution in rural areas.

To develop knowledgeable positions on issues requires that the governors have technical resources at their disposal. It is the responsibility of governors to insure that the strategies and objectives of these organizations are consistent with state goals and strategies. This can only be done by linking them up in a coalition that elected state officials can guide and direct. It is my hope that in addition to national organizations, each area will develop strong regional organizations with a water quantity and water quality resource capacity. Not unexpectedly, this capability exists in a mature form only in the West, where the Western States Water Council provides a dependable and influential voice for western water interests. I am convinced that strong regional positions on water are essential in order to sharpen the issues and better define the interests at risk. It was through such a process that the basic outline for the agreement that became the National Governors' Association (NGA) policy position on water emerged. This policy was adopted by the NGA without a dissenting vote early in 1978 and has become the basis for our discussion and negotiations with the federal government. The central premise of that position as stated in the preamble is that "the States have the primary authority and responsibility for water management."

I have no doubt that the NGA effort materially influenced the tone and direction of the president's water message that was sent to Congress on June 6, 1978. The president emphasized that he envisioned comprehensive changes in water policy requiring development of "a new, creative partnership" between the federal government and the states. The president further stated that his proposals were designed "to enhance the role of the states, where the primary responsibilities for water policy must lie. . . . States must be the focal point for water resource management."

These were reassuring words to those of us in the West for whom the idea of state sovereignty in water use and management is rooted in the development of our water laws. But preemption is seldom blatant and often appears in subtle guises as in the implementation of the recommendations on water conservation.

The options that the administration wants to pursue in the name of conservation not only could preempt the states in their traditional role in conserving water but would also emasculate the state's prerogatives in allocating water resources. Conservation has long been recognized as essential in the arid West. The basic legal concept of the western states that prevents waste in water use is that beneficial use determines the scope of the water right. Beneficial use is measured by the reasonableness of the purpose of water use. It requires reasonableness not only with respect to the amount of water but also in the efficiency of the facilities diverting and transporting the water. The measure of reasonableness is often quantified by specifying the duty of water or the amount beneficially needed for particular uses. Thus, mechanisms are available under present state laws to identify wasteful practices and to prevent them. New federal mechanisms in the form of federally enforceable conservation requirements are unnecessary and would preempt traditional state prerogatives.

I remain confident, however, that the man charged by the president for management of the federal effort in developing a national water policy will listen to any appeal on potential preemptions of state prerogatives that occur in the implementation of the policy. That man is Interior Secretary Cecil Andrus who enjoys the trust, confidence, and affection of his former colleagues in the nation's statehouses.

A more clear and present threat to the states' water rights comes not from the water policy review but from the proposal to create an Emergency Mobilization Board with broad powers to supersede state laws when it is determined that they pose an impediment to the completion of priority energy projects. I find it amusing that the federal government deems this radical legislation necessary in order to break the alleged log jam of state bureaucratic barriers to energy development. Except for the notorious and oft-cited SOHIO pipeline in California, there are precious few examples of state recalcitrance in energy development.

My fears are that the fast-track legislation that is presently being considered could, under the pretense of an overriding national interest, trample state procedural and substantive laws underfoot. I have joined with my colleagues in opposing both House and Senate versions of this legislation. I find it particularly ironic that the sponsor of the House preemption bill is Representative John Dingell who was the sponsor of the National Environmental Policy Act that established the environmental safeguards that he now seeks to supersede. There is no doubt in my mind that the momentum behind the fast-track legislation poses a far greater threat to state water laws than any aspect of the water policy review. It disregards experience and it disdains custom, both of which are the hallmarks of western water law. The emergence of this body of law is unique to the West and dramatically illustrates the primary role of the state in the management of its water resources.

Western water law has developed through the accretion of custom and experience and reflects the realities of life in an arid region. Water rights can be acquired only by beneficial use of water, and they can be lost by nonuse. Under the western appropriation doctrine, the first to make beneficial use of water is protected to the extent of his use. The appropriation doctrine enables the state through definition of "beneficial use" to prevent waste and mismanagement of its waters, and therefore, in contrast to the riparian doctrine, vests the state with broad control over its waters.

State water laws evolved during the nineteenth century, when federal policy stressed disposition of the public domain to encourage homesteading and settlement. By a series of acts in 1866, 1870, and 1877, Congress approved the western appropriation policy and declared that rights to water on public land could be obtained under the laws of the states and territories. Even government patentees had to acquire water rights in accordance with state law.

Congress also passed the 1902 Reclamation Act to encourage development of the West. As with the earlier acts, western congressmen secured provisions that reserved to the states broad control over water resources. Section 8 of the 1902 Act provides:

> That nothing in this Act shall be construed as affecting or intended to affect or to any way interfere with the laws of any state or territory relating to the control, appropriation, use, or distribution of water used in irrigation, or any vested right acquired thereunder, and the Secretary of Interior, in carrying out the provisions of this Act, shall proceed in conformity with such laws.

The 1902 Reclamation law thus established a true partnership between nation and state: the federal government would build and operate reclamation projects; the states would control the acquisition, distribution, and use of water.

While state laws may not override congressional objectives expressed in the federal reclamation laws, where state laws and federal laws do not conflict, state law is applicable. Congress, in the reclamation laws and the earlier public land disposal acts, clearly evinced a policy of deferring to state law on the acquisition, control and distribution of water.

As you can see, water projects and water rights run in tandem in the western mind, and President Carter took them both on, first with his assault on western water projects and then with his subsequent announcement of a national water policy review, which was seen as an attempt to preempt state water rights. As I indicated to you earlier, the states succeeded in modifying and limiting the intent and scope of the water policy review and when finally announced by the president, the policy listed four basic objectives:

1. to improve planning and efficient management of federal water programs,
2. to establish a new national emphasis on water conservation,
3. to enhance federal/state cooperation in water policy and planning, and
4. to increase attention to environmental quality.

I would like to elaborate on the objective of federal-state cooperation because it is in keeping with the thrust of my remarks to you today. Two aspects of this objective have provoked the most controversy and presented the clearest delineation of state-federal divergence: cost sharing on federal water projects and federal reserved rights.

First, as to cost sharing, legislation has been introduced at the request of the administration proposing to establish shared financing of federal water projects built by the Army Corps of Engineers, the Bureau of Reclamation, the Soil Conservation Service, and the Tennessee Valley Authority by requiring states to contribute in advance and in cash a variable percent of the project cost depending on whether the products of the project are "vendible" or "nonvendible."

The National Governors' Association policy supports the concept of cost-sharing, but it is not specific on what the percent of cost share should be or whether it should be retroactively applied. The NGA policy position on cost-sharing urges that it be consistently and uniformly applied to structural and nonstructural alternatives as well as among federal agencies. It also recommends that when a state cannot provide its front-end share there should be a provision for recoverable loans.

The administration's cost-sharing legislation is intended to winnow out the so-called bad water projects. There is a provision in the bill for voluntary cost-sharing of projects that have been authorized by Congress but for which no money has yet been appropriated. Under the terms of the administration's bill, this $38 billion backlog of projects would be subject to additional cost sharing. Suffice it to say there has been little enthusiasm for the administration's proposal either from the Congress or the states.

A more intriguing approach to cost sharing is the legislation that has been introduced by Senator Peter Domenici of New Mexico and cosponsored by Senator Patrick Moynihan of New York, entitled the National Water Resources Policy and Development Act of 1979. As Senator Domenici said, upon introduction of his legislation, the goals of a federal water policy should be "to increase state responsibility to move projects ahead to earlier completion and to establish an effective system of project priorities." I believe his bill goes a long way toward achieving the NGA objective that has been set forth in our policy statement. It establishes a block grant approach to water resource development based upon land area and population. It would require a 25 percent state match that could be paid back through the life of the project, but it would guarantee certainty of funding within the block grant category. There is another category of projects of "national significance" that would be exempted from cost sharing entirely. These would be projects with multi-state impacts and benefits of the sort originally contemplated by the Reclamation Act of 1902.

This two-tiered approach to water project funding achieves

two important objectives. First, it allows a state more discretion in the management of its water resources by allowing it to establish project priorities, and second, it broadens the base of support for water project appropriations. This second point is crucial because those of us who are interested in water resource development should fully appreciate the significance of the failure of Congress to override President Carter's veto last fall of the public works bill which contained water projects that had been on his original hit list. As a result there have emerged new realities in water politics that require a new consensus, and if the price of that consensus should include doing something about the water resource needs of other regions of the country, then so be it. But whether it be the Central Utah Project or the Third City Water Tunnel in New York City, we must be about the business of building them before spiraling costs and interminable delays bring water resource development in this country to a complete stand-still.

Despite the conceptual audacity of Domenici-Moynihan, there is some resistance to it, particularly in the West. Western reticence centers on the 25 percent up-front cost share and concern over replacing a tried-and-true system for water project funding with something new and untried. As a western governor I understand these concerns, but I am apprehensive that the old system will not complete the reclamation agenda of the West so that we can develop our vast natural resource reserves in a timely fashion. There will be another attempt to reach an accommodation among the states represented on the NGA water subcommittee when they meet in Salt Lake next week.

An even more difficult question presents itself in the federal reserved water rights issue as it relates to both the reserved water rights of Indians and the reserved water rights attaching to federal lands. Indian reserved water rights were specifically exempted from the jurisdiction and schedule of the national water policy review and have been developed separately by the assistant secretary of interior for Indian affairs. The federal reserved rights portion of the national water policy was issued in an opinion delivered by the solicitor of the Department of the Interior to a special meeting between western governors and Secretary Andrus in Salt Lake City in May of this year.

While the states are still scrutinizing that document in order to be able to respond definitively to it, it appears that the solicitor's opinion devises a new theory upon which to base a claim for a nonreserved federal water right. As a brief prepared by the Western States Water Council states in response:

> The reasons for development of this new theory by the Solicitor can also be surmised. The Supreme Court in the New Mexico case denied the government's claims to reserved rights for instream uses on forest lands for aesthetic, recreation, wildlife-preservation, and stock-watering privileges. Besides being a vital source of timber, national forest system lands are considered the most important watershed areas under any agency of the United States. In the eleven western states, more than half of the stream flow comes from national forests.
>
> Having lost the effort to claim such instream rights through the reservation doctrine, it is not difficult to conceive that federal agencies will try again in light of the Solicitor's opinion to claim that such instream non-consumptive uses have been "appropriated" by the federal government for congressionally authorized purposes and therefore should be upheld without reference to state substantive law. Such claims could be anticipated not only from the Forest Service, but also from the National Park Service, the Fish and Wildlife Service and the Bureau of Land Management as well.

The New Mexico case that is referred to was a significant decision handed down by the Supreme Court last year that limited the application of the federal reservation doctrine. In tandem with *California* v. *U.S.*, decided the same day, it portends a dramatic shift in the court's attitude in favor of greater state discretion in water management. If this judicial trend continues it will easily surpass in importance and long-run significance the administration's water policy review. It has emboldened state water lawyers, which explains their immediate and militant reaction to the solicitor's opinion.

As long as the solicitor's opinion does not harden into an official position of the Department of the Interior on this issue, there is still an opportunity for an accommodation, but clearly the concept of a nonreserved federal water right is unacceptable to the states.

Similar sentiments exist among the states on the issue of Indian reserved water rights. Although this issue is not addressed within the context of the administration's water policy review, I want to consider it in concluding my remarks to you. In an article that appeared this summer in the Yale Law Journal analyzing the implications of the Indian reserved water rights issue, the author argues that the definition of Indian rights should be achieved through adjudication rather than legislation, and that adjudication through the courts is preferable to adjudication by federal agencies. While I cannot agree with his preference for federal courts over state courts in the resolution of these rights, the rationale the author develops in justifying adjudication over legislation reveals a process that I want to expand upon: Any definition of the Indian reserved right must be judged by its workability; legislative standards would lack the benefits of decentralized decision making. Given the diversity of Indian reservations and the variety of their claims, fine-tuning and flexibility is essential in defining the scope of Indian reserved rights.

The alternative to legislative definition of Indian reserved water rights is development of standards through case-by-case consideration of reservations. Such consideration requires close scrutiny of the legal instruments and circumstances surrounding the creation of the reservation as well as thorough evaluation of the tribe's economic possibilities at the time. Because the definition of Indian reserved rights is currently undeveloped, a court or agency adjudicating these rights has great flexibility to ensure that the result is equitable under the circumstances of each case. Decentralized decision makers would be permitted to learn by experience. This familiar process of common law evolution would develop outer boundaries for Indian reserved rights that could be tested in a variety of contexts and adversary proceedings and could then be applied to particular situations. Reliance on adjudication thus involves significantly less potential than the legislative approach for unwanted rigidities in defining the extent of Indian reserved water rights.

Notions like "decentralized decision makers" and "common law evolution" that describe a process rather than an outcome remind me of the way Justice Curtis solved a problem before the U.S. Supreme Court involving the Commerce Clause over 120 years ago. He devised a uniformity-diversity test in *Cooley v. Board of Wardens* as a standard for determining when laws should be applied uniformly and therefore enacted at the federal level, and when laws should recognize local diversity and therefore be enacted at the local level. It was a singularly creative act in constitutional law and one that expresses clearly the reason the federal system was devised. This is the genius of the federal system; and as in the case of the free enterprise system, we forget how simple and how well it can work. What is needed in the search for a national water policy is a good measure of both.

8
Western Water Resources: Means to Augment the Supply

Theodore M. Schad

Introduction

Other speakers in the symposium have been charged with the responsibility for reporting on the dimensions of the water resources problems of the western United States, both as to quality and quantity. In this paper I shall set forth some ideas as to how supplies can be augmented to meet demands in terms of water quality as well as quantity and will go on to discuss policies to cope with the water resources problems that must be faced in the future if the West is to continue to prosper. The water supply-demand background upon which this presentation is based, in the absence of prior knowledge of what the earlier speakers will be presenting, is the recently published first volume of the Second National Assessment of the Nation's Water Resources, 1975–2000, prepared by the U.S. Water Resources Council under the authority of the Water Resources Planning Act of 1965, Public Law 89-80.

The Water Supply

For the purposes of its assessment, the Water Resources Council has divided the United States into twenty water resources regions. Ten of these are wholly or partly included within the seventeen contiguous western states that comprise the West, as commonly defined. River basins, of course, are not cognizant of political boundaries, so to be strictly accurate the summarized data for the ten water resources regions should be adjusted by deleting that portion relating to the easternmost portions of the Souris-Red-Rainy, Missouri, Arkansas-White-Red, and Texas Gulf regions. For the purposes of this paper, however, such refinement is not necessary, and for the sake of simplicity, the streamflow and water use figures for the entire basins are used.

The Second National Assessment shows a total mean annual runoff from the ten western water resources regions of 459 billion gallons a day (bgd). In 1975, base year for the assessment, there were substantial overdrafts of ground water resources, primarily in the Arkansas-White-Red, Texas Gulf, and lower Colorado regions that augmented the available supply by about twenty bgd. Such augmentation cannot be sustained for more than another decade or so, because of the rising costs of pumping and the finite capacity of the aquifers.

The Demand

Against this water supply, the Water Resources Council has estimated that 175 bgd were withdrawn in 1975, the base year for the study, and has projected, under a variety of assumptions, that this will increase to 187 bgd by 1985, and then decrease again to 177 bgd by the year 2000 as the cost of water and environmental regulations increase. The "bottom line" in water demand, however, is not withdrawal, but consumptive use: the amount of water that is not returned to the stream or ground water aquifer, but is evaporated, transpired, incorporated into a manufactured product, or polluted to such an extent that it cannot be reused. The Water Resources Council estimates consumptive uses in the ten western water resources regions at 88.7 bgd in 1975, or about 19 percent of the supply, and projects increases to 96.8 bgd by 1985, 21 percent of the supply, and to 100.7 bgd, 22 percent of the supply, by the year 2000.

The Water Resources Council data is summarized in Table 1, which shows that water use in the various water resources regions bears little relationship to the indigenous stream flow. For example, water use in the lower Colorado water resources region in 1975 was almost three times the mean stream flow, the excess use being provided by inflow from the Upper Colorado and

TABLE 1
Streamflow and Estimated Consumptive Uses of Water Western Water Resources Regions
(in billion gallons per day)[a]

Water Resources Regions	*Mean Streamflow (runoff)*	*Groundwater Overdraft in 1975*	*Consumptive Uses*					
			1975	*Percent*	*Est. 1985*	*Percent*	*Est. 2000*	*Percent*
Souris-Red-Rainy	6.0		.112	1.9	.204	3.4	.446	7.5
Missouri	44.1	2.6	15.469	35.0	19.206	43.5	19.913	45.0
Arkansas-White-Red	62.6	5.5	8.064	12.9	8.769	14.0	8.887	14.2
Texas-Gulf	28.3	5.6	11.259	39.8	10.227	36.3	10.529	37.3
Rio Grande	1.2	.7	4.240	353.0	4.320	360.0	4.016	336.0
Upper Colorado	10.0		2.440	24.4	3.018	30.2	3.232	32.3
Lower Colorado	1.6	2.4	4.595	288.0	4.754	297.0	4.708	294.0
Great Basin	2.6	.6	3.779	145.0	3.765	144.0	4.036	155.0
Pacific Northwest	255.3	.6	11.913	4.7	14.610	5.7	15.196	6.0
California	47.4	2.2	26.641	56.5	27.932	59.0	29.699	62.8
Total, 10 western regions	459.1	20.2	88.714	19.3	96.805	21.0	100.662	22.0

[a] One billion gallons per day = 1,120,000 acre-feet per year.

ground water overdraft in central Arizona. An even greater disparity is shown in the Great Basin, but similar ground water overdrafts and importation into the Arkansas-White-Red water resources region are hidden in the table by the fact that the region includes areas of heavy precipitation in the eastern part of the basin.

Supporting volumes of the Second National Assessment, not yet published, show these variations in more detail by dividing the ten western water resources regions into fifty-four aggregated subareas. Use of this data would permit more accurate consideration to be given to water resources shortfalls and deficiencies in localized areas of the West. The Water Resources Council data are not always consistent with other water supply and use data. More recent studies by Bruce Bishop at Utah State University are more optimistic as to the availability of water in the Colorado River Basin.

Along with the uses summarized in Table 1 (which include uses for agriculture, domestic and commercial purposes, manufacturing, energy production, and the mineral industry), there are substantial instream uses of water, such as for preservation and propagation of fish and wildlife, outdoor recreation, hydroelectric power generation, and navigation. These are difficult to quantify. There is rarely enough water in a stream to satisfy all uses, or else there is too much. Under federal and state laws, use of water for hydroelectric power generation and for navigation in states lying wholly or partly west of the ninety-eighth meridian is subservient to beneficial consumptive uses. Recent court decisions with respect to use of water for fish and wildlife have tended to exacerbate conflicts between federal and state water rights, so the situation is indeterminate. Recreational use of water is not recognized under most state water rights laws, but the importance of recreational use to the economies of the western states is well enough understood that it is generally accepted as an important use of water. Thus, in spite of the fact that the bare statistics may show only about one-fifth of the water in the western water resources regions is actually consumed, there are very real shortages now in several regions, and the likelihood of greater shortages as the West continues to grow is certain. New energy technologies (such as coal gasification and liquefaction and producing oil from abundant oil shale resources of the Upper Colorado Basin) will undoubtedly increase demands for water in the Upper Colorado and the western portions of the Missouri Basin water resources regions.

Associated economic development and continuation of recent population growth will increase demand for water in the Lower Colorado, Great Basin, Rio Grande, and the western portion of the Arkansas-White-Red water resources regions. Some method must be found to meet the demands in order to prevent stagnation of the economy of the West due to lack of water in the twenty-first century.

Alternative Means of Meeting Demands

Demand for water can be satisfied in a variety of ways, including increasing the supply, making better or more efficient use of existing supplies, or by reducing the demand. Among the obvious ways of increasing supplies are creating impoundments or storage reservoirs, either above or under ground, to more completely develop existing water resources, transferring water from areas of surplus to areas of deficient water supply, water harvesting through land and vegetation management, precipitation augmentation, and desalting. Less obvious but potentially possible ways include such practices as better forecasting of hydrologic events, augmenting fog drip, snow and icefield manipulation, iceberg towing, undersea aqueducts, and collapsible bladders for transport of large quantities of fresh water through the ocean. Some of these techniques would obviously be applicable only in coastal areas, but could benefit water-short areas in interior regions through exchange.

When the costs of augmenting water supply through any of the above techniques are considered, the advantages of increasing efficiency of use or otherwise reducing demands become evident. There are numerous ways of doing this, including institutional changes such as revisions in state water rights laws where they impede or deter efficient water use, pricing systems to motivate more efficient water use, integration of ground and surface water, and reuse of water. The following sections of this paper cover these points in more detail.

Additional Impoundments

Construction of dams and storage reservoirs has been the most frequently used method of augmenting water supplies. Capacity of storage reservoirs in the United States has increased from 33 million acre-feet in 1920 to 273 million acre-feet in 1953 and 450 million acre-feet in 1975. About 20 percent of this is in the Colorado River Basin. It should be obvious that full offstream use of the average annual streamflow in any water resources region as shown in Table 1 could not be achieved without sufficient holdover storage in reservoirs to equalize the flow over a long period of years. Even with the tremendous storage capacity in the Missouri River main stem reservoirs, it is not possible to operate the system without some spills during floods, so that full regulation has not been achieved. An even smaller portion of the Columbia River system is regulated by reservoirs, but the immense snowfields and glaciers in the headwaters of the river system in Canada achieve somewhat the same purpose as reservoir storage, holding back winter precipitation for gradual release as they melt during the summer months. Complete control of a major river system in an arid climate cannot be achieved without going past the point of diminishing returns, however, as the increase in evaporation from the surface of the reservoirs as complete control is approached will exceed the increase in yield resulting from the addition of another reservoir. This condition has been reached in the Colorado River Basin, according to an analysis in U.S. Geological Survey Circular 409, and probably in the Rio Grande Basin. Storage in small reservoirs and farm ponds, while tending to equalize flows in small drainage basins, also has an adverse effect on streamflow because of increased evaporation and greater infiltration into groundwater. If the groundwater reservoir can be pumped, the loss of surface runoff may be offset. With the ever-increasing difficulty of reaching agreement on construction of new reservoirs because of environmental objections, the possibility of securing more complete regulation of river basin systems through construction of additional storage reservoirs in the West becomes increasingly remote.

Interbasin Transfers

Augmentation of water supply in one river basin through transfer of water from an adjacent river basin is a technique that has been used in the United States for more than two centuries, since water was imported from an adjacent basin to run a mill in the Charles River Basin in Massachusetts. In the past century more than a hundred interbasin transfers have been accomplished, some of which move substantial quantities of water. In the eastern part of the United States, the cities of Boston and New York depend on water supplies from adjacent basins for part of their drinking water. The Chicago River diversion from Lake Michigan, which reversed the flow of a river, transfers over 2 million acre-feet a year from the Great Lakes to the Mississippi River for pollution abatement. In the West, interbasin transfers are even more prevalent. Los Angeles went to the Great Basin for part of its water supply more than sixty years ago, to the Colorado Basin some forty years ago, and to the Sacramento River Basin in more recent years. Denver went across the continental divide to the Colorado River via the Moffat Tunnel for part of its water supply more than fifty years ago.

As the federal government assumed a larger role in U.S. water development, the scale of interbasin transfers increased, with irrigation a major purpose to be served. Projects such as the Colorado–Big Thompson diversion in Colorado and the Central Valley project in California were begun in the 1930s. It is ironic that the Colorado River Basin, which drains some of the nation's more arid areas and has the lowest run-off per square mile of any major river basin, is the exporting basin for such a large number of interbasin transfers. In addition to those already mentioned, the San Juan-Chama diversion in New Mexico, the Frying Pan–Arkansas project in Colorado, and the Central Utah project in Utah convey or will convey a substantial part of the Colorado River Basin runoff into other water resources regions. In a report published in the *Geographical Review*, Volume 58, pp. 108-132, Frank Quinn has tabulated 146 interbasin transfers in the western United States as of 1965 that transfer a total of more than 18 million acre-feet per year.

Starting with proposals made in 1950 in the Bureau of Reclamation's United Western Study, preliminary studies were made of even larger interbasin transfers until a moratorium on such studies by federal agencies was legislated in 1968. A summary of these developed by C. C. Warnick and published by the University of Arizona in *Arid Lands in Perspective,* 1969, is included as Table 2. The last project shown on the table is the Texas Water Plan, studied by the Bureau of Reclamation and the Corps of Engineers under a special Congressional authorization between 1967 and 1973. This proposal would have transferred over 10 million acre-feet annually from the Mississippi River or its tributaries to the high plains of Texas and New Mexico to sustain agricultural production after the Ogallala aquifer is pumped out. Cost of water delivered on the high plains was estimated to be well over $300 an acre-foot with the cost of energy for the 5,000-foot pump lift computed at pre-1973 price levels. Since that report was completed there has been less interest in interbasin transfers.

It is dubious whether any of these plans involving diversions across state lines can be undertaken, even if funds for construction could be made available. No state will be willing to sell its water "birthright" unless the consideration is so high as to increase the cost of the project to such an extent that it would not be economically justified.

International water transfers might have some possibility of being effected if the benefit from water development in the exporting country, which would be Canada, could be made high enough, and since the water for export would probably always flow north into the Arctic unused. However, the environmental disruption would be huge, and if the environmental movement develops in Canada as it has in the United States, it would be very difficult to negotiate the necessary treaty and enact the implementing legislation in the two countries.

Groundwater Management

There are an estimated 180 billion acre-feet of water in underground aquifers within a depth of 2,500 feet under the forty-eight contiguous United States. About one-fourth of this, 46 billion acre-feet, is usable with present technology; this is

TABLE 2
Summary of Information on Conceptual Plans Proposed for Regional Water Transfer

Project Name	*Agency/Company Sponsor Author of Plan*	*Approximate Date of Proposal*	*River Basin(s) for Source*	*River Basin(s) of Use*	*Countries Involved*	*States Involved*	*Proposed Diversion: (a) 10^6 acre-ft/yr; (b) cfs; (c) mgd.*
United Western	U.S. Bureau of Reclamation Rep. R. J. Welch—Calif.	1950	Columbia River North Pacific Coastal Streams	Great Basin South Pacific Coastal Plain Colorado River	United States Mexico	11 Western States	6.0 9,100 5,900
California Water Plan	California Department of Water Resources	1957	Northern California Rivers	Central Valley California South Pacific Coastal Plain	United States	California	
Pacific Southwest Water Plan	U.S. Bureau of Reclamation W. I. Palmer	1963	Northern California Streams Colorado River	Lower Colorado River South Pacific Coastal Plain	United States Mexico	California Arizona, Nevada Utah, New Mexico	1.2 1,660 1,070
Snake-Colorado Project	Los Angeles Department of Water & Power S. B. Nelson	1963	Snake River	Colorado River South Pacific Coastal Plain	United States Mexico	Idaho, Nevada Arizona California	2.4 3,320 2,140
North American Power & Water Alliance (NAWAPA)	Ralph M. Parsons Company	1964	Alaskan & Canadian Rivers, with Columbia River	Great Lakes Basin South Pacific Coastal Plain Colorado River Texas High Plains	United States Canada Mexico	Western States Texas Lake States	110.0 152,000 98,000
Yellowstone-Snake-Green Project	T. M. Stetson Consulting Engineer	1964	Yellowstone River Snake River	Green River Colorado River	United States	Montana, Idaho Wyoming, Lower Colorado States	2.0 2,770 1,780

TABLE 2 (continued)
Summary of Information on Conceptual Plans Proposed for Regional Water Transfer

Project Name	*Agency/Company Sponsor Author of Plan*	*Approximate Date of Proposal*	*River Basin(s) for Source*	*River Basin(s) of Use*	*Countries Involved*	*States Involved*	*Proposed Diversion: (a) 10^6 acre-ft/yr; (b) cfs; (c) mgd.*
Pirkey's Plan Western Water Project	F. Z. Pirkey Consulting Engineer	1964	Columbia River	Colorado River Sacramento River South Pacific Coastal Plain	United States Mexico	Oregon Washington California Utah, Arizona Nevada	15.0 20,800 13,400
Dunn Plan Modified Snake-Colorado Project	W. G. Dunn, Consulting Engineer	1965	Snake & Columbia Rivers	Great Basin Snake River South Pacific Coastal Plain Colorado River	United States Mexico	Idaho, Oregon Washington Utah, Arizona Nevada California	5.0 6,900 4,450
Sierra-Cascade Project	E. F. Miller, Consulting Engineer, Maryland	1965	Columbia River	Oregon Valleys Central Valley, California South Pacific Coastal Plain	United States	Oregon, Nevada California	7.0 9,700 6,250
Undersea Aqueduct System	National Engineering Science Company F. C. Lee	1965	North Coast Pacific Rivers	Central Valley South Pacific Coastal Plain	United States	Oregon California	11.0 15,200 9,800
Southwest Idaho Development Project	U.S. Bureau of Reclamation, Region 1	1966	Payette River Weiser River Bruneau River	Snake River	United States	Idaho	
Canadian Water Export	E. Kuiper	1966	Several Canadian Rivers	Western States (indefinite)	United States Canada	All Western States	150.0 208,000 134,000

Central Arizona Project	U.S. Bureau of Reclamation	1948, 1967	Lower Colorado River Basin	Colorado River	United States Mexico	Utah, Nevada Arizona California	1.2 1,660 1,070
Central North American Water Project C3 NAWP	E. R. Tinney Washington State University, Professor	1967	Canadian Rivers	Great Lakes Entire Western States	United States Canada Mexico	Great Lakes Western States	150.0 208,000 134,000
Smith Plan	L. G. Smith Consulting Engineer	1967	Liard River McKenzie River	All river basins of 17 western states	United States Canada Mexico	17 Western States	40.0 55,500 35,750
Grand Canal Concept	T. W. Kierens Sudbury, Ontario	1965	Great Lakes and St. Lawrence River	Canadian rivers flowing to Hudson Bay	United States	Great Lake States	17.0 23,600 15,200
Beck Plan	R. W. Beck Associates	1967	Missouri River	Texas High Plains	United States	South Dakota Nebraska Kansas, Colorado Oklahoma, Texas	10.0 13,800 8,930
West Texas and Eastern New Mexico Import Project	U.S. Bureau of Reclamation & U.S. Corps of Engineers	1967 (1972 due)	Mississippi and Texas Rivers	High Plain of Texas and New Mexico	United States	Oklahoma, Texas New Mexico Louisiana	16.5 22,900 14,700

Source: C. C. Warnick, "Historical Background and Philosophical Basis of Regional Water Transfer," in *Arid Lands in Perspective*, McGinnies and Goldman, Eds. (Tucson: The University of Arizona Press, 1969), pp. 340–351.

about thirty-five times the annual surface runoff. Annual recharge may approximate one billion acre-feet, more than twice the amount that can be stored in all the man-made reservoirs in the United States, but much of this spills out of the aquifers to become part of the surface runoff if the aquifers are not pumped.

Availability and magnitude of this resource are well understood by the water resources professions in the United States but are not too well understood by the layman. Over 20 percent of all the water withdrawals for use in the United States are from ground water, a quantity estimated by the U.S. Geological Survey in 1975 at 83 bgd. This is less than 10 percent of the estimated recharge capability of 900 bgd, so there would appear to be room for a considerable increase in the use of ground water in many areas of the United States. Not all areas are favorably situated for the use of groundwater, however, and some of the heaviest uses of groundwater, as shown in Table 1, are in areas where there is insufficient recharge to provide a sustained yield anywhere near the present demand. Furthermore, in some areas, pumping of groundwater results in a direct reduction of surface stream flow.

Capacity of aquifers could be increased by increasing their water holding capacity through fracturing rocks by blasting or underground explosions, or by creation of underground barriers to temporarily store water, restrict the rate of flow, or divert the water along more desirable paths. The advantages of using ground water aquifers to a greater extent are minimization of evaporation losses, decrease in adverse environmental effects of construction, lower cost than construction of surface storage facilities, and decrease in pollution hazards. While recharge of aquifers has been practiced with varying degrees of success for many years in many places, it is not always successful. Recharge wells tend to become clogged with silt, and aquifers may become polluted. Nevertheless, the prognosis for recharge of aquifers and increased use of ground water for augmentation of water supplies in the West is probably more favorable than development of surface supplies. More states are recognizing the interrelationships between surface and ground water, and policies are being adapted to provide for conjunctive management of water resources from the two sources, which is an essential step before full use can be made of ground water to augment present supplies.

Water Harvesting Through Land Management

Land management through control of vegetation on watersheds and along water courses can be an important tool in augmenting water supplies. Typically, from 25 to 100 percent of precipitation is lost through evaporation or transpiration near the point where it falls. By modifying vegetal cover on watersheds, replacing dense forest with grass and scattered trees, or replacing brush and shrubs with grass, present water supplies in some watersheds can be increased by 10 percent or more. The soil surface itself can be treated to increase infiltration or to increase runoff into collection areas; either technique might be beneficial in augmenting water supplies in some areas of the West.

Removal of phreatophytes–water-loving plants such as salt cedars or cottonwood trees whose roots reach all the way down to the ground water–is another technique that can be used to increase usable water supplies. A number of projects having this objective have been undertaken along water courses in the Rio Grande and Lower Colorado River basins. Phreatophyte removal must be accompanied by substitution of other vegetal cover, to prevent erosion and environmental objections that can be expected if wildlife habitat is destroyed in the process. Removal of phreatophytes through chemical defoliation also may have adverse side effects.

Desalinization

Substantial amounts of research funds have been expended on desalinization technology since 1952 when the federal research program was initiated. A number of demonstration plants have been built and operated by the U.S. government, and a sizeable industry has been developed, dominated largely by European firms. Costs of distillation projects are high and going higher as energy costs increase. Efforts have been made to finance large scale dual purpose desalting plants, in which heat is used for electric power generation as well as desalting, but the economics, based on the distillation process, have not been favorable.

Recent advances in development of processes for desalting of brackish water have centered on the reverse osmosis process, which uses less energy. A large plant is being built on the lower Colorado River to improve the quality of the water delivered to Mexico under the 1945 U.S.-Mexico Treaty and subsequent agreements. The need for the project is still being debated and costs are expected to be at least three times higher than the estimates on the basis of which it was authorized.

While solar distillation would appear to show some promise of reduced costs, the immense area required and substantial construction cost of the facilities required offset the savings in cost of energy.

Coupling of a desalting plant with a geothermal resource of hot brine is a possibility and may prove economic in such areas as the Imperial Valley of California, which is underlain with an immense reservoir of saline water at high temperature. Geothermal heat would be used in a dual purpose plant to produce electric power and to produce fresh water from the brine.

Precipitation Augmentation

Meteorologists believe that only about 10 percent of the water in the atmosphere actually reaches the earth. Laboratory experiments conducted by Langmuir in 1946 established a scientific basis for concluding that under favorable circumstances precipitation can be increased by seeding clouds with silver iodide crystals. If precipitation could be increased at the times and the places where there is need for additional water supply, this would appear to be an extremely valuable technique for augmenting water supplies in the western United States.

The processes and potential of precipitation augmentation as a means of augmenting water supply are not yet fully understood. Research so far appears to have established that cloud-seeding techniques may be used to increase precipitation from winter orographic clouds (clouds that are forced upward as they pass over mountains) without significant adverse environmental effects. The additional snowfall produced creates problems in highway maintenance costs, increases danger from avalanches, and may decrease precipitation elsewhere, but the skiers should love it. A research and demonstration program conducted by the Bureau of Reclamation in the San Juan Mountains of southern Colorado over a four-year period led to the conclusion that seeding produced increases in precipitation of about 10 percent during a winter of average snowfall, with a resulting potential increase in the flow of the San Juan River of about 19 percent.

Progress toward developing a scientific basis for increasing precipitation from warm season convective clouds has been much slower, but many atmospheric scientists believe that we know enough to conduct a full scale field experiment. Environmental problems may be greater; too much rain in the summer months may have adverse economic effects. So far there is no way to show that increased precipitation in one area may not result in a decrease in other areas. An environmental impact statement based on the results obtained to date and the comments of concerned individuals, agencies, and interest groups has been filed, and the Bureau of Reclamation is continuing research in the high plains regions of Montana, Kansas, and Texas, with cooperation of the states and the universities. It may be decades before we know enough to be able to count on augmenting water supplies by artificially increasing precipitation.

Better Forecasting of Hydrologic Events

Research on precipitation augmentation may lead to increased knowledge of atmospheric processes that may make it possible to make better forecasts of both long- and short-term precipitation. Accurate forecasts could make it possible to manage reservoirs in such a way as to increase usable water supplies. Reliable and accurate short-term forecasts would permit use of flood-control storage for water conservation, while accurate long-term forecasts would permit modification of agricultural programs so as to decrease water demands and minimize drought losses.

Augmenting Fog Drip

When low-lying clouds or fog intercept the earth's surface, condensation of water occurs, and the ground and the vegetal cover becomes wet. This is sometimes referred to as horizontal precipitation, cloud condensation, or fog drip, and occurs naturally in many places, including the forests along the coastal shores and mountains of California and Oregon. An experiment in Hawaii consisting of planting Norfolk Island Pine trees on a cloud swept ridge on the island of Lanai in Hawaii has demonstrated that the technique may be useful. The estimated increase in water supply of 400 acre-feet annually is used for supplemental irrigation on pineapple plantations in neighboring valleys. Other development possibilities for the use of fog drip include planting crops under trees so the crops could utilize drip water, or using impervious surfaces under trees to collect the fog drip water for delivery to crops. More research into such techniques as inducing electrical charges in the fog particles and chemical seeding might develop more efficient ways to harvest water from fog drip.

Snow and Icefield Management

A number of techniques involving manipulation of snow and ice resulting from winter precipitation have been advanced. Application of snow melt retardants on high mountain snow fields might be useful in prolonging the period of spring runoff in many areas of the West. Deliberate avalanching of selected snow fields so as to create deep piles that would melt slowly late in the spring to meet water demands or to replenish reservoir storage might promote more efficient use of snow melt retardants, as they could be applied to a reduced area of denser snow. Care would have to be taken that the avalanche snow is not in a warmer area that would induce more rapid melting than at the unavalanched site. Likewise, it is necessary to insure that the avalanched snow does not block a live stream.

Creation of artificial ice fields has also been mentioned as a means of delaying spring runoff to augment usable water supplies during the late spring or summer. Water released from reservoirs on winter nights and sprayed onto shaded terraces or north-facing slopes would freeze as it falls, forming an ice field that would melt in the spring to augment water supply. If the water would have spilled anyway and been lost downstream, this would have the effect of increasing the yield of the reservoir, but in a fully controlled river system no new water supply would be created. Environmental impacts and costs have not been assessed.

Iceberg Towing

Discussion of snow and ice leads naturally to the subject of iceberg towing—capturing or quarrying floating icebergs and towing them to a suitable offshore point where they could be broken up into manageable pieces that could be hauled on shore by a conveyor belt or other system to provide cooling and water supply. The technique has been much talked about but never put into practice. It has been ascertained that the icebergs from the Antarctic would be more suitable than those from the Arctic, since the latter are irregularly shaped because they come from mountain glaciers. This tends to make them dangerously unstable.

Icebergs from the great Antarctic ice shelf tend to be larger and of a more regular shape so they can be more safely towed. Ocean currents that flow northward from the Antarctic continent also favor use of icebergs from the south, even though they would have to be towed across the tropics. It has been estimated that five or six of the largest tugboats could move an iceberg of 100 million tons at a speed of one knot with a loss of only about 20 percent of its volume, if suitable protection against erosion is provided.

An international conference on this subject held in October 1977 at the University of Iowa concluded that the problems posed were within the reach of existing technology and that water produced from icebergs would cost less than fresh water produced by desalinization. If the technique is to be tried it would appear that Saudi Arabia would be the logical place, as the needs are great and there are fewer alternative sources of water. Until such a test is made, there is little reason to look to towing icebergs as a means of augmenting the water supplies of the western United States.

Undersea Aqueducts

One of the potential sources of augmenting water supplies in southern California that was considered in the Bureau of Reclamation's United Western investigation was an undersea aqueduct carrying fresh water southward from the mouth of the Columbia River. The principle involves laying a large-diameter, flexible or semirigid plastic pipe leading from a pumping station at the source, which is at the mouth of the river, taking the water at a point where it is no longer of use to the basin of origin. The Bureau of Reclamation report concluded in 1950 that a conventional interbasin transfer would be more economical. Since then other proposals have been advanced, but they appear to be more in the realm of science fiction than that of a serious alternative source for augmentation of water supply in the West.

Collapsible Bladders for Transport of Liquids

Petroleum products can be transported through waterways and the sea by using large watertight bags or bladders fabricated of synthetic rubber or some type of plastic film. The same technique could be used with water. The empty bladder could be easily transported to a place where there is an excess of fresh water, immersed, and loaded with fresh water, then towed by ship to the point where the water is needed. Such a method might be used to provide for reuse of some of the vast quantities of fresh water that flow out to sea from the mouth of the Columbia River.

Evaporation Reduction

The possibility of increasing water yield by controlling evaporation from land surfaces has been touched on briefly earlier in this paper. Similar results could be achieved through spreading a layer of an insoluble chemical coating, such as hexadecanol, on reservoirs. The technique is not effective in areas of high winds that break up the layer or drive it up on the shore. At the time extensive tests and research were conducted by the Bureau of Reclamation, it appeared that the cost of the treatment was equal to or greater than the value of the water saved.

Demand Reduction

Thoughtful consideration of the alternatives discussed heretofore tends to lead one to the almost inescapable conclusion that the most economical solution to the problem of satisfying demands, at least over the near term, is demand reduction. All of the methods heretofore discussed involve costs, both economic and environmental. On the other hand, some forms of demand reduction actually create savings. Savings in pumping costs and savings in pipe sizes and the size of the facilities are a few of the obvious ways in which savings may accrue. Savings may be offset by the cost of the more careful engineering and more intensive water management techniques that may be required.

Pricing

Water has been so abundant that it was assumed in the past to be a "free good" available for the taking. The importance of water availability as a stimulus to the economy has led to subsidies that were deemed to be necessary to achieve various social purposes, such as the encouragement of development in the West. The time has come for the need to subsidize the price of water for agriculture to be reexamined. Pricing of water at levels which repay costs of development in full would be a powerful stimulus to more efficient use of water and reduction in demand.

Water Reuse

Rising costs and increasing environmental regulation have led to an increase in recycling and reuse of water in industrial plants. This stretches the use of existing water supplies and reduces demand for new supplies. The use of effluent from municipal sewage treatment plants for industrial purposes is quite prevalent in the East, and extension of the practice in the West could reduce demands for development of new supplies. A demonstration project right here in Denver is pointing the way.

Recycling of effluents back through the primary drinking water system cannot be recommended at this time and does not appear to be necessary yet. Research is under way that should clear up some of the unknown questions about what happens to the pathogenic bacteria and viruses and other impurities which may persist through the treatment process. At some time in the future, it may be possible to reuse and recycle some of the water that now passes once through the municipal systems, thus effecting a substantial reduction in demand.

Increased Efficiency in Irrigation

Experience with some crops during the California drought a few years ago showed that yields actually increased when a smaller amount of water was applied. While this is not a condition of general applicability for most crops, it is true that there are many instances in which irrigation diversion can be reduced. For example, the flooding of high mountain meadowland to create forage for livestock may result in unnecessary evaporation losses. Application of irrigation water under controls related to soil moisture conditions, rather than water rights, also might result in savings. Very specialized techniques, such as trickle irrigation, are also available, but at a considerable cost. As water shortages in the West become more prevalent, we can expect some reduction in demand of water for irrigated agriculture, if our institutions can be updated to meet the new conditions.

Improved Institutions for Allocating Water

This subject is to be discussed by several speakers at the Friday morning session, so it will not be covered here.

Conclusion

In the available time it has been possible to touch only briefly on the many ways of augmenting water supplies in the western states. A great deal of additional research is underway that has not been possible for me to assimilate in the available time. No attempt has been made to compare the costs of various alternatives for augmenting supply or reducing demand, since the estimates contained in the literature are based on different assumptions, not always clearly stated. On the basis of my experience, I would reiterate my view that the most economic way to bring supply and demand into balance is by reducing demand.

References

Bishop, A. Bruce and Narayanan, R. "Competition of Energy for Agricultural Water Use," *Journal of the Irrigation and Drainage Division*, American Society of Civil Engineers, September 1979, p. 317.

Langbein, Walter B. *Water Yield and Reservoir Storage in the United States*, U.S. Geological Survey Circular 409, Washington, D.C., 1959.

McGinnies and Goldman, editors. *Arid Lands in Perspective*, University of Arizona Press, 1969.

Murray, C. Richard and Reeves, E. Bodette. *Estimated Use of Water in the United States in 1975*, U.S. Geological Survey Circular 765, Arlington, Va., 1977.

National Academy of Sciences Committee on Technologies and Water. *Potential Technological Advances and Their Impact on Anticipated Water Requirements*, National Technical Information Service, PB-204-053, Washington, D.C., June, 1971.

Quinn, Frank. *Water Transfers; Must the West Be Won Again?*, Geographical Review, vol. 58, 1968, pp. 108–132.

U.S. Bureau of Reclamation. *Project Skywater*, Fiscal Years 1975–78 Reports on the Atmospheric Resources Management Program, Denver, Colorado, March 1979.

U.S. National Water Commission. *Water Policies for the Future*, Washington, D.C., June 1973.

U.S. Water Resources Council. *The Nation's Water Resources, 1975-2000*, vol. 1, Summary, Washington, D.C., December 1978.

Victor, Paul-Emile. *Will Deserts Drink Icebergs?* UNESCO Courier, Paris, February 1978.

Commentary

Keith A. Henry

My discussion of Theodore M. Schad's paper is going to be amicable. I have no quarrel with the facts on which he bases his arguments and I agree with his conclusions, although I may be a bit more pessimistic than he is about the future at least until we make some difficult decisions. I think the most useful contribution I can make to our deliberations here is to tell you how some of the points made by Mr. Schad appear to a Canadian, which may indicate that we put a different emphasis on some of them.

I must admit that having worked with Americans nearly all my professional life in cooperation on river systems (such as the Niagara, St. Lawrence, and Columbia) and then having served with the International Joint Commission for several years, I occasionally suffer a lapse into confusion about what I mean by "we" and "you." Sometimes "you" are Americans and "we" are Canadians, but often "we" are engineers and scientists, and "you" are those who disagree with "us."

May I make it clear that I speak in my private capacity as a professional engineer, and that while I am not aware that Canadian government has a different point of view or policy than I will be expressing, still I am not pretending to be giving you an official Canadian viewpoint.

First of all I would like to emphasize a point about water use that occasionally is forgotten. Sometimes accidentally and sometimes deliberately, confusion arises about the nature of consumptive use of water, which we speak of as the "bottom line" in water demand. Consumptive use is overwhelmingly for irrigation. Irrigation use is at least a full order of magnitude larger than other consumptive uses. For instance, the use by all the people of California, for domestic and industrial purposes, would only be about 15 percent of the consumptive use in the state. That is the withdrawal, mind you, and usually two-thirds of municipal withdrawals are returned to the water cycle at a point not far removed from the point of withdrawal. Municipal consumptive use therefore amounts to something in the order of 5 percent of the total. Other consumptive uses are also normally small so that when we talk about water supplies and water shortages and water demands, we are in the main talking about water for irrigation. This point needs to be kept in mind.

Of course there are specific concentrations of other consumptive uses that may raise some local difficulties. These usually occur in large cities where industries and municipalities use large quantities of water. However, conservation practices are very effective in reducing consumption, generally through on-site treatment and reuse in industry, and through pricing in municipalities. The important point to remember is that the shortages we face are basically for irrigation.

Mr. Schad's review of various possibilities for augmentation of the supply clearly makes the point that while we may tinker with the established system, there is little hope of significant results in the next couple of decades. One can go further and say that even after that period there is little ground for hope that anything significant will occur until we can make a quantum leap in energy supplies to a point where pumping and desalinization can be undertaken on scales not presently viable. In addition, we will have to achieve a better understanding of environmental impacts and methods of protection.

The greatest changes we have brought about in water supplies are by means of dams and canals. The impoundments behind dams transfer water in time, from one part of a year to another, or even to another year. Canals (and tunnels and pipelines) transfer water in space, from one part of a valley to another or even to another valley or another basin. These two mechanisms are combined to make water available to dry areas at times of need. However, I believe we have passed the heyday of dam-building and interbasin transfer. Recreation and environmental concerns have created a whole new concept of what has to be considered in deciding on whether or not to carry out such projects.

I do not think we should decry what we have done in the past. Those projects which I am familiar with such as the Niagara developments and the St. Lawrence, the Ottawa River, the Peace, and the Columbia (in Canada) have to my mind had benefits far outweighing the costs. But the most beneficial and least harmful projects have naturally been done first, and the costs of those left tend to be high. This becomes more apparent when we begin to recognize and count certain types of costs that have been ignored in the past, such as loss of recreational opportunity or aesthetic values.

Mr. Schad says quite rightly that interbasin transfers across state lines are dubious today. We now recognize that the selling of our water birthright is a very doubtful transaction under the best of circumstances. It is difficult to assess what new uses and priorities will arise in the future. This is important because I believe that such a sale has to be considered as being in perpetuity. It is well nigh unthinkable to cut off a supply on which an agricultural industry and a significant social complex has developed. I am not suggesting that no more interbasin transfer schemes will be carried out, but I do suggest that the colossal concepts such as NAWAPA will not be practicable with the technical, economic, energy, and political constraints under which we presently live, and even smaller schemes are going to present great difficulties.

To a Canadian it seems as if the most logical source of water for the western United States is the Columbia. In that river we generously allow an annual average of some 90,000 cfs (nearly 60 bgd) to flow unimpeded across the forty-ninth parallel for your use. In fact, we have even allowed you to build, or at least pay for, three very large dams in Canada that markedly improve the flow distribution throughout the year—to our mutual advantage. We have our own critics who claim that under the Columbia Treaty, we have sold our birthright. This I do not believe. I am satisfied that the Columbia River development in Canada has been to our advantage and we will long enjoy substantial benefits from it. But these developments and the many more in the United States make the Columbia a very large water resource within your own jurisdiction.

I recognize that the economics of moving this water to areas of shortage are doubtful, but they must be just as doubtful for our Fraser River, if not more so. Indeed, I think there is very little sympathy in Canada for any transfers of water out of Canada west of the Great Divide until the United States has devised some method of making use of its own share of Columbia River water.

On the Great Plains the situation is different. There we are both short of water for irrigation. On our own southernmost river system of the prairies, the Saskatchewan, we built a major impoundment in the 1960s: Diefenbaker Lake formed by Gardiner Dam. Its storage is not yet fully utilized but it will be eventually, and this means that it is not a source for export. Unfortunately, this particular situation demonstrates very explicitly the international contiguity of water-short areas that makes the likelihood of international water transfer minimal.

I would like to remark parenthetically at this point that the Garrison Project is an example of the problems we can expect to have to cope with in the future when we consider interbasin transfers. It also shows how much more complex such transfers become when an international boundary is involved in the transfer. Finally, it demonstrates how necessary a mechanism such as the Boundary Water Treaty and the International Joint Commission is in preventing a local difficulty from exacerbating national emotions and in bringing a sense of reasonableness to the resolution of serious problems.

To realize how fortunate we are, we need only look at the unfortunate situation in which Nepal and India find themselves. The huge Ganges River, which is the life line of hundreds of millions of people in India, rises in substantial measure in Nepal. Nepal would like to derive some benefit from development of this resource, but without any mutual agreement with India there is no easy way to proceed. India is nervous about any sort of change to river flows unless she is in control. The rivers all cross the boundary one way and so the shoe is always on the same foot. When the final complication of having Bangladesh downstream of India is added, I think a picture is presented that ought to make us thankful that our problems are only between states or between provinces, and between two countries who are good neighbors.

North of the Saskatchewan Basin, the Athabasca-Peace-MacKenzie system flows to the Arctic. Mr. Schad speaks of it as probably always flowing north into the Arctic unused. Canadians look at this differently, as a presently undeveloped resource, and feel that while it presently flows unused to the north it does not do so unusefully. Our scientists are uncertain about the fragile Arctic ecology and the effect of the large flow of fresh water, of sediments and of heat on the MacKenzie Delta and the Arctic Ocean itself. At the moment the river is also an important navigation link. This is not an exhaustive list of concerns about our northern-flowing rivers but the concerns are very real and make even consideration of a transfer very difficult at the present time.

On another subject, the use of Canada as a corridor to transport water from Alaska to the contiguous continental states depends on the size of the transfer. A pipeline might be politically and technically possible but it is economically ridiculous as evidenced by the cost of the oil pipeline financing. I suppose when water is worth \$22 a barrel or say \$133,000 an acre-foot then we can look at it again. A system of canals and lakes in the Rockies such as that proposed under NAWAPA is technically feasible and might some day be an economic possibility. It is not, however, a political possibility in British Columbia where flooding of the Rocky Mountain Trench and other comparable projects would inundate a very large percentage of our habitable land, undeveloped though it may be at this time.

Indeed, to some of us in Canada it seems that when the western United States begins to look to Canada for water it is not because you do not have it in the United States but because you have a lot of political problems between your states in transferring water from the Columbia system. Believe me, there are just as great political problems in Canada where water resources are the property of the provinces, and in addition there is the even more difficult one of international transfers.

Mr. Schad has spoken of some of the more exotic ideas of augmenting the western water supply. Unfortunately, most of them can only be thought of in terms of uses other than for agriculture. For instance, the best available technology at present indicates a cost of over \$1,000 per acre-foot for desalting water. Iceberg towing has an indicated cost of between $100 and $200 per acre-foot to bring it up from the Antarctic to a coastal point in the United States, but it is certainly going to be expensive to get it to where it's needed.

The idea of reducing evapotranspiration to increase groundwater supplies by changing forest areas to grass may indeed have possible applications. It needs, however, to be measured against the value of the biomass production of the forest that may have a future, not only as pulp and timber, but also as a renewable resource to produce liquid fuels.

One is led by all this to Mr. Schad's pretty well inescapable conclusion. The most practical, economically viable action we can presently undertake is to reduce our water demands. The capital costs involved will be relatively small and the results will be immediate. The first step that appears prudent to an outsider is to move gradually but effectively to a system where users pay the true cost of water. This means that subsidizing water supply schemes on a permanent basis must gradually be discontinued. For uses other than agriculture, actual savings will unquestionably accrue as reuse becomes general and waste is reduced. As far as agriculture is concerned it means that a more realistic evaluation will occur as to what is the most economic means of filling our food requirements. It seems to me that two aspects need consideration.

First, the institutions and laws that govern water appropriations, transfers, and uses must be changed to take into account the priorities that our society now places on use of water. The uses considered must include energy production, navigation, industrial and domestic use, mining, agriculture, and commercial fishing, as always. But it must now also include recreation and aesthetics, which have often been ignored or at best considered as incidental. Mr. Schad mentions the allocation of irrigation water on an as-needed basis rather than according to the rights held by a user. This seems eminently reasonable, but it is going to be difficult to implement. Second, all the techniques we have developed to increase agricultural efficiency that we can characterize as best management practices must become standard practice.

I would (somewhat diffidently) suggest that a minimum of

legislative revision to enable the necessary changes be made and combined with a maximum of inducement through gradually improved pricing systems for water. This, I believe, is our best hope to reduce the demand.

As a last thought, may I suggest it is time for us to accept the fact that fresh water is a finite resource. In many places in the western United States we are far along the way to making the maximum withdrawals from all available sources. Now we must make sure that our institutions and our technology are used efficiently to plan the most satisfactory developments in accord with our priorities, thereby maximizing the benefits we can obtain from our water resources. An acceptance must be engendered of the fact that there is a limit to the expansion of irrigated agriculture and other high consumptive uses of water. Where mining of groundwater or salinization is taking place it may be necessary to cut back. But these are the realities and we will be better off when they are understood not just by our technical people but by commercial operators, businessmen, politicians, and the public.

9 Financing Water Resources Development

Leo M. Eisel
Richard M. Wheeler

Introduction

In theory, cost sharing and financing are distinct: financing refers to the provision of funds enabling the implementation of a project, while cost sharing refers to the agreements made among involved parties to assume responsibility for the payment of incurred expenses. In practice, however, the distinction between cost sharing and financing tends to blur and becomes less distinct. For example, a local government may seek federal cost sharing as one of several alternative methods of financing a local project. The cost-sharing policies and programs of the federal government profoundly affect the financing arrangements of local and state governments and the private sector for water resources development and management. Consequently, in the discussion which follows, some effort is made to separate financing and cost sharing, but in general, the two concepts merge.

The role of financing and cost sharing in water resources development has received relatively little attention in the past. Compared to the attention given to benefit-cost analysis, the role of financing and cost sharing in water resources development has been ignored. This lack of attention probably results because cost sharing does not rest on an elegant theoretical basis and is politically sensitive. Furthermore, only minimal data on cost sharing and financing local, state, and federal government and private water projects and programs exist.

In the following sections, a brief survey is made of past and present financing practices for water resources development and the roles of federal and nonfederal governments and private interests in financing. A more detailed look at the varied assortment of existing federal and nonfederal cost sharing provisions is then presented along with a sampling of some emerging issues. The focus here is on policy questions that are currently arising due to competing interests for water and water project funding. Next, several proposed strategies for dealing with these issues are discussed including the current administration's proposal resulting from the president's water policy review. Finally, some closing remarks are made concerning the substantial changes necessary to bring about consistent, equitable, and efficient cost sharing and financing arrangements in water development.

Federal Financing and Cost Sharing

Federal Interest and Involvement

Historically, the federal government has had a major interest and involvement in financing and managing water resources development. This federal interest and involvement stems from the close association between national goals and water resources and is fundamentally based on the constitutional provisions of the Preamble, the Commerce Clause, war and treaty powers, and interstate compacts. In practice, however, it is through taxing and spending that the federal government can allocate financing resources to specific water problems. The underlying motivation is often a national interest such as national defense, economic development, environmental quality, or general social well-being. According to North (1978), justification for federal involvement in water resources can be summarized in four functions:

1. Meeting national priorities, either constitutionally specified or jointly agreed upon by federal and nonfederal interests.
2. Providing and allocating public goods or services associated with water development.
3. Providing reservations for the future.
4. Providing a response to emergency and critical needs.

National priorities motivate the federal government's involvement in many areas, and water is no exception. These priorities change from time to time and emphasis has been placed on such aspects of development as navigation, irrigation, flood control, energy, and the environment. Attention is focused on these areas of water development as possible means to achieve more general national goals such as defense, economic development, full employment, wage and price stability, and income redistribution.

Over the years, important water-related congressional acts have provided explicit areas and means for federal involvement in water resources development and management. In general, the intent has been to assign the cost of providing benefits to the direct recipients. However, the Rivers and Harbors, Flood Control, Reclamation, and Water Resources Development acts and amendments have dealt with this principle inconsistently, due in part to the difficulty in identifying beneficiaries.

The Reclamation Act of 1902 required the beneficiaries of irrigation water to repay the capital costs of irrigation and to assume responsibility for operation and maintenance costs (P.L. 161, 1902). The Rivers and Harbors Appropriation Act of 1884 prohibited any cost burden to be placed on users of navigation channels (C. 224, S. 4, 23 Stat. 147). The Rivers and Harbors Act of 1902 recognized that local benefits derived from federal investment in rivers and harbors and provided for local cooperation in return (P.L. 154, 1902). This cooperation has typically been in the form of lands, easements, and rights-of-way. Another manifestation of federal financing and cost sharing came into being with the Flood Control Act of 1936 (P.L. 738, 1936). Under the act, extent of federal cost sharing varies, but in general it includes all implementation excluding lands, easements, and rights-of-way that must come from nonfederal project sponsors. On the average, the federal financing share for local flood control projects amounts to about 80 percent of the total first cost (National Water Commission, 1973). Although the original 1936 Flood Control Act included major flood control reservoirs in the cost-sharing provisions, later amendments in 1938, 1941, and 1944 excluded nonfederal cost sharing of reservoirs. The rationale behind that decision included such factors as interstate problems, the national interest, and the inability to identify beneficiaries. Federal involvement in municipal and industrial water supply has been a more recent development. The Water Supply Act of 1958 (P.L. 85-500, Title III) provides for federal financing of water supply storage in federal reservoirs for municipal and industrial purposes but requires 100 percent reimbursement of capital and operating maintenance costs.

Quantitative estimates of federal financial involvement in water resources development and management as a result of these various federal acts are displayed in Tables 1 and 2. Table 1, from the Report of the National Water Commission (National Water Commission, 1973), presents estimated historic federal expenditures for water resources development for the period 1900–1970. Table 2 presents a summary of federal water-related obligations by purpose, by major agency, and by type of financing for 1974. With the exception of expenditures for water quality as detailed below, little change in relative funding levels has occurred since 1974.

With the passage of the Water Quality Act of 1965 (P.L. 89–234) and the Federal Water Pollution Control Act Amendments of 1972 (P.L. 92–500), the federal government became heavily involved in the financing of water-quality projects. To achieve the goals of the 1972 act, $18 billion was authorized for planning, design, and construction of wastewater treatment facilities. These funds are administered by the Environmental Protection Agency under a cost-sharing arrangement that provides for a federal share of 75 percent of construction costs, with the remaining 25 percent to come from state and/or local contributions. As a result of "midcourse corrections," the Federal Water Pollution Control Act Amendments of 1977 (P.L. 95-217) extended the deadlines set in 1972 and authorized an additional $24.5 billion for the EPA Facilities Construction Grants Program, covering the period 1978–1982. While the full Fiscal Year 1978 authorization of $4.5 billion was appropriated, the annual appropriations of $4.2 billion (FY 1979) and $3.4 billion (FY 1980) have fallen short of the $5 billion annual authorizations. However, federal financing of water quality is

TABLE 1
Estimated Historic Federal Expenditures for Water Resources and Related Activities
(billions of 1972 dollars)

	Indexing Factor[a]	*Navigation*	*Flood Control*	*Irrigation*	*Power*	*Water Supply & Pollution Control*	*Watershed Protection*	*Fisheries & Wildlife*	*Multiple Purpose*	*Total*
1900	18.7	.35	–	–	–	–	–	–	–	.35
1905	18.6	.43	–	.09	–	–	–	–	–	.52
1910	17.5	.55	–	.14	–	–	–	–	–	.69
1915	18.2	.85	–	.18	–	–	–	–	–	1.03
1920	6.8	.28	.06	.04	–	–	–	–	–	.38
1925	8.1	.53	.12	.07	–	–	–	–	–	.72
1930	8.3	.66	.35	.07	.04	–	–	–	–	1.12
1935	8.6	1.48	.38	.18	.11	–	–	–	–	2.15
1940	7.0	1.02	.74	.24	.23	.01	–	–	.11	2.35
1945	5.5	.28	.40	.08	.14	–	–	–	.07	.97
1950	3.3	.44	.90	.48	.53	.03	.01	–	.84	3.23
1955	2.55	.29	.38	.19	.44	.02	.02	.01	.66	2.01
1960	2.03	.59	.69	.17	.46	.15	.03	.02	1.07	3.18
1965	1.73	.70	.92	.16	.61	.23	.06	.02	.49	3.19
1970	1.22	.23	.36	.11	.55	.56	.08	.02	.40	2.31

[a]The indexing factor is the multiplier used to convert current dollars to 1972 constant dollars.

Source: Adapted from John B. Legler et al. (1971). A Historical Study of Water Resources Policy of the Federal Government, 1900–1970, prepared for the National Water Commission. Mimeo, Washington University, St. Louis, Mo., pp. 397–398.

TABLE 2
Summary of Federal Water Related Obligations by Purpose, by Major Agency and by Type of Financing, 1974

Purpose	*Total (mil $)*	*(%)*	*By Major Agency (mil $)* SCS	*Corps*	*BuRec*	*EPA*	*Other*	*By Type Financing (mil $)* Direct	*Grant*	*Loan*
Urban flood damage reduction	796	11	<1	364	-0-	-0-	432	404	107	285
Rural flood damage reduction	564	8	64	355	17	-0-	128	434	-0-	130
Drainage	27	<1	5	1	-0-	-0-	21	27	-0-	-0-
Agricultural water supply	172	2	28	19	126	-0-	-0-	160	-0-	12
Erosion and runoff control	120	2	-0-	26	-0-	-0-	94	120	-0-	-0-
M&I water supply	397	6	3	43	40	-0-	311	85	20	293
Water quality management (P.S.)	3008	42	-0-	1	<1	2662	345	22	2805	181
Recreation—general	325	5	9	149	10	-0-	157	198	127	<1
Fishing and hunting	114	2	1	16	19	-0-	78	72	41	1
Boating—berthed and launched	10	<1	-0-	7	-0-	-0-	10	10	-0-	-0-
Natural areas	28	<1	-0-	<1	<1	-0-	28	25	3	-0-
Historic and cultural sites	<1	<1	-0-	-0-	-0-	-0-	-0-	<1	-0-	-0-
Ecological systems	2	<1	-0-	<1	-0-	-0-	2	2	-0-	-0-
Navigation	660	9	-0-	660	<1	-0-	-0-	660	-0-	-0-
Hydroelectric power	419	6	-0-	206	130	-0-	83	419	-0-	-0-
All other	483	7	34	32	78	57	282	313	143	26
Total	7125	100	144	1879	420	2719	1963	2951	3246	928

Source: Taken from "Financing Water Resources Planning, Implementation, Management: The Unsolved Problems," 1978, by Ronald M. North; the information comes from U.S. Water Resources Council, *Planning and Cost Sharing Policy Options for Water and Related Land Programs*, "Current Situation," Part II, Washington, D.C., November 1975.

by far still the largest single component of total federal expenditures for water resources development and management.

Since the 1972 amendments, $28.2 billion has been appropriated for EPA grants (through FY 1979). About $21.2 billion of this total has been obligated in contracts and approximately $11 billion has actually been outlaid (U.S. Environmental Protection Agency, 1979a). In comparison, under the 1956 Water Pollution Control Act Amendments, which first authorized federal financial assistance in the construction of municipal treatment plants, a total of $5.2 billion was granted for projects between 1956 and 1972.

Cost Sharing

Federal interest and involvement in financing of water resource development is closely related to, and in some cases identical to, the federal interest and involvement in cost sharing. The National Water Commission articulated a clear statement of goals for federal cost sharing (National Water Commission, 1973):

- To provide adequate supplies of water and water-related services for the nation developed at least cost over time.
- To promote the efficient use of water and water-related services by users.
- To encourage improved management of land and other related resources in conjunction with water.
- To promote harmony of water developments with other national policies and programs.

A central element in any notion of cost sharing is that of an equitable distribution of costs. This goal is deceptively easy to state, but a widespread agreement on what is equitable is difficult if not impossible to obtain. While requiring the beneficiaries to bear the cost of providing received benefits is conceptually sound, it is in the identification of the beneficiaries that the problem lies. First, the benefits from a water project may be so widespread that beneficiaries can be identified in only general terms. Flood control projects illustrate this problem in that the resulting flood protection can be enjoyed by residents of states and towns as well as by industries over a considerable area. Another difficulty lies in the traditional approach of allowing the federal government to underwrite public benefits but assessing to private beneficiaries the portion of costs allocated to the provision of private benefits. The problem here is to define clearly what is meant by the terms public and private. For example, the costs of irrigation projects have customarily been transferred to the recipients of the water, indicating a private benefit. However, in many cases the water is not priced at market value; hence the agricultural water supply has, in effect, been subsidized, indicating some sort of public benefit.

Current Practices and Policies

The current cost-sharing situation for water resources development reflects the lack of consistent or uniform policies. Cost sharing in practice involves a wide variety of participants, methods, and timing schedules. The Section 80(c) Study, the most detailed analysis of federal cost sharing to date, summarized the current situation for 1974 and a brief discussion of that summary lends useful insight into the complexity of the issue (U.S. Water Resources Council, 1975). At the federal level, cost-sharing participants in water resources include seven cabinet departments encompassing eighteen agencies and seven independent agencies, commissions, and authorities. Methods of cost sharing at the federal level include grants, loans, and direct investment in programs and projects. At the nonfederal level, shares can be borne through contributions in cash or in kind, responsibility for operations and maintenance, user charges, reimbursement contracts from user fees, or assessments. Regarding timing of the cost-sharing arrangement, a distinction must be made between implementation costs and operating, maintenance, and replacement costs. The federal share for implementation can occur either during construction or as a reimbursement, while the nonfederal share can appear in either of these forms or through contracted periodic payments or market-based direct payments (made when, as, and if used). For operation, maintenance, and replacement costs, the federal share can be appropriated as required or contributed through a reimbursement arrangement. The nonfederal share can appear currently as required or as repayments derived from user charges.

To further complicate the cost-sharing picture, there exists a wide variety of water resource development purpose categories. Twelve major purposes were defined in the Section 80 Study and included such areas as urban flood damage reduction, agricultural production, water quality management, navigation, etc. (see Tables 3 and 4). Furthermore, it is possible to separate cost-sharing arrangements according to the measures employed (such as construction of levees, dams and channels; flood warning systems; and sewage treatment plants). Finally, cost-sharing arrangements apparently vary among the twenty-one water resources regions of the nation (see Table 3). For example, in the case of recreation, the nonfederal percentage varies from 8 percent in the Arkansas and Upper Colorado regions to 70 percent in the Tennessee region. For irrigation, the nonfederal share varies from 10 percent in the Missouri region to 66 percent in the Alaska region.

Before analyzing some specific examples that illustrate aspects of the current situation, it is necessary to develop a definition of cost sharing. To merely say that cost sharing is the agreement concerning cost allocation among federal and nonfederal interests is not adequate. For example, a 50 percent share contributed at the front end is not the same as a 50 percent share distributed over a specific repayment period, interest free, or a 50 percent share paid back over time with interest. For this purpose, the Section 80 Study used the concept of "effective composite" cost sharing. The term "effective" refers to the result of adjustments made for the impacts and implications of the major exceptions, provisions, and conditions which make the nonfederal actual cost share different from the stated cost share. Specifically, an effective cost share considers

- timing of the nonfederal contribution to the project, whether initially or by reimbursement,
- the interest rate on the reimbursable balance,
- the number of interest-free years,
- the length of the repayment period,
- the interest during construction,
- the magnitude and terms of transfer accounts, and
- the value of contributions in kind.

TABLE 3

Water Resources Council Options for Cost Sharing: Cost Sharing Issues–
Dimensions, Current Situation and Options Summary of the Mean, Effective, Composite
Nonfederal Cost Sharing for All Programs and Projects by Purpose, by Region (in percent)[a]

Purpose	NE 01	MA 02	SAG 03	GL 04	Ob 05	Tn 06	UM 07	LM 08	SRR 09	Mo 10	Ark 11	TG 12	RG 13	UCo 14	LCo 15	GB 16	CNP 17	CSP 18	Al 19	Ha 20	PR 21	22 22	USA 23
URBAN FLOOD DAMAGE REDUCTION	16	29	30	26	8	56	24	5	5	11	11	40	15	*	28	8	3	34	6	2	–	13	20
Rural Flood Damage Reduction	32	20	13	33	9	46	13	8	21	9	6	7	14	9	22	6	10	21	–	21	44	–	11
Drainage	37	47	53	53	43	34	47	41	47	35	41	56	34	34	54	41	50	54	33	35	63	–	46
Agricultural Water Supply (Irrigation)	34	42	27	39	35	34	34	52	37	10	18	37	19	10	32	59	11	34	66	47	50	–	19
Erosion and/or Runoff Control	83	75	78	69	82	67	79	88	82	7	16	87	89	68	89	73	48	63	2	90	89	–	34
RURAL FLOOD DAMAGE REDUCTION AND AGRICULTURAL PRODUCTION	37	32	23	43	13	48	18	10	34	9	11	11	24	13	31	33	12	30	4	27	53	–	16
Commercial Fisheries	*	33	1	–	–	–	–	10	–	–	–	–	–	–	–	–	2	1	–	*	–	*	5
Services	–	–	–	–	–	–	–	–	–	–	–	–	–	–	–	–	–	–	–	–	–	*	–
AQUACULTURAL PRODUCTION	*	33	1	–	–	–	–	10	–	–	–	–	–	–	–	–	2	1	–	*	–	33	8
M&I Water	94	52	86	96	79	90	63	72	91	56	50	67	70	75	72	57	61	53	88	–	92	–	64
Streamflow Regulation	*	13	*	–	4	–	4	31	–	–	*	–	–	–	–	–	*	–	–	–	–	–	2
WATER QUANTITY MANAGEMENT	39	46	82	96	71	90	51	62	91	56	24	67	70	75	72	57	59	53	88	–	92	–	54
Point Source	66	64	65	65	64	65	65	67	70	66	63	64	64	78	66	65	63	64	59	65	64	61	64
Non-Point Source	–	1	*	–	3	–	2	33	–	4	–	5	–	–	–	–	–	5	–	–	–	30	3
WATER QUALITY MANAGEMENT	65	62	64	65	39	65	59	65	68	49	62	63	64	77	63	64	57	64	59	65	64	60	60
General	47	27	19	47	21	75	20	19	25	16	8	16	15	6	8	44	13	20	*	35	12	50	19
Fish and Wildlife	38	27	11	33	12	27	16	39	27	11	7	9	6	10	19	30	8	19	23	58	25	–	14
Boating (Berthed and Launched)	41	24	28	39	*	50	29	50	50	50	50	50	50	50	50	50	49	52	32	50	50	50	38
RECREATION	44	27	19	42	20	70	20	25	26	15	8	16	11	8	13	41	11	22	19	42	14	50	19
Natural Areas	7	1	2	6	55	23	2	54	2	1	4	4	13	22	55	62	2	15	11	87	*	*	*
Historic & Cultural Sites	–	–	–	–	–	–	–	–	–	–	–	–	*	–	–	–	–	–	–	–	–	–	–
Ecological Systems	51	41	38	35	55	88	2	59	62	35	68	48	82	88	82	79	30	43	38	83	*	–	26
NATURAL AREAS & CULTURAL RESOURCES	13	2	5	11	55	39	2	57	4	3	5	9	18	39	73	74	4	24	18	85	*	*	6
Commercial Harbors	5	19	2	41	–	–	19	13	–	–	–	12	1	–	–	–	2	23	1	7	–	–	16
Waterways	–	9	10	13	1	94	2	6	–	3	6	6	–	–	–	–	7	20	–	–	–	–	6
Services	–	–	*	*	–	–	–	30	–	9	30	12	–	–	–	–	25	–	–	*	–	–	10
NAVIGATION	5	16	8	27	1	94	2	6	–	6	6	10	1	–	–	–	7	21	1	7	–	–	7
HYDROPOWER GENERATION	101	61	55	*	41	123	56	23	*	57	27	*	*	70	72	*	63	73	85	*	*	*	64
AREA REDEVELOPMENT BENEFITS	65	52	66	56	52	64	36	62	61	61	68	65	64	56	56	58	65	61	76	–	81	47	60
GENERAL SUPPORT OR UNALLOCATED	2	12	1	2	12	9	4	16	21	18	52	4	17	18	15	17	3	100	–	50	*	2	23
OTHER	100	21	46	50	–	–	–	13	–	9	18	2	6	4	19	–	1	28	–	*	–	–	25
REGION MEAN, ALL PURPOSES	55	42	29	47	18	70	17	10	23	21	16	33	24	37	38	39	40	42	40	32	51	23	30

[a]Weightings for the major purpose such as Water Quality Management may reflect programs that were unallocated to the subpurposes shown but included in the major purpose aggregate; (*) means there is a program or project activity for that purpose but no cost sharing was reported; (–) means there is no program or project activity reported for that purpose.

Source: U.S. Water Resources Council, *Planning and Cost Sharing Options for Water and Related Land Programs* (Washington, D.C.: U.S. Government Printing Office, November 1975.

TABLE 4

Water Resources Council Options for Cost Sharing: Cost Sharing Issues—Dimensions, Current Situation and Options

Summary of the Mean, Effective, Composite Nonfederal Cost Sharing for All Programs and Projects by Purpose, by Agency (in percent)[a]

Purpose	*ASCS*	*FmHA*	*FS*	*SCS*	*COE*	*EDA*	*NOAA*	*EPA*	*CPD*	*FIA*	*FDAA*	*BLM*	*USBR*	*BOR*	*FWLS*	*NPS*	*CG*	*FPC*	*TVA*	*SBA*	*USA*
URBAN FLOOD DAMAGE REDUCTION	–	–	–	*	17	–	–	–	–	13	*	–	*	–	–	–	–	–	94[b]	47	20
Rural Flood Damage Reduction	–	80	–	27	7	–	–	–	–	–	–	–	10	–	–	–	–	–	60	–	11
Drainage	34	–	–	58	35	–	–	–	–	–	–	–	–	–	–	–	–	–	–	–	46
Agricultural Water Supply (Irrigation)	34	–	–	54	19	–	–	–	–	–	–	–	18	–	–	–	–	–	–	–	19
Erosion and/or Runoff Control	34	–	*	89	5	–	–	–	–	–	–	*	–	–	–	–	–	–	–	–	34
RURAL FLOOD DAMAGE REDUCTION AND AGRICULTURAL PRODUCTION	34	80	*	47	8	–	–	–	–	–	–	*	18	–	–	–	–	–	60	–	16
Commercial Fisheries	–	–	–	–	5	–	*	–	–	–	–	–	–	–	–	–	–	–	–	–	5
Services	–	–	–	–	–	–	*	–	–	–	–	–	–	–	–	–	–	–	–	–	–
AQUACULTURAL PRODUCTION	–	–	–	–	5	–	33	–	–	–	–	–	–	–	–	–	–	–	–	–	8
M&I Water	–	91	*	100	54	–	–	–	–	–	–	–	71	–	–	–	–	–	–	–	64
Streamflow Regulation	–	–	–	–	2	–	–	–	–	–	–	–	–	–	–	–	–	–	–	–	2
WATER QUANTITY MANAGEMENT	–	91	*	100	40	–	–	–	–	–	–	–	71	–	–	–	–	–	–	–	54
Point Source	–	92	*	–	3	–	–	62	79	–	–	–	82	–	–	–	–	–	102	–	64
Non-Point Source	–	–	–	–	3	–	–	–	–	–	–	–	–	–	–	–	–	–	–	–	3
WATER QUALITY MANAGEMENT	–	92	*	–	3	–	–	62	79	–	–	–	99	–	–	–	–	–	102	–	60
General	–	–	*	63	17	–	–	–	50	–	–	*	18	*	–	*	–	–	94	–	19
Fish and Wildlife	–	–	–	57	11	–	–	–	–	–	–	*	13	–	25	–	–	–	–	–	14
Boating (Berthed and Launched)	–	–	–	–	38	–	–	–	–	–	–	–	–	–	–	–	48	–	–	–	38
RECREATION	–	–	*	62	17	–	–	–	50	–	–	*	15	*	25	*	48	–	94	–	19
Natural Areas	*	–	*	–	–	–	–	–	–	–	–	–	4	–	4	–	–	–	–	–	4
Historic & Cultural Sites	–	–	–	–	–	–	–	–	–	–	–	–	*	–	–	–	–	–	–	–	*
Ecological Systems	–	–	–	–	–	–	*	–	–	–	–	–	–	–	51	–	–	–	–	–	26
Other	–	–	–	–	*	–	–	–	–	–	–	–	–	–	–	–	–	–	–	–	*
NATURAL AREAS & CULTURAL RESOURCES	*	–	*	–	*	–	*	–	–	–	–	–	4	–	9	–	–	–	–	–	6
Commercial Harbors	–	–	–	–	16	–	–	–	–	–	–	–	–	–	–	–	*	–	–	–	16
Waterways	–	–	–	–	6	–	–	–	–	–	–	–	7	–	–	–	7	–	94[b]	–	6
Services	–	–	–	–	1	–	–	–	–	–	–	–	–	–	–	–	*	–	–	–	*
NAVIGATION	–	–	–	–	7	–	–	–	–	–	–	–	7	–	–	–	5	–	94[b]	–	7
HYDRO-POWER GENERATION	–	–	–	–	61	–	–	–	–	–	–	–	65	–	–	–	–	*	123	–	64
AREA REDEVELOPMENT BENEFITS	–	–	–	–	2	66	–	–	–	–	–	–	*	–	–	–	–	–	*	–	60
GENERAL SUPPORT OR UNALLOCATED	–	–	–	18	13	–	–	–	–	–	–	–	100	*	3	*	–	–	9	–	23
OTHER	–	–	–	–	30	–	–	–	–	–	–	–	17	–	–	*	–	–	–	–	25
AGENCY MEAN, ALL PURPOSES	34	89	*	49	20	66	33	62	73	13	*	*	37	*	20	*	8	*	76	47	30

[a]Weighting for the major purpose such as Water Quality Management may reflect programs that were unallocated to the subpurpose shown but included in the major purpose aggregate; (*) means there is a program of project activity for that purpose but no cost sharing was reported; (–) means there is no program or project activity reported for that purpose.

[b]Upon review, TVA indicates that this rate is virtually zero. Consult TVA before use.

Source: U.S. Water Resources Council, *Planning and Cost Sharing Options for Water and Related Land Programs* (Washington, D.C.: U.S. Government Printing Office, November 1975.

"Composite" refers to the combined total of implementation costs plus the capitalized present value of the estimated annual operation and maintenance costs. The concept of an effective composite cost share is a logical basis from which to compare cost-sharing provisions among purposes, agencies, measures, and regions. It is a true indication of the ultimate cost burdens borne by both federal and nonfederal interests.

A useful basis for assessing the current situation is to look at the variation of cost-sharing provisions among agencies for the same purpose. Tables 3 and 4 are included as summaries of the situation as determined by the Section 80 Study for Fiscal Year 1974. Since little revision of cost-sharing rules has taken place since then, these results should give a reasonably accurate picture of the situation in 1979. Table 4 lists each subpurpose and gives the nonfederal effective composite cost share as a percentage as it exists for each agency involved in that purpose. Where more than one provision exists within an agency for a single purpose, the figure given is the mean value of all such provisions. For example, in rural flood damage reduction, the nonfederal cost share in the three major federal construction agencies ranges from 7 percent for the Corps of Engineers to 10 percent for the Bureau of Reclamation to 27 percent for the Soil Conservation Service. In irrigation projects, the respective percentages are 19, 18, and 54. Other variations among agencies for the same purpose can be seen in Table 4.

The current situation in navigation has changed substantially since the Section 80 Study. Historically, the federal government has borne the full cost of construction, operation, and maintenance associated with navigation on inland waterways, with nonfederal contributions primarily in the form of land, easements, and rights-of-way. Using the mean effective composite cost-sharing concept, the nonfederal share in navigation was estimated to be 7 percent in 1974. The National Water Commission recommended full cost recovery of operation and maintenance costs on existing navigable waterways through a combination of fuel taxes and lockage charges. Under this recommendation, both passenger and commercial vessels would be subject to charges and for future projects all costs, including construction costs, would be borne by nonfederal interests except in cases where national defense benefits are derived. In October 1978, Congress passed the Inland Waterways Revenue Act, which incorporated a "user-pay" principle (P.L. 95-502). While lockage charges were not included and passenger vessels were exempted, the act authorized a tax on fuel for commercial waterway transportation. A trust fund was established that will consist of fuel tax revenues and provide the funding source for appropriated construction and rehabilitation expenditures. While it remains to be seen what the ultimate cost recovery will be, the new act does provide some implementation of the fundamental user pay principle in cost sharing.

In summarizing the current situation, it is apparent that significant differences exist among water resource purposes, among agencies for similar purposes, among water resources regions for similar purposes, and among repayment arrangements. On a national average, including all purposes, agencies, and regions, the estimated effective composite nonfederal cost share is about 30 percent of the total cost of the federal and federally assisted water and related land programs (see Tables 3 and 4). Federal cost-sharing policy today is a complex web of approximately 185 separate rules that have been developed over the years by congressional acts and administrative decisions. Past studies of cost sharing, including the Cooke Commission (The President's Water Resources Policy Commission, 1950), the second Hoover Commission (Commission on Organization of the Executive Branch of the Government, 1955), President Eisenhower's Cabinet Advisory Committee (the Secretary of Agriculture, the Secretary of Defense, and the Secretary of the Interior [Chairman], 1955), the National Water Commission (National Water Commission, 1973), and President Carter's Water Policy Review (Carter, 1978) have all recommended reform in these areas. The current situation is evidence that these recommendations have generally gone unheeded.

Nonfederal Financing of Water Development

State and Local Governments

In general, the largest portion of water resources financing and management lies in the domain of state and local governments, including special districts (North, 1978). However, there is a lack of data concerning nonfederal financing of water projects and programs for urban flood control and drainage; water supply, treatment and distribution; sewage treatment; and recreation. Existing data are generally only available for limited and scattered geographical areas and various purposes which are not consistently defined. Table 5 presents some aggregated estimates prepared by the National Water Commission. This lack of data on nonfederal financing of water projects and programs creates problems in determining appropriate federal and state water development and management policies. In response to this problem, the Water Resources Council recently sent legislation to Congress requesting authority to survey and compile historical expenditures by federal, state, and local governments and the private sector for purposes of water resources development and management (H.R. 4608, May 1979).

Excluding federal aid in the form of grants and revenue sharing (and state aid in the case of local projects), the two basic means of state and local financing are current revenues and proceeds derived from assuming a debt obligation. Current revenues at the state level consist primarily of tax revenues (e.g., sales, licenses, individual, and corporate income and property). In 1976, the total general revenues from state sources for all states was about \$107 billion (U.S. Statistical Abstract, 1978). In comparison, local governments received about \$109 million in general revenues for the same year.

Debt financing at both the state and local level continues to increase rapidly. Table 6 shows the increase in gross outstanding debt for states and localities from 1950 to 1976 (U.S. Statistical Abstract, 1978). In recent years, there has been a marked trend toward increasing the portion of revenue bonds issued relative to the total bond issuance. In 1970, new issues totaled \$18.2 billion of which \$11.9 billion was in general obligations and \$6.1 billion was in revenue bonds. By 1977, total issue had increased to \$46.8 billion of which only \$18.0 billion was in general obligations, while \$28.7 billion was in revenue. The explanation for this trend lies in the constitutional and statutory limitations on the debt incurred by state and local governments.

Such limitations are applicable in most states only to general

TABLE 5
Total Historical Expenditures for Water Resources Development

	Period of Estimate	Cumulative Expenditures (billions of 1972 dollars) Federal Ownership or Financed	State & Local Ownership and Financed	Private Ownership and Financed	Total
Instream Uses					
Hydro Power	Total to 1968	9.3	3.2	6.2	18.7
Flood Control	Total to 1969	25.3	2.0	1.3	28.6
Navigation	Total to 1969	16.8	1.6	–	18.4
Recreation	Total 1956–65	1.1	1.9	3.3	6.3
Fish & Wildlife				–	
Waste Treatment	Total to 1971	11.3[a]	62.8	no est.	78.7
Sanitary Sewers	Total to 1971			4.6[b]	
Storm & Combined Sewers	Total to 1971	–	36.3	3.2[b]	39.5
Out-of-Stream Uses					
Municipal Water	Total to 1971	6.6	78.5	9.3[b]	94.4
Industrial (except cooling water)	Total to 1965	6.6	4.6	13.3	24.5
Cooling Water	Total to 1969	.1	.1	1.4	1.6
Irrigation	Total to 1968	10.6	3.4	13.9	27.9
Total		87.7	194.4	56.5	338.6

[a] Includes $6.6 billion at Federal facilities.
[b] To 1966 only.
Source: NWC staff estimates.

TABLE 6
Debt Outstanding: 1950 to 1976
(in billions of dollars)

Year	*Total*	*State*	*Local*
1950	24	5	19
1955	44	11	33
1960	70	19	51
1965	100	27	72
1970	144	42	102
1975	221	72	149
1976	240	84	156

Source: U.S. Statistical Abstract, 1978, p. 287.

obligation bonds. Hence, by turning to revenue bonds, the limitations can be avoided. Other means of circumventing such limitations are available. One method is to shift increased responsibility for debt financing from more restricted to less restricted governments. This can be either from state to local or from local to state. Another method is to lease the required facilities initially with the ultimate intention of purchasing them. The creation of special districts with individual debt and taxing limitations has enabled project financing to avoid local debt and property tax restrictions. As a way of reducing local borrowing costs, state financing authorities have been created which provide for state purchase of bonds issued by local governments. To provide the required funds, the state then issues its own bonds.

The Private Sector

In general, private investment in water projects represents merely another form of capital investment, financed in the usual ways by selling stock, issuing bonds, drawing from retained earnings, and incurring long-term debt. However, data are not generally available concerning total investment by the private sector in water projects.

Following the passage of water pollution control legislation, even industries not involved in water resources development have been forced to consider water-related capital expenditures in the area of wastewater treatment. Industrial approaches to this problem vary considerably among industries as well as among companies within an industry. The two basic options are to use a municipal treatment plant or to build an individual plant that will treat only the company's wastewater. In the case of sharing the use of a municipal plant, a company's role in financing is well defined. In order to receive a federal grant authorized by P.L. 92-500, a municipality must comply with the requirements concerning industrial cost recovery and user charges. Industrial cost recovery provisions require industrial users to repay over a thirty-year period that portion of the federal share of capital costs that is allocated to the treatment of their wastewater. This repayment is interest-free and as such amounts to a federal subsidy on capital. According to a staff report to the National Commission on Water Quality, this subsidy amounts to about 44 percent of the capital costs (National Commission on Water Quality Staff, 1976). This feature, in addition to the favorable economies of scale that an industrial user can enjoy (up to 80 percent reduction of treatment costs for small users), makes the use of publicly owned treatment works very attractive to industry. The 1977 Amendments (P.L. 95-217) placed a moratorium on the industrial cost recovery provision to allow for review of the program. The review found the program to be ineffective and recommended an extension of the moratorium, which is now being considered by Congress. For industries building their own systems, incentives exist through accelerated depreciation and the use of tax-exempt municipal bonds. The latter arrangement allows a state or local government to issue tax-exempt bonds that finance a pollution control facility for a local industry. The bonds are backed by the credit of the industrial corporation, not by the issuing government (National Commission on Water Quality Staff, 1976).

Cost Sharing and Financing Issues

Many controversies and issues surround present financing and cost-sharing arrangements for water projects and programs.

Some of these have been discussed for years, such as the inconsistency in federal cost sharing among federal agencies, programs, and purposes. Some are relatively recent; for example, proposed federal cost sharing for rehabilitation of urban water supply systems.

Within the constraints of this paper, it is impossible to make a complete review of the many issues involving cost sharing and financing of water projects at the federal, state, and local levels. A few selected issues, however, are presented and discussed: (1) proposed federal cost sharing for rehabilitation of urban water supply systems, (2) the role of present federal cost-sharing policies in the energy/agriculture competition for western water, (3) proposed federal cost sharing for assisting local governments in complying with the Safe Drinking Water Act of 1974, (4) the problem of inconsistency in federal cost-sharing policies, (5) who will ultimately pay for poor groundwater management practices, and (6) extension of federal cost sharing to "multiple-purpose" water quality projects.

Rehabilitation of Urban Water Supply Systems

This problem is particularly acute in some eastern cities where water supply and distribution systems have been in place for up to 100 years. The antiquated distribution systems are known to lose significant amounts of water through leakage, possibly as much as 50 percent of the supply (GAO Draft Report, 1979). Also, many current supply systems are simply not adequate in size to provide for increased water usage. The costs of upgrading such systems are generally high. New York City, for example, has partially completed a water supply tunnel for which the total cost is estimated to be $2.5 billion. That city also is spending $20 million annually on replacement of distribution lines but would require twice that amount to keep from falling behind in its replacement schedule (GAO Draft Report, 1979). In Denver, the additional supply and treatment facilities required to meet projected needs will cost an estimated $1.7 billion (GAO Draft Report, 1979). Boston can either rehabilitate its current system or divert a new supply from the Connecticut River at an estimated cost of $100 million for either option (Wilson, 1978). Although water supply, unlike other public services, is revenue producing, it is extremely capital intensive. Approximately $10 in assets is required to generate $1 in annual revenues (Environmental Protection Agency Study, 1977). The financing of rehabilitation programs has prompted several cities to call for federal assistance.

The basic federal policy question is whether a federal interest exists in assisting cities and towns in the solution of what previously has been primarily regarded as a strictly local problem—the provision, treatment, and distribution of a safe public water supply. Eastern cities point to the West and argue that the federal government has for years provided a source of supply of municipal and industrial water to western urban areas and that it is time that eastern cities and their system rehabilitation problems receive comparable federal assistance.

If the federal government should decide to cost share in this area, a secondary issue is whether a new program should be created or whether an existing program such as general revenue sharing or Community Development Block Grants (administered by the Department of Housing and Urban Development) could provide for rehabilitation needs. As noted earlier, cost estimates for rehabilitation are very large and existing programs would not be able to contribute significant amounts. While general revenue sharing allows any legal distribution of funds within a state, provided two-thirds of the funds go to local governments, a state may not be able or willing to channel most of this federal source into only one or two of its cities. Furthermore, the amount of revenue sharing available is limited, the allotment for Fiscal Year 1979 amounting to $6.8 billion.

Western Energy-Agriculture Conflicts

In contrast to the primarily urban problem of rehabilitation of water distribution systems is the problem of western agriculture. Nowhere is water more scarce, yet more essential, to production. At present, there is increasing pressure on agriculture, which accounts for about 90 percent of consumptive use in the West, to yield to competing uses of available water. In particular, large-scale energy development in the form of shale oil development, coal gasification, and thermal electric generation will require large amounts of western water, which can only be provided at the expense of irrigated agriculture. The economic position of agriculture has worsened as agricultural price increases have not generally kept pace with rising costs. Much cropland has gone out of production as groundwater levels have dropped in some places as much as ten feet per year (U.S. Water Resources Council, 1978). Falling groundwater levels combined with rapidly increasing electric rates have increased the cost of irrigating with groundwater by several hundred percent since 1973 (Washington Post, June 18, 1979). Technological improvements have responded to the need for improved irrigation efficiency, but they tend to be highly capital intensive, further complicating the question of who will finance future agricultural production.

The cost-sharing issues underlying this competitive situation include:

- Are future federally developed irrigation projects in the national interest or will they produce benefits only to agricultural interests?
- Should the federal government continue to provide irrigation water at less than market value from existing and proposed projects in order to maintain western irrigated agriculture?

1974 Safe Drinking Water Act

Another financing and cost sharing issue results from the 1974 Federal Safe Drinking Water Act (P.L. 93-523), which established monitoring and regulation standards for community water supply systems. Amendments to the act in 1977 are expected to result in increased costs to certain communities for water supply. According to the American Water Works Association (AWWA), the total annual capital cost (amortized over fifteen years) directly associated with the implementation of the act is expected to be between \$150 and \$250 million (American Water Works Association, 1976). The AWWA estimates the annual operating and maintenance costs will be about \$263 million. Furthermore, it is estimated that the monitoring required to comply with the act will cost local governments an additional \$17 to \$35 million annually (American Water Works

Association, 1976). These increased costs will be felt by both publicly-owned and investor-owned systems and each must deal with the financing question.

The basic cost sharing and financing policy question is whether the federal government should cost share with local governments and private water companies in meeting certain requirements of the Safe Drinking Water Act.

Consistency of Federal Cost Sharing

Where should inconsistency in federal cost-sharing policies be eliminated, and where is there little cause for concern? This general question produces additional, more specific, questions. Should cost sharing for the same purpose be consistent among all agencies? Should cost sharing for a specific purpose be uniform among agencies even if the federal share may be in a variety of forms or if different measures are used? Should all regions be required to cost share at the same level even though different regions may have different needs? The consistency issue is particularly difficult since it is closely related to the equity problem in cost sharing. Despite this problem, however, it is probably desirable to seek consistency among agencies for similar purposes as a desirable feature. Also, there should be some consistency among purposes to avoid having projects planned and built on the basis of favorable cost sharing for a purpose rather than economic justification of the project. Finally, it is evident that inconsistencies among different measures to achieve the same purpose (e.g., structural vs. nonstructural flood control measures) must be overcome.

Who Pays for Inadequate Groundwater Management?

Depletion and mismanagement of groundwater resources is one of the most serious water resources problems facing the nation today (U.S. Water Resources Council, 1978). Someone will eventually pay for this—either the residents of the depleted groundwater basins through displacement of agriculture and industry, or the nation as a whole. In brief, should the federal government eventually pay to resolve this problem either by construction of major projects to import surface water or industrial development to replace the declining agricultural base in the depleted ground water basins?

For example, consider the Ogallala aquifer under the high plains of the Midwest and Southwest, which is a major supply source for parts of Colorado, Kansas, New Mexico, Oklahoma, Texas, and Nebraska (Wilson, 1978). Since this region depends on irrigated agriculture for much of its economic activity, water is of primary concern. However, present pumping rates are exceeding recharge rates, and the groundwater reserves are diminishing (U.S. Water Resources Council, 1978). Unless other sources of water are explored and more efficient use of water is made, the ultimate result must be a decline in irrigated agriculture. A Resources for the Future study concludes that "The viability of hundreds of small towns and, indeed, the entire economic and social base of the area will be threatened by rapid decline in irrigated agriculture" (Frederick, 1976). The extent to which the federal government will become involved in the resolution of this situation is not yet determined. Even if it is decided that the high plains water problem is of national concern, it is not clear whether federal involvement will be in water development or in economic development through the stimulation of nonagricultural activities with less dependence on water. If water development is pursued, should federal cost sharing recognize ineffective management at the local level?

Multipurpose Water Quality Projects

Water quality has been the focus of recent debate involving cost sharing. The question is whether the federal government should help pay the costs of controlling pollution in both wastewater and water supply. In wastewater treatment, the 75 percent federal share (85 percent for projects using "innovative/alternative" technology) appears likely to remain as policy through 1983. There is a current move among planners of wastewater treatment systems to incorporate more than the single purpose of wastewater treatment into the design of a project. Additional purposes of primary interest include reclamation and reuse, energy generation, urban drainage, and recreation. The proponents of the additional purposes argue that the entire project should be grant eligible and not just the wastewater portion. Current EPA cost sharing policy does not cover the wide range of multipurpose projects proposed, even though the innovative and alternative technology encouraged in the Clean Water Act is in many cases multipurpose in nature. In addition, current EPA policy is based on the assumption that achieving multiple purposes simultaneously should be less costly than achieving them separately, and all purposes should share in the cost savings. This can mean that funding for a multipurpose project is less than it would have been had the project been designed for the single purpose of pollution control. The net result is that fewer federal grant dollars are provided, thus discouraging a multipurpose approach.

Some data on the magnitude of potential cost sharing for multipurpose water quality projects exist. Urban drainage in combined sewer overflow is the most expensive purpose that can be combined with pollution control. The 1978 EPA Needs Survey estimates the cost of including this purpose to be about $103 billion, compared to a pollution control only cost in the same area of $25.7 billion (U.S. Environmental Protection Agency, 1979a). The same survey estimates the total cleanup costs (including, for example, secondary treatment, new collector and interceptor sewers, and combined sewer overflow), excluding urban drainage, to be $106 billion. The implication of these estimates on federal cost-sharing obligations if multipurposes are made eligible is clear—the inclusion of urban drainage in combined sewer overflow areas alone would increase the required grant dollars by $58 billion (75 percent of $77.3 billion).

Several observations are in order. EPA concludes that if the grants appropriation level remains roughly constant, then the pollution control needs alone will never be met because of inflation. Further, if any significant funds are reallocated to other purposes, then some pollution control needs must be sacrificed. Finally, by making multipurpose projects eligible, the needs levels among the states will change, resulting in a reallocation of funds among the states. For example, making urban drainage eligible implies a relative shift in funds to the Northwest and the Great Lakes states (U.S. Environmental Protection Agency, 1979b). On the other hand, making reclamation and reuse more eligible will result in more funds available to the West.

Strategies for Dealing with Emerging Issues

Issues have been discussed in the context of both financing and cost sharing. While attempting to approach the two areas separately, in theory, it is acknowledged that practically the separation is much less distinct. The pursuit of certain cost-sharing policies can profoundly affect the financing issues and the resulting financing methods employed. Consequently, alternative options in both financing and cost sharing will be discussed together.

Basic philosophical changes in cost-sharing policy have been proposed as means of improving the current situation. Shortly after the initiation of the president's water policy review in 1977, five cost-sharing options reflecting a broad range of philosophy were presented in an Issues and Option Paper published in the *Federal Register* (U.S. Water Resources Council, 1977):

1. *The current situation.* This option would continue the existing cost-sharing arrangements without change. It presumes that the inconsistencies in repayment terms and variations among agency programs and purposes that now exist are supported by valid reasons.
2. *Cost-sharing floor.* This option would modify existing cost-sharing arrangements to achieve greater consistency among agencies and measures providing similar benefits. It provides that cost sharing be expressed in terms of effective composite rates.
3. *Joint venture.* This option provides that 50 percent of the initial capital implementation or financing costs of projects would be provided by the federal government and the other 50 percent would be provided by state, interstate, or local governments, or by public nongovernmental entities.
4. *Block grant.* This option provides for grants to states as a replacement for the federal direct water resources development programs and projects. Initially, each state would receive grant funds equivalent each year to the annual federal water resources investment in that state

for the past several years. Eventually, grants would be distributed on a formula basis reflecting population, economic, and other factors related to state investments and expenditures in water resources.

5. *Full recovery.* This option calls for the federal government to plan, finance, implement, and operate projects and programs as it does today. However, in the case of projects authorized in the future, the cost-sharing terms for each project purpose or service provided by a project would require 100 percent repayment of all costs involved, including operation, maintenance, and replacement costs, interest during construction, and interest at the project evaluation rate for all repayment obligation schedules over a period of years.

Of the five options, several are under active consideration for implementation. Option 2 above emphasizes the elimination of inconsistencies among agencies and measures serving the same purpose. This incorporates the effective composite concept of cost sharing and results in moderate increases in the ultimate nonfederal share. In effect, it endorses the recommendation of the Section 80(c) Study, which set minimum levels for a variable nonfederal share depending on the purpose in question (U.S. Water Resources Council, 1975). Option 5 above has attracted little nonfederal support since it would require ultimate recovery of 100 percent of all associate project costs, including interest. The three remaining options from the 1977 Issue and Options Paper are presently receiving active consideration. Considerable support exists for maintaining the current situation based on the premise that the existing inconsistencies are justified by legitimate reasons.

Option 3, the joint venture approach, as detailed in the 1977 report of the president's water policy review, originally called for a uniform 50 percent federal, 50 percent nonfederal sharing of implementation costs for all projects (U.S. Water Resources Council, 1977). A modified version of this option was adopted as one of the president's water policy initiatives and was recently submitted by the administration to Congress (H.R. 4135). The proposal calls for an up-front state contribution of 10 percent of the implementation costs associated with projects yielding vendible outputs (e.g., municipal and industrial water supply, irrigation, and power). For other projects, the outputs are considered nonvendible and a 5 percent contribution would be required. The administration proposal requires that the mandatory state 5 and 10 percent contribution be approved by the state legislature. Revenues received from vendible outputs would be shared with the states in proportion to the investments made. To prevent an undue burden on a state, an upper limit equal to one-quarter of 1 percent of the state's revenues would be placed on a state's contribution to any project. This 5 percent and 10 percent contribution would apply to projects of the Corps of Engineers, Bureau of Reclamation, and Tennessee Valley Authority that are not yet authorized, but would not apply to Soil Conservation Service projects. The SCS projects were excluded because of the large number of very small projects. For interstate projects, the states' cost and revenue shares would be based on the portion of benefits each state receives as a result of the project. If a state chose not to cooperate, the remaining states could provide that state's share and hence enable the project to proceed. The proposal would not apply to projects already authorized, but if a state volunteered to cost share on such projects, it would receive expedited consideration for implementation.

This proposal also addresses the consistency question in cost sharing with respect to flood control. A 20 percent nonfederal contribution (in addition to the 5 percent share) would be required for all flood control projects regardless of whether structural or nonstructural measures are used. This provision would apply to projects and programs of the Bureau of Reclamation, the Corps of Engineers, the Tennessee Valley Authority, and the Soil Conservation Service.

The administration has proposed this variation of the joint venture strategy as a means to: (1) involve the states more significantly in water project decisions by requiring state legislative involvement in deciding whether to build a water project; and (2) eliminate some of the conflicting inequitable rules governing cost sharing—especially with regard to structural and nonstructural flood damage reduction measures.

It should be noted that the proposed legislation is technically both a financing reform and a cost-sharing reform. If a project under present policy calls for full federal front-end financing, but with full reimbursement by the nonfederal interest involved (appropriate interest included) then the ultimate cost shares would not be changed under the new policy. However, in many cases, repayment is interest-free and distributed over as many as 50 years, reducing the ultimate nonfederal share from a nominal level of 100 percent to an effective level of perhaps 20 to 30 percent. The new policy in these cases will result in a decreased effective federal share by eliminating some of the advantages enjoyed by nonfederal interests due to interest-free reimbursement.

The administration's proposal has been subjected to criticism. A commonly expressed concern is that, in spite of the stated goal, there is no increased state involvement in planning and managing of water resources development. However, while not necessarily opening up new areas for state involvement in water resources development, planning, and management, the proposal should provide incentive for states to take better advantage of existing opportunities. In addition, calling for formal cooperation among states in carrying out interstate projects is viewed by many as an unworkable provision of the proposal. Review of recent federal water project authorizations, however, indicates that relatively few are interstate projects. Interstate cooperation should be possible to meet the state cost-sharing requirements for the relatively few projects that have multistate benefits. Another objection raised by several states is that their ability to pay the front-end amounts is limited either by statute or state constitution. This problem already exists with some current cost-sharing requirements for federal projects. Under Section 221 of the Flood Control Act of 1970 (P.L. 91-611), a written agreement to repay construction costs is required prior to construction of Corps of Engineers projects. However, this has been interpreted so as not to commit states to bind future legislatures to assume the terms of previous agreements. It is also argued that the proposed cost sharing does little to eliminate the inconsistencies among purposes, programs, and agencies. In fact, the proposal does eliminate these inconsistencies for flood control, a category for which total federal investment is only exceeded by water quality improvement. With the exception of flood control, the new proposal does not alter any of the existing cost-sharing provisions, although due to 5 or 10 percent front-end contributions, the reimbursement amounts would be correspondingly less. Finally, it has been suggested that an effect of the proposal will be to deter states from initiating projects less able to compete in the marketplace, but which may nonetheless provide substantial benefits such as environmental programs. In spite of the above objections, the administration proposal represents a much needed step in the direction of long overdue cost sharing reform.

The block grant approach, Option 4, has also been proposed as an alternative to the current situation. This option would provide block grants to states, allocated by a formula based on relevant factors such as population, economic variables, and land area. This concept forms the basis for a bill currently under Senate consideration (S. 1241) and represents a significant change in federal water resources development cost sharing. S. 1241 calls for assessment by the states of their individual water needs and the subsequent preparation of a priority list of projects. These projects would be subject to public hearings and agency review but would not require economic justification. The concept proposed by S. 1241 would consequently significantly decrease the existing emphasis on benefit-cost analysis for project justification.

To finance the cost of such projects, the bill calls for first-year funding of $4 billion to be allocated to the states by a formula based strictly on population and land area. The states then would be free to spend their allotments as they felt appropriate, provided that they make a contribution of 25 percent of the construction costs of any project undertaken and 50 percent of the operating and maintenance costs. The 25 percent contribution could be made over the life of the project, subject to a "reasonable rate of interest." The effect of this strategy would be to give the states the primary role in water resources planning and development. Each state could then tailor the expenditure of its annual allotment to meet its individual needs.

An initial objection to this strategy is that the water needs of the states are not adequately reflected by population and land area alone. The allocating formula as it stands would result in an inequitable distribution of the total amount spent nationally on water resources. States are also concerned that the nonfederal share of 25 percent is too high. It is difficult to predict the impact of this 25 percent obligation on a given state until its needs and its allocation are evaluated and compared. However, a general impact expected by the bill's sponsors is a reduction from current levels of the flow of funds to southern states and an increase in flow to northeastern and northcentral states.

Much of the preceding has dealt with proposed financing and cost-sharing arrangements for major water resources development involving federal and state governments. In addition to this area of concern is the financing and cost sharing for development of major municipal and industrial water supply systems by both public and private entities. One strategy calls for the establishment of a Federal Water Bank that would provide a vehicle for water companies and municipalities to issue long-term debt at reasonable interest rates (Joint American Water Works Association–National Association of Water Companies Committee on Financing Water Industry Projects, 1979).

The Water Bank would issue debt and use the revenue to purchase the securities of local water systems. Among the features of such a system would be:

- Private companies as well as municipalities would be eligible to use the Bank's services.
- All size of utilities would be eligible for loans.
- The Bank would eventually become privately owned.
- A provision could be made for giving loan preference to taxpaying investor-owned utilities to balance the grant/low-interest federal programs available to publicly-owned systems.

Another proposal for generating investment capital for private companies involves the establishment of a fund by local government through the sale of bonds (Symonds, 1978). Water companies then borrow from this fund for plant investment. The government then taxes the companies to recover interest and principal. The tax represents an expense to the companies and thus can be recovered through increased water rates. The plant thus financed would qualify for a depreciation allowance enabling it to be replaced as required. A feature of this scheme is that each company would have its own financial program and would not have to compete with publicly-owned systems for scarce public dollars.

EPA is currently investigating alternatives to assist water utilities, especially small systems, in complying with the Safe Drinking Water Act (P.L. 93-523). EPA estimates the capital costs required to comply with the act would be about $1.5–2.0 billion (EPA Staff estimate). Strategies under consideration involve possible expansion of existing programs. For example, something similar to Small Business Administration loans for private companies is being considered. For publicly-owned systems, programs like the loans and grants of the Farmers Home Administration could represent a viable form of federal assistance without creating a new multibillion dollar federal grant program.

Conclusion

An attempt has been made to survey and analyze a few of the key issues involving financing and cost sharing in water resources development. These issues are complex for many reasons—evolution of national goals, political sensitivities, vested interests, financing requirements of nonfederal interests, and cost-sharing inconsistencies, to list a few.

It is evident that financing and cost sharing are implicit issues in every water resources development question. The conceptual differences between the two issues must be acknowledged in order to design policies to achieve national goals and strategies to implement those policies.

The survey and analysis herein suggest that some present federal cost-sharing policies have resulted from conditions that are no longer applicable. The emerging issues discussed indicate trends in contemporary national priorities that must be recognized in water resources development and management. Primary areas of present concern include energy production, maintenance of existing water supply infrastructure, and water quality and related environmental problems. As priorities change, national cost-sharing policies must be either modified or reformulated to remain effective. Without such reform, financing obligations can become inequitably allocated.

Several strategies have been proposed as a basis for the acknowledged need for reform. To be successful, such strategies must not only be theoretically sound, they must be politically sound. Practical solutions must be sought through the existing political structure since any realistic solution generally requires the transfer of a subsidy from one interest to another. Until sufficient political support for transfer of this subsidy exists, the existing imperfections in cost-sharing policy for water resources development will remain.

References

American Water Works Association, Fact Sheet, April 1976.

Carter, Jimmy. "Water Resources Policy Reform Message," June 6, 1978.

Commission on Organization of the Executive Branch of the Government, *Report on Water Resources and Power: A Three Volume Report Prepared by the Task Force on Water and Power,* June 1955.

General Accounting Office Draft Report, "Urban Water Problems: An Overview," 1979.

Joint American Water Works Association—National Association of Water Companies Committee on Financing Water Industry Projects, Draft Report, May 1979.

National Commission on Water Quality Staff, *Staff Report to the National Commission on Water Quality,* U.S. Government Printing Office, Washington, D.C., April 1976.

The National Water Commission, *Water Policies for the Future: Final Report to the President and to the Congress of the United States,* U.S. Government Printing Office, Washington, D.C., June 1973.

North, Ronald M. "Financing Water Resources Planning, Implementation, Management: The Unsolved Problems." Presented at the Engineering Foundation Conference, New England College, Henniker, New Hampshire, June 16–21, 1978.

The President's Water Resources Policy Commission, *Volume 1: A Water Policy for the American People (General Report); Volume 2: Ten Rivers in America's Future; Volume 3: Water Resources Law,* U.S.

Government Printing Office, Washington, D.C., 1950.

Rivers and Harbors Appropriation Act of 1884, c. 229, s. 4, 23 Stat. 147, July 5, 1884.

P.L. 154, June 13, 1902, 57th Congress, 32 Stat. 331.

P.L. 161, June 17, 1902, 57th Congress, 32 Stat. 388.

P.L. 738, June 22, 1936, 74th Congress, 49 Stat. 1570.

P.L. 85-500, July 3, 1958, Title III, 72 Stat. 319.

P.L. 89-234, October 2, 1965, 79 Stat. 903.

P.L. 91-611, December 31, 1970, Title II, 84 Stat. 1818.

P.L. 92-500, October 18, 1972, 86 Stat. 816.

P.L. 93-523, December 16, 1974, 88 Stat. 1660.

P.L. 95-217, December 27, 1977, 91 Stat. 1566.

P.L. 95-502, October 21, 1978, Title II, 92 Stat. 1696.

The Secretary of Agriculture, Secretary of Defense, and the Secretary of the Interior (Chairman). *A Report by the Presidential Advisory Committee on Water Resources Policy,* December 22, 1955.

Symonds, Robert T. "Thoughts About Our Industry: Mainly Financing," National Association of Water Companies, *Quarterly,* vol. 19, no. 1, Spring 1978.

U.S. Environmental Protection Agency, Clean Water Fact Sheet, June 1979a.

U.S. Environmental Protection Agency, Office of Water and Waste Management, "Strategies for Funding of Multiple-Purpose Projects," June 1979b.

U.S. Environmental Protection Agency Study, *Survey of Operating and Financial Characteristics of Community Water Systems,* April 1977.

U.S. Statistical Abstract, 1978.

U.S. Water Resources Council, Section 80(c) Study, "Planning and Cost Sharing Policy Options for Water and Related Land Programs," U.S. Government Printing Office, Washington, D.C., 1975.

U.S. Water Resources Council, *The Nation's Water Resources: 1975–2000,* vol. 1: Summary, U.S. Government Printing Office, Washington, D.C., December 1978.

U.S. Water Resources Council, *Water Resource Policy Study; Issue and Option Papers,* Federal Register, Friday, July 15, 1977, Part VI.

Washington Post, "Agriculture Losing Contest for Western Water," June 18, 1979.

Wilson, Leonard U. "State Water Policy Issues," The Council of State Governments, Lexington, Kentucky, November 1978.

Commentary

B. Delworth Gardner

Leo Eisel and Richard Wheeler (EW) have presented a useful and broad-gauged paper on financing water development projects. Quite appropriately, they have touched on the legal, institutional, and political as well as economic aspects of the developing situation. My consideration of their arguments will be admittedly narrower and unabashedly more partisan, i.e. from a strictly economic point of reference. I have chosen this course, knowing that I will not be quite fair to them, to get many of the more controversial issues squarely before us where they can be debated.

In their opening paragraphs on financing and cost sharing, EW argue that in theory cost sharing and financing are distinct, whereas in practice they are blurred. Then, in the second paragraph, they assert that cost sharing does not rest on an elegant theoretical basis. I have several comments that in general take issue with these assertions.

Yes, there is an important distinction in principle between financing and cost sharing. Financing has to do with who provides the up-front financial resources to get the project built, whereas cost sharing determines who bears the ultimate burden of giving up real resources incorporated in building and managing the project. The reason the distinction becomes blurred is that the federal government often finances the entire project, including, of course, its share of the real resource costs. The share ultimately assumed by the water users and beneficiaries of the project is usually paid at a later time when the government is reimbursed for the share of project costs assigned to the users. It can be argued that this process is economically both efficient and equitable. It is efficient because were it not for the tremendous financial reserves that are available for project construction to the federal government through taxation and borrowing, projects that meet rigorous benefit-cost tests might never be built. It is equitable, because the project beneficiaries do not reimburse the government until the flow of benefits from the project enhances their income and wealth positions.

It is possible that we accept these arguments without subjecting them to sufficient scrutiny. First, what about the necessity of federal financing? Few, if any, water projects require such enormous up-front financial resources as the Alaskan pipeline, a project financed largely with private sector funds. Many private firms, such as public utilities, finance projects running into the hundreds of millions of dollars. It may not be the size of the projects per se that requires federal financing so much as it is the class of users from whom it may be difficult to collect large sums of up-front money. For example, it could be argued that even if an irrigation project is economically feasible, it may be prohibitively costly—if possible at all—to collect the necessary front-end financial resources from hundreds of farmers, to say nothing of thousands of recreationists or water consumers. Once again, it may be a mistake to jump to this conclusion without some investigation. It is conceivable that lending agencies in the private sector, such as the commercial banks and insurance companies, would be quite willing to lend money on project development that offered potential profits. Projects that are heavily into electric power production obviously could be privately financed if they were economically feasible since so many already are.

My own speculation for why federal financing of water projects exists is quite different from the "size of project" and "capital rationing" issues. There are two basic reasons: (1) many of the proposed projects are not economically feasible and therefore the private market would not generate the funds because losses would ensue and private firms cannot stay in business and make a habit of incurring losses, and (2) some of the outputs from water projects are "collective" goods and thus entrepreneurs in the private market will not have sufficient incentives to invest. I will elaborate more on this second point below.

It is quite true that the question of economic feasibility is very complex when it is removed from the stratosphere of economic theory and made operational. Quite apart from the collective good issue, there is the question of national goals that EW raise. Their discussion implies that the existence of national interests justifies federal involvement in water development. Is this supposed to mean that private investment does not also further national goals, or that some incompatibility exists between private economic activity and national interests? Does it even suggest that governmental activity is more efficiently directed towards national goals than private activity is? I believe these notions are fundamentally mistaken. We must not forget that the nation is simply the sum of the individuals composing it and that individual interests are the nation's interest. Policies and projects that on balance enhance individual interests are by definition in the national interest. This is really what we mean by economic feasibility of a project—that having it enhances the sum of individual interests and thus the national interest more than not having it.

Perhaps these issues can be more easily analyzed and understood in a different context. What rationale can be given for governmental intervention in financing and bearing the real resource costs of water development? We might begin answering this question by asking another one: if water were expropriable and firm property rights in its use were created so that incentives for private investment in development and use were present, which of North's justifications for federal involvement mentioned by EW would be valid?

I have already indicated why I believe that "national priorities" per se do not justify governmental as opposed to private actions. If the national priority represents a commitment to provide a collective good, however, then a case for governmental action can be made. Collective or public goods are those that are nonrival in consumption (meaning that person A's consumption does not diminish the amount available to person B) and individual consumers are not excludable from the consuming population. A good example is national defense.

It must be obvious that many outputs that result from the use of water are not public goods: food and fiber, power, most industrial products, and the utility derived from domestic water consumption. Thus the public good argument cannot justify their production. Flood control, navigation, some forms of recreation, and environmental goods are public goods, however, and the private market cannot be relied upon to allocate water to those uses in socially optimal quantities. Some governmental decision to provide them may be therefore required.

The question of providing reservations of water for the future and in times of emergency and critical needs are not of a different class from national priorities. There is no reason, in principle, why the private sector would not adequately provide if water were market allocated, providing the goods that are produced are private goods, and no other classes of market failure are found to be significant.

But, as we all know, water is not market allocated and therefore is not this entire discussion sterile conjecture? I do not think so. We probably have federal financing of water development because we have never created property rights in water as we have in land. Part of the reason for this is that water is a fugitive resource and moves from place to place unless it is consumptively used. This interdependence of water use creates external effects: the use by one party affects the availability and value of water to other users. These effects are difficult to include in normal water transactions that a water market would entail. Some have concluded, therefore, that these effects can be more adequately considered in political allocations than they possibly could by a market. A complete evaluation of this issue would take us far afield. Suffice it to say, political allocations of water by our water rights law have been shown to be economically highly inefficient and thus it is not obvious that political allocations that supposedly take explicit account of externalities have induced more efficient water allocation than would a water market.

A second reason for the absence of water markets is even more fundamental. Because land in the West is of limited value without water, particularly irrigible land, agricultural development and successful settlement could only occur if water were applied to the land. At the time of settlement no great urgency existed to conserve water or to worry about its efficient use. It was rather security of tenure that was needed to induce development and the water right doctrine of prior appropriation admirably met this need. No doubt the "ability-to-pay" doctrine of cost sharing that came into use by the Bureau of Reclamation was justified in the same way. Irrigators would not be willing to put developed water to use if they had to pay more for it than it was worth. Therefore, even if water charges had to be set below supply costs, the important thing was to get it used so the region could become developed.

Regardless of whether or not this policy was once justified (I doubt it ever was) the situation is far different today. Most of the best dam sites and irrigible land have been developed, and in many places competing uses for water have made it scarce and very valuable. A set of water allocation institutions is needed now that can come to grips with scarcity. Nothing would serve us better, in my opinion, than a change in institutional rules that would permit a water market that could be responsive to changing demand and supply conditions. What we have instead is a set of obsolete institutions bequeathed to us from another time, established to accomplish goals no longer valid. Indeed, federal financing of water development and ability-to-pay cost-sharing rules are an important component of these obsolete institutions. Thus, to induce development the federal government assumed the financial responsibility to build projects. It then allocated (sold) the water to classes of users through long-term contracts, and the question became, How much should be charged? Where the beneficiaries could be identified and use resulted in private marketable goods such as power and food, the users paid, although because of the ability-to-pay rule the irrigators have seldom paid the full separable costs. The beneficiaries of collective goods have generally paid nothing. Thus, the Reclamation Act of 1902 and the Water Supply Act of 1958 have cost sharing provisions consistent with their emphasis upon private good supply, whereas the collective good statutes, the Rivers and Harbors Act of 1884, and the Flood Control Act of 1936 do not require cost sharing.

The goals of federal cost sharing get major treatment in EW

as well they should. I heartily agree with the National Water Commission statement that cost sharing should "promote the efficient use of water and water related services by users." Presumably, if all goods derived from water use were private goods, water users would pay the full supply costs of water rather than go without it, providing they valued water more than its cost. In fact, one way of insuring that resources would be efficiently utilized in water development would be to sell contracts that would obligate the users to pay the full supply costs in advance. If they were unwilling to pay these charges there would be at least prima facie evidence that resources were not being efficiently utilized in the proposed development. Introducing collective goods does not alter the logic as applied to private goods and their separable costs. In reality, irrigation water users have not been required to pay the full separable costs of irrigation development. It is not surprising, therefore, that allegations of wasting resources cannot be put to rest.

In this connection, there is a very mysterious paragraph in the paper. EW argue that requiring the beneficiaries to bear the cost of providing benefits is conceptually sound, providing beneficiaries and benefits can be properly identified. They then say: "For example, the costs of irrigation projects have customarily been transferred to the recipients of the water, indicating a private benefit. However, in many cases the water is not priced at market value; hence the agricultural water supply has, in effect, been subsidized, indicating some sort of public benefit." The term "subsidy" could have various meanings, but usually society would be subsidizing irrigators if they pay less for the water than the supply costs, particularly if the water is worth more than the supply costs. It is the difference between user charges and costs that represents a transfer from the taxpayers to the water users and can be aptly called "subsidy." Of course, any surplus of water value over water charges will constitute a "rent" on water use that will probably be capitalized into land values, but it is confusing to call this "rent" a subsidy. In any case, comparisons of water charges, costs, and values tell us absolutely nothing so far as I can see about whether or not any public benefit exists.

The data in the EW tables are very revealing. It is one thing that cost sharing might vary as between different water uses. As argued above, this might be expected given that some goods produced are purely private while others are largely public. But how can such geographic variation be justified for identical classes of use? For example, in the case of irrigation the nonfederal share varies from 10 percent in the Missouri region to 66 percent in Alaska. The reason might be the extreme variation in costs between areas, since projects were built in different time periods, as well as the application of the ability-to-pay rule that has little or no relation to cost.

The data in Table 3 are particularly interesting and provocative. I would like to see an analysis of these data that would attempt to explain these extreme differences among agencies and among geographic areas in the percent of costs covered by nonfederal entities. No doubt much of the explanation must be sought for in the political market where votes are traded.

The discussion of industrial use of municipal waste water plants appears to be incomplete. On the one hand, EW point out that there is a significant subsidy captured by industrial firms to the extent of about 44 percent of the capital costs of waste water treatment, and this, coupled with favorable economies of scale, means that publicly owned treatment works are very attractive to industry. Presumably, industry would be eagerly participating. Yet a review of the program found that it was ineffective and recommended a continual moratorium on the cost recovery provision. It isn't at all clear why the program review found it to be ineffective given its apparent popularity.

I will close this discussion with several brief comments on the section in EW dealing with cost sharing and financing issues. Probably paper length constraints prevented EW from treating these issues as extensively as they would have liked. My focus will be on economic efficiency and overall resource allocation implications of the issues raised.

EW's discussion of rehabilitating urban water supply systems indicates the huge sums needed for this work. Perhaps some justification for federal financing can be found, although I for one, as discussed above, am skeptical. If the federal government does assist, however, it ought to be on the basis of full-cost recovery, and that includes interest over the period of the loan. Furthermore, the local governments should obtain the repayment resources through direct charges on the water users. Only by following these rules are truly economically feasible investments likely to be made. All of these comments also apply to the need for federal involvement in developing water under the 1974 Safe Drinking Water Act.

I believe that EW somewhat overstate the competition over water likely to arise in the West between agriculture and energy. It is true that energy development could require large amounts of water. Still, many empirical studies indicate that there is high potential for finding the water for energy.[1] Where flexible transfer institutions exist, water rights can be purchased from farmers through purely voluntary transactions, leaving both farmers and energy developers better off. Other studies[2] show vast underground aquifers, presently underutilized, that could be tapped and carefully managed to yield valuable economic output. Most importantly, we must not overlook the possibilities for conservation that would follow increases in water prices. I hearken back to my earlier point that it is the rigidity of our water allocation institutions that prevents new and higher users from getting water, not an absolute shortage of it.

As for water pricing and agriculture, following my discussion of urban pricing above, efficient resource allocation would be enhanced if new irrigation water were priced at full cost. Only if this is done can premature and inefficient development of agricultural water be prevented. I will hasten to add, however, that full-cost pricing of newly developed water has very different efficiency and equity implications from the after-the-fact full-cost pricing of water from existing projects. In the case of existing projects, real resources have already been sunk into project development, and water rents resulting from underpricing have already been capitalized into land values. Many of these lands have changed hands, and thus the wealth losses suffered in the form of reduced land values resulting from increased water prices may be imposed on a different set of irrigators than those who captured the original wealth gains resulting from pricing water below its value.

The section in EW on the need for consistency in federal cost sharing policies raises the relevant questions. What is required to answer them meaningfully, however, is an intellectual framework where the questions can be systematically analyzed. I believe the economist has a framework that offers great promise although space constraints will prohibit a full development here. The two important concepts in the framework are *economic efficiency* and *income distribution equity.* The latter may involve a perceived federal responsibility to alter the existing distribution of income and wealth via (1) transfer programs, such as unemployment compensation, welfare, medicare, etc., through a long list; and (2) federally financed and subsidized production activities, such as building weapons for national defense or building multipurpose dams. Transfer activities usually are negative sum games since the transfer itself involves use of scarce resources, only one of the reasons they are so vigorously opposed. Production activities will also be inefficient and negative sum unless they pass rigorous benefit-cost tests.

The real problem is that efficiency and equity goals will often, if not usually, be in conflict. If water development projects are utilized to redistribute income and wealth, among users of different classes or among geographic areas or both, and user charges are set below costs in order to accomplish some equity goal, the resulting resource allocation will almost always be inefficient. Simply stated, efficiency requires that resources be allocated in such a way that the net value of the resources at the margin be equal as among all areas and users and that the marginal benefits of expansion of production equal the marginal costs. Thus, large transfers from the taxpayers to western irrigators in the form of subsidized water may well result in premature and overextended (and thus inefficient) water development.

On the issue of who pays for inadequate groundwater management, EW state that either the residents of the depleted groundwater basin will pay, or the nation as a whole will. It is not clear what the national interest is in this issue. If common property use of the aquifer leads individual pumpers to take more water than is optimal in an efficiency sense, and there is every reason to believe this will ultimately happen, the aquifer will be utilized until it is no longer profitable to pump. Irrigated agricultural production will cease, land values will decline, and resources will need to move. The waste is obvious. The primary losers will be the producers and the owners of land in the area. Of course, there may be many indirect effects regionally and even nationally such as small impacts on food prices and factor prices utilized in agriculture, but these are likely to be negligible in most instances. There could also be some national impact if declining water tables are used as an excuse to initiate new, costly, and inefficient water-replacement development projects at taxpayer expense. Perhaps this is what EW have in mind when they state that the nation will pay for groundwater depletion.

The root problem causing over-exploitation of groundwater is clearly the common-property ownership issue.[3] This is inadequately dealt with in the paper. It is an issue that local district managers of groundwater aquifers must come to grips with. Groundwater pumping must be curtailed if the aquifer is being utilized beyond the socially optimal level. Many states have statutes now that attempt to deal with the problem. The two largest groundwater users, California and Texas, do not, however.

I found the discussion of the water bank immensely interesting. If there is a case for government providing up-front financing, the bank would serve the purpose and still provide a mechanism for full-cost reimbursement of loans along the lines needed to insure efficient water development.

Finally, I return to the plea made earlier that what is most urgently needed is an intellectual framework within which the need for federal intervention and alternative strategies for dealing with emerging issues can be evaluated. In my view, to justify governmental intervention in financing and cost sharing there must be demonstrable evidence of one or more of the following conditions: (1) significant externalities that negotiating parties cannot consider, (2) public goods that provide no incentives for private production, (3) common-property ownership of resources, (4) inefficient private monopolistic or monopsonistic control of resources. In addition, if there is to be federal cost sharing to provide private goods such as irrigation water, municipal and industrial water, and power, the likelihood is great that overinvestment will occur. This is tantamount to saying that if the state and local governments were required to pay the full costs of providing water for these purposes, we would have greater assurance that uneconomical projects would not be built. If the federal government must redistribute income and wealth, then at least it should do so in the most efficient way possible. Given the present value of water and current levels of economic development, I seriously doubt that new subsidized water is an efficient redistribution mechanism. Efficient development and utilization of water should be given a higher priority as it becomes increasingly valuable.

Notes

1. For example, see B. D. Gardner, K. Lyon, and R. O. Tew, "The Effects on Agriculture in Utah of Water Transfers to Oil Shale Development," PRJAE-028-1, Utah Water Research Laboratory, June 1976, pp. 1–57.

2. J. Noel, B. D. Gardner, and C. V. Moore, "Optimal Regional Conjunctive Water Management." Unpublished paper, Ag. Econ. UCD, June 1979.

3. B. D. Gardner, "Economic Issues in Groundwater Management." Paper presented at Twelfth Biennial Conference on Groundwater, Sacramento, California, September 20–21, 1979.

10
The National Perspective

Guy R. Martin

I am honored to be here with you today; it is an honor to attend, let alone have the opportunity to speak to such a distinguished gathering of experts. According to the program, my task here this evening is to add to your discussions by offering a "national perspective" on the water resource issue. I'm happy to see that a distinction has been drawn between the "national" perspective and the "federal" perspective. I can assure you that while I will probably talk about both, I have a profound appreciation for the distinction between "national" and "federal," and will attempt to reflect it.

Because of my respect and admiration for those attending and speaking here, I make the following introductory statement cautiously but truthfully. I believe I am qualified by recent experience to discuss the perspective I have been assigned. As most of you know, as a result of actions taken by the president and Secretary Andrus–and at their directive–I've taken the lead role in the president's water policy reforms. I chaired the policy review process, the coordination of the actual formulation of the policy, and the actions that have been instrumental in its implementation. As a result of this responsibility, I think I can make a respectable claim to having taken an active role, over the last two and a half years, in more meetings, hearings, symposia, conferences, annual conventions, and down-home arguments on water policy than just about anyone I know.

Throughout this process, I've gained a number of impressions:

- I have witnessed both brilliant discussions and indescribably stupid and petty conflicts between federal water agencies.
- I've walked into congressional hearing rooms where the atmosphere was angry but the concerns legitimate, and into hearing rooms where the agenda was unabashed political theatrics.
- I've been to meetings of water groups from every region, and covering virtually every perspective on the issue.
- I've heard city councilmen from urban areas in the East tell me that their water system has totally deteriorated but that the federal government should pay to fix it because the last time they tried to raise water rates, someone got recalled.
- I've been told in Wyoming that, in the West, "water is like sex." Everyone is sure there is more of it around than there really is and sure that everyone is getting more of it than they are.
- I've heard dozens of times—East and West—that there is no problem, and the best federal role regarding water policy is to "leave well enough alone."
- I've gone through the fight to sustain a presidential veto of the public works appropriations bill and experienced the not-very-satisfying feeling of winning, but understanding that such a symbolic up-or-down vote doesn't give people on either side much chance to reflect the substantial consensus on values and objectives that I sincerely believe exists.
- I've been privileged to have quality learning experiences with Governor Matheson, Senator Gary Hart, and many others who thoughtfully represent the West, and are unstintingly honest and specific about the items where we do and don't agree.

In short, I have had tremendous opportunity to get a very broad perspective on all the issues surrounding water policy, both as the policy was developed, and as individuals and groups have reacted to it.

For some of you, the next question probably is: "If you've

got so much perspective, why the hell don't you start doing something right, then?" I guess the answer is that a central element of the national perspective is, like it or not, there are a good number of changing ideas today about what is right, what the priorities are, and how a national or federal policy can best address them.

First, it might be useful to put the present national discussion of water in some historic perspective. Certainly, we are in a discussion of water policy on a national scale that is at least the equal of any before. I don't want to overrepresent this because many of you know that, almost on a quadrennial cycle, we have a national "study" relating to water resources, and an attempt to institute new policy. Most of these studies have involved substantial debate, but most of them have gone on the shelf. There are some significant differences this time, and they are well worth noting here:

- In the past, virtually every water policy review has resulted in good ideas and controversy. What has always been missing, however, was leadership and commitment. Without it, good ideas have simply been filed away. This time, the president asked to formally adopt the policy and to pursue it vigorously. It can't be filed away, and won't be while Jimmy Carter is president.
- This time, the interest in water policy goes far beyond the national level. The national action we stimulated has created or complemented genuine reassessments of water policy at the state and regional level, and the sweeping reassessment I see occurring is fueled by interests very close to home in every area of the country.
- There is a far greater sense of regional identity and strength in the water discussion than ever before. While the West has always had a strong sense of regional interest and identity, the existence of a growing water coalition in the urban Northeast is a strong indication that other regions will be heard from far more than ever before, and on a sustained basis.
- And finally, this debate on water policy is taking place, for the first time, in an atmosphere that suggests a poten-

> tial crisis in water. The last national assessment provides the documentation for such a sense, and while the crisis is clearly not yet one of an absolute shortage of water, it can certainly be regarded as a growing crisis in water management systems.

Nationally, very few issues or institutions are escaping the sweeping reassessment of traditional water solutions which is now underway. Consider some of the basic, traditional policies, programs, institutions and issues that are under serious reconsideration and change:

- The basic structure and responsibilities of the Water Resources Council (WRC) are undergoing significant change; until this policy review, it had remained unchanged since Congress created it in 1965.
- The Reclamation Act of 1902 is now being altered dramatically after decades without change. This is one of the fundamental programs of the federal water program and its most basic elements are under review.
- The basic structure for financing most federal water projects is being seriously reconsidered. New ideas, some radically new, are under active consideration.
- A presidential veto, sustained by Congress, of the public works appropriations bill last year, and another seriously considered this year, have led to a redefinition of the congressional-executive relationship and the strengths of various regional areas as they affect federal water programs.
- An active attempt on the part of urban areas to seek a greater share of federal funds for water supply has begun to shift the political balance that has existed for funding water projects for decades.
- The demands of new water uses are being assessed, and existing systems analyzed for their capability to meet new, high priority needs. In this region, there can be no doubt that energy uses are the new demands to consider and seek ways of accommodating.

Obviously, the list goes on, but the point is clear, this is a time when many of the fundamental, traditional water resources solutions are, at the minimum, being reassessed, and more likely, being changed. I can easily understand this as a period of deep concern and dislocation for those who genuinely believe that no change is necessary in the existing national water policies and institutions.

I can also understand that, depending on your perspective, much of the credit, or the blame, for the dynamic status of national water policy issues can be attributed to the president's policy and his continued interest in water issues. Putting this feeling in perspective, however, I believe that the more accurate judgment is that the president only accelerated a debate that was in most areas both imminent and inevitable anyway. Inevitable or not, however, the early stages of the water policy discussion were not well handled. I believe Governor Matheson's identification of the "hit list" as the worst way to start is painfully accurate. I think I can say now, however, that we are steadily leaving the period of rhetorical confrontation behind us and focusing on the real issues.

The real issue, from the national perspective, is not preemption of state water rights systems.

- The president's policy agrees that "the states have primary authority and responsibility for water resources."
- We assiduously avoided those actions in the policy that went fundamentally to the basic state systems. While there will be continuing concern about protecting the state systems, it is in most respects fading as an issue in the president's policy because we kept our promise in this area, and most western leaders recognize this. In those specific areas where it remains an issue, we remain open to discussing it.
- In some cases, the strict avoidance of this fundamental federal/state conflict was in the face of strong evidence that individual states were not fully coping with some elements of that basic state system. Groundwater control comes readily to mind as an example of where problems

> exist—where state responsibility is basic, but where in some areas that responsibility is not being carried out very well.
>
> Even in energy, it has been our position not only to honor state water systems regarding slurry lines, but to require gubernatorial approval. Some confusion has recently emerged about the position of the administration on protecting state water prerogatives in the debate on the Energy Mobilization Board. I can assure you, despite what you may have heard, the administration supports the right of states to retain preeminent authority over water rights, and nothing in the president's proposal is intended to alter the basic state systems.

If "states rights" is not the issue, what is? From the national perspective, I believe federal programs are a large part of the issue. There are few better examples of this than the attention the president has given to the issue of federally-financed construction of water projects.

Here, what has been traditional for decades is now very much at issue, not only because of presidential action, but because there is a national demand for better programs. The items at issue are basic.

- How projects are planned (at a time when the appropriate state and federal roles are under intense discussion).
- How they should be evaluated, both economically and environmentally (at a time when costs are rising and fewer acceptable sites can be found).
- How projects are financed (at a time when the competition for budget dollars is tougher than ever before).
- How priorities for competing projects should be set (considering both old objectives, such as irrigation, and new ones, such as energy and urban water supply).

Every one of these issues is forcefully emerging, and there is no question that, with or without President Carter's actions, each would have to be addressed in the next few years. As it is, the president did not wait; he set the agenda, and it is being taken up in virtually every quarter. Governor Matheson complimented the president for not vetoing this year's public works appropriations bill, and I'll accept that compliment for the administration. But some perspective on it might help:

1. Overall, it was a better bill than last year's. We believe the veto of last year's bill has impressed upon the Congress the need for restraint and judgment. You will note there are no hit-list projects this year and the number of unbudgeted new starts is lower than any year in memory.
2. The governor takes the failure to veto as a good sign. I agree, and perhaps that will help convince people that the administration is *not* anti-water development. The accomplishments of federal water programs should be—and are—well recognized. The federal water programs can properly claim important accomplishments in settling the West and creating a new agriculture, in limiting flood losses, and in contributing to substantial economic development of all kinds. This record continues today, however, it is at a diminishing pace.
3. This action does not end the president's or the national concern about the quality of federal water programs or the projects they construct. Those concerns, on the part of the president, the secretary and myself are as deep and as real regarding the federal programs as they were in 1977. They are as strong where we can do a better job of efficiently using water (housing, water treatment, and others) as they are for planning the right solution, the lowest cost solution, to a water problem or insuring we build the most important and best project first.

From the national perspective, I believe the real question is whether we will continue to rely on the traditional programs, or whether we will recognize their shortcomings in the modern context and boldly make the reforms that are essential to modernize them. Although I have suggested that the debate, and even the agenda, are to some extent inevitable, the real answers on reform of the traditional system are still outstanding.

Today, the federal government still spends between \$2 and

$3 billion per year on water through more than 25 agencies (not including EPA). The system for spending this massive amount of money has competing and sometimes conflicting objectives, inconsistent standards, overadministration, and, in many cases, a range of solutions that is simply too narrow for the complex water problems that exist today.

These are the problems to which the president's water policy is addressed. There is no question that the response to much of the policy has been controversy, but that is accepted so long as we move forward to better solutions to contemporary water resources problems. Perhaps the best sign of the success of the policy is the debate it has provoked and the alternative policies suggested by others on issues where, in the past, the status quo was acceptable to so many. As I said, the verdict is not yet in, but results thus far are encouraging regarding the policy. Let me turn to a report on the implementation of the policy itself.

In the area of improving planning:

1. The standard planning manual for federal agencies under the Principles and Standards (P&S) will be finalized this fall. The goal–a more efficient, uniform approach to planning.
2. The independent project review is still under congressional consideration (with mixed reviews) but the administration intends to send to Congress no further projects until this issue is further resolved. I believe we will ultimately reach a compromise on this issue.
3. Revisions to the P&S for water conservation and nonstructural solutions are in final review and will be final this fall.
4. Congress is actively considering the future structure and role of the WRC. The most likely outcome, in my view, is an expanded and more effective council.

In the area of improved state-federal cooperation:

1. While neither of the new proposed state grant programs is completely through congressional consideration, both are getting favorable consideration. Both the state planning grant and water conservation programs will likely pass this

year, and this will improve the ability of the federal government to work with stronger state water systems nationwide. nationwide.

2. The cost-sharing proposal has provoked major debate, but has also inspired an alternative proposal that would make sweeping changes in all federal water programs. While we continue to favor the president's proposal, we consider the debate extremely useful, and far from closed.
3. The water policy message and subsequent agency actions have also begun to resolve a problem of major proportions for some states—the nature and extent of federal water rights. A recent Department of the Interior policy document released as part of the water policy implementation effort proposes to clarify these rights for the first time, beginning action to remove the cloud which now hangs over the limited supplies of water in the western states. Specifically, the report proposes to (1) quantify all federal water rights and to establish a date after which no new rights would be claimed; (2) attempt to negotiate rather than litigate most conflicting claims; and (3) utilize state courts and state administrative procedures wherever possible. It is useful to note in the midst of conflict over federal water rights and this solicitor's opinion that this is the first time any administration has overruled the objections of the Department of Justice to specifically spell out these rights. This is the result the states strongly sought. While it was predictable that there would be disagreement about the federal rights, once specified, we can now move toward resolution based on a better sense of the issue than ever before.

In the area of water conservation: For the first time, the conservation of water will be a stated principle in the future development of water resources. Significant progress in implementing this has already been made through the revision of many agency practices and procedures. The Environmental Protection Agency will require flow reduction of all recipients of wastewater treatment grants; the Department of Agriculture will tie some agricultural assistance funds to water conservation efforts; the Department of Housing and Urban Development will fund water conserving devices in publicly subsidized residences; and the Farmer's Home Administration will require water conservation efforts from its grant recipients. In addition, upcoming agency budgets are being revised to reflect greater emphasis on water conservation and reuse.

In the area of environmental quality: Much of the concern over the present methods of developing water projects has been generated by growing dissatisfaction with the impact of those projects on the nation's other natural and cultural resources. The issuance of an executive order on floodplain management is a good example of how this concern has been addressed through the president's water policy message. Almost seventy-five federal agencies conduct activities that have an impact on floodplains, often in harmful or wasteful ways. By the end of this year, every one of those agencies will have adopted improved agency practices designed to reduce adverse impacts on floodplains, an activity that will not only reduce environmental losses but also the damage to property and communities caused by floods. The president has also directed in his message that each new project proposal consider a primarily nonstructural alternative in order to reduce the disruption and destruction of natural and human communities. The president's message has also resulted in the issuance of the first regulations ever to implement the Fish and Wildlife Coordination Act and the Historic Preservation Act, two laws that will help preserve and promote our environmental and historic resources. In summary, the implementation of the president's policy remains active and enthusiastic. As with any broad national policy, some elements are being accepted more easily than others.

Major issues, such as joint federal-state financing of water projects should be debated in detail before a change is made. Significantly, however, much of the debate is now on the type of cost sharing that will work best, rather than an all-or-none debate on cost sharing itself.

Overall, our general feeling at this time is favorable given realistic rather than idealistic expectations for so large and difficult a policy area. Contrary to some feelings that the policy has slackened, I suggest that there are real changes occurring at a rapid pace, and all sectors of the water community should remain active and constructive in the process. For my part, I will be most happy if we can improve all federal programs so that they are water and cost efficient, honest and modern in their economics and selection of solutions, and publicly credible in the priorities chosen for use of the budget. I believe these things, and more, are possible. Generally, I see our approach as continuing to be one of intense presidential interest in water. I believe it is crucial that the dialogue be continually improved so that whatever the political outcome, there exists a growing capability for federal water programs to serve the West.

Part 3

Improving the Water-Allocation Process

11 Water Law, Policies, and Politics: Institutions for Decision Making

Frank J. Trelease

A Decision Is Made

The application of the water resources of the northern great plains to the task of developing the area's energy potential must be preceded by many decisions. Many individuals and public and private organizations must resolve conflicts, undertake actions, make choices, give approvals. The institutional framework for these decisions includes not only the organizational structure of the bodies that make them but also the law that guides and shapes them.

Perhaps the best lead-in to the topic is to tell of a fairly recent decision and examine its framework and other attributes. There is a great deal of coal in the sparsely populated northeastern quadrant of Wyoming. There is a great need for electric power in the heavily populated and industrialized area of southeast Texas. Early this year, Texas Eastern Transmission Corporation sought a decision that would permit it to appropriate 20,000 acre-feet of water per year from the Little Bighorn River in northern Wyoming and use it in a coal slurry pipeline to transport 250,000,000 tons of Wyoming coal to Houston, Texas, there to be used in several steam-electric power generation plants. The Little Bighorn is a small stream rising in the Big Horn National Forest. It flows northward through a small canyon to the Montana state line and is then joined by several other tributaries as it flows fifty miles through the Crow Indian Reservation to the Custer Battlefield National Monument. No irrigable lands lie alongside it in Wyoming, and no Wyoming appropriator takes its waters. When interest in coal mining spurred a search for water, the TR 12 Corporation filed for and obtained a permit to appropriate the water for coal development. The permit calls for intercepting part of the water almost at the state line and piping it to an offstream reservoir with a capacity of 42,580 acre-feet. Texas Eastern acquired this permit, but under the statutes of Wyoming, the legislature must approve any taking of water out of the state for use as a medium for transportation of mineral products to another state.[1] When Texas Eastern sought this permission, the legislature found too many variables and unanswered questions to allow it to act decisively, so it gave a conditional approval to be effective if the governor of Wyoming was able to work out a satisfactory contract with the company within 90 days.[2] The contract was to require Texas Eastern to undertake a feasibility study and, upon a favorable result, to give the state three options. Under the first, Texas Eastern would construct the project and the state would buy all the water in excess of 20,000 acre-feet per year for a share of costs and sell it to irrigation, municipal, and industrial users within Wyoming. Under the second option the state itself would construct the project, finance it with revenue bonds, sell Texas Eastern a firm supply of 20,000 acre-feet per annum, and sell the balance as it pleased. Under the third option Texas Eastern would finance and construct the project. No industrial use other than slurry would be made by Texas Eastern, but the state, municipalities, and water districts would have an opportunity to buy into the water pipeline at the incremental cost of enlarging it beyond 20,000 acre-foot capacity for these additional uses. Under all the options, Texas Eastern was to promise that if it did not build the coal slurry preparation plant in Wyoming it would still pay to state and local entities a sum equivalent to property taxes on the plant. Under the first and third options, the project and related water rights would be conveyed to the state without cost after the use of water for slurry pipeline transportation was permanently terminated.

The governor and Texas Eastern entered into negotiations. The governor held public hearings. He got a lot of advice—the project was vociferously opposed by several environmental groups, the railroads, the railroad brotherhoods and other labor unions, the State Democratic Central Committee, the Crow Indian Nation, and the state of Montana.

After eighty-five days the governor threw up his hands and refused to sign any contract. The legislature had put the cart before the horse, he said, and many questions ought to be resolved before, not after, the state was bound by the contract. Would it be in the best interests of the state of Wyoming "to export its precious water resources to Texas"? How much water would be available to the state after the pipeline received its 20,000 acre-feet? What were the social, economic, and environmental effects of the project? What were the chances of agreeing with the Indians?[3] He did not indicate who was to make these studies. While there is still a chance that Texas Eastern might get its water at some future date, the present decision denied permission.

This decision is unique, the process by which it was reached is most unusual. I have been teaching water law for a third of a century. Most of my students would not recognize these proceedings as having any relations to what they have been taught. This is not water law as we have known it in the past. The governor and the legislature are newcomers to the decision-making process. A short review of the traditional institutions, policies, and processes will help to identify and emphasize the change.

Traditional Institutions and Policies

Initiating Water Uses

The law of prior appropriation is said to be a western invention adapted to pioneer needs.[4] If Texas Eastern's project had occurred in the early days of western settlement, the company merely would have physically seized the water, and as the "first taker" (to translate the Latinate English into Anglo-Saxon) it would have acquired a property right to continue its use, a right that would be superior to the rights of "later takers."[5] The right was self-initiated. If the company's hydrologist found the amount of water needed in the stream in the average year and its civil engineer found a dam site with sufficient capacity to even out the lean years and the fat years, the company would have been the only decision maker involved. True, had a neighbor challenged it in court the appropriation would have had to meet one policy: it would have had to stand the test of "beneficial use." Did it fulfill some need or desire of man; did it produce wealth?[6] There seems little doubt that coal transportation could qualify. The pioneers placed no limit on the place of use, and the fact that the water would be used out of its valley and would cross a state line was of no moment.[7]

This era of self-created rights gave way to a second stage in the growth of the law of prior appropriation. Administrative law was superimposed upon property rights. In 1889 the territorial engineer of Wyoming, Elwood Mead, persuaded the pioneer framers of the state constitution to adopt state ownership of water as the basic rule.[8] In the following year the first session of the Wyoming legislature implemented this concept with a permit system for initiating appropriations.[9] No longer were rights to be created *ministerio legis,* no longer solely at the will of the appropriator. Now the state had to concur in the decision. The appropriator had to apply for a permit to construct the works and use the water. A government agency was to decide whether there was unappropriated water for the use, dole out the share of water needed for the use, and oversee the construction of the works. Most important, this 1890 legislation declared a new policy: the state agency was to withhold the grant of a property right, to deny the application, if to grant the permit would be "contrary to the public interest."[10]

Although there are not many cases that call the public interest limitation into play, the courts have made it into a very important policy under which water use has been controlled by employing surprisingly modern and sophisticated economic concepts. As early as 1910 the New Mexico territorial court held that it incorporated the economist's maximization or efficiency principle and required the water officials to choose from competing projects the one that would produce the greatest net benefits.[11] In 1915 and 1929, social costs were recognized as grounds for denying permits that would have very bad external effects on others.[12] In 1943 the Utah Supreme Court employed the notion of opportunity costs in preventing a single-purpose appropriation from cutting the heart out of a great multipurpose project.[13] In none of these cases did the judges use the economic terms, but they had no difficulty in recognizing and applying the economic concepts. In recent years legislators have embroidered on these themes; the Alaska and Washington water appropriation statutes incorporate express cost-benefit formulas,[14] and several states identify specific recreational, fish, wildlife, and environmental values that must be considered or guarded.

Very recently it has been found that these ad hoc procedures do not exhaust the public interest concept. The state need not wait until activity in the private sector initiates an application for an appropriation. A modern water planning process can be integrated with the permit procedure and provide policy guidelines for determining the public interest. The proposed project may be a needed unit in the plan, but the plan can assist water officials in disposing of an individual case even though the project was not specifically contemplated by the plan. The plan can provide standards for construction of works, tests for waste and inefficient use, and narrow the range of acceptable uses. The plan's description of the resource, identification of possible uses and alternatives, analyses of conflicts and problems may reveal the externalities of a particular project, identify the choices that have to be made, and indicate the proper choice.[15] A recent case in North Dakota makes this procedure mandatory. A group called the United Plainsmen Association sought an injunction that would prevent the state water officials from issuing future water permits for coal-related power and energy production until a comprehensive plan for conservation and development of the state's natural resources was undertaken. The North Dakota Supreme Court upheld this claim and stated that since the water officials had to act in accordance with the public trust in which the state holds the water resources, planning by appropriate state agencies and officers was an essential and necessary part of the allocation of public water.[16]

The permit system and its public interest limitation was adopted in sixteen of the continental western states. Colorado still maintains common-law self-created appropriations with an overlay of judicial control.[17] Montana had a somewhat similar system until 1973, when it adopted a permit system *without* the public interest feature.[18] In these states the same results could be reached by expansion of the beneficial use concept. The cost-benefit formula could be incorporated, since if a new use were to cause more harm than good it could hardly be said to be beneficial.[19] The maximization principle could be found in a slight extension of the notion that beneficial use was to some extent a relative concept.[20] One use could be denied the beneficial tag if a competing use was found to be more beneficial. Cases like this have seldom if ever arisen, just as there have been very few cases construing "public interest." This is for a very good reason—practically all the farmers, miners, power companies, manufacturers, and cities who put to use the waters of the West had a practical, wealth-producing, "beneficial" use in mind, all advanced the development of the resources of the country, each was an increment toward maximization of the welfare of the people, the states, and the nation, and hence each was in the public interest. There was very little direct competition for water in the sense that simultaneous demands were made on the streams, and there was little need to allow some projects and deny others. The law of priority settled each right in turn. If the new user was left an insufficient or insecure supply, he could seek another source or store seasonal floods. The waters were appropriated as the land was settled, the developers made the decision, and state concurrence was seldom withheld. Today the land is quite well settled, the pioneer notion that all development is good is fading, and available waters have so dwindled that the state takes a more active interest in seeing that what little remains is really put to its highest and best use.

Reallocation of Water

As each appropriator was awarded a water right, the supply soon dwindled and newcomers found no water available for them, at least no inexpensive, easily obtainable water. Obviously the best uses of water did not always arise first and get the earliest rights, so it became necessary to reallocate the water. Since farming had taken the largest share, this meant that the use and place of use had to be changed from irrigation, often of low-value crops, to industrial and municipal uses that would produce greater wealth or command greater income.

The institutions that evolved for reallocating water were the transferable property right and the market. The decision makers were the parties to the transaction. In theory, the process was much like the reallocation of rights in land. A farmer has a fee simple title to his land, running "to him and his heirs forever," but when an encroaching city makes the land more valuable for residences than for crops, a subdivider, who will get greater value from the land than the farmer, will offer the farmer a price that will compensate him for his lost farm income and give him enough profit to induce him to sell. Although the "land right" lasts forever, the land use is flexible and can meet new and changing demands.

The process is much the same for water. A permanent, stable water right guarantees the farmer irrigation water, but if the water would be more productive in a slurry pipeline or synthetic fuel plant, a transfer of the water to the new use can be made by a sale of the right.[21] Some think that flexibility requires intervention of the state, but it can be achieved without sacrificing security. The property right insures that the gainers pay the losers; it does not prevent the reallocation of the resource.[22]

The state takes a hand in making a decision to reallocate water just as it does in the original allocation. The rule allowing an appropriator to sell his water has always been subject to the policy limitation that the transfer must not injure other appropriators. Most irrigation is quite inefficient in the engineering sense. Only a portion of the water diverted and applied to the field evaporates or is consumed by plants; the remainder seeps back into the stream where it becomes available downstream. Since the water can be used and reused, many irrigators have rights to the same molecules of water. The water right is usually phrased in terms of the diversion of a specific quantity of water, so if an irrigator sells his right to a coal developer for use out of the watershed, he will have sold some molecules of water that belong to his downstream neighbor. To avoid this type of social cost, the rule was early developed that the transferee can take only the amount consumed by the original use, not the amount diverted from the stream. The early cases announcing this rule were often decided after the fact and the sale was made. Then if injury occurred a lawsuit was begun and the transfer was blocked or the amount reduced.[23] Nowadays all states have a procedure for making an advanced determination of whether or not sufficient injury will occur to prevent the sale, whether conditions can be imposed upon the new user that will avoid the harm, and whether the amount of water that can be transferred should be reduced.[24]

In practical fact this transfer mechanism has not always worked well. Proceedings to approve the change are cumbersome and time-consuming. The parties cannot be sure at the time of striking the bargain just what is being sold and what will be received. Defects in water titles, poor descriptions, the possibilities of abandonment and forfeiture, and other uncertainties and unknowns impede the process.[25] Yet it seems to have worked well enough. Cities have been able to expand, industry has moved west, and there are no signs that the growth of the West has been impeded because all the water is being used for irrigation.

The Politicization of Water Law

When the "coal rush" to the northern high plains started a few years ago the people seemed to lose faith in these long-used economic, judicial, and administrative mechanisms for allocating and reallocating water. The first changes came in the laws for initiating projects.

Slurry pipelines attracted particularly vigorous opposition. Some water was apparently available for them. Water for the iron horses of the first transcontinental railways had been one of the earliest uses in these states, so the transportation of coal sounded very much like a beneficial use. Cost-benefit ratios and net benefit comparisons seemed undoubtedly favorable to the pipelines. But the public reaction to slurry lines was very negative. They would take some of the last unappropriated water out of the state, and this ran counter to local claims that even unappropriated water was "our water," not to be taken away by strangers. This feeling had long ago resulted in some states placing restrictions on the appropriation of water within the state for use outside it.[26] There were also some fears that the exporting states would be stripped of their coal resources without the production of much local wealth. In addition, these rural states had long had one strongly unionized industry, the railroads, and their present and future prosperity could be affected if coal were transported in pipelines instead of in railroad cars.

The matter was first brought to a head in Wyoming by a coal company's applications for a large number of wells into the state's largest untapped groundwater aquifer. The ultimate use was for coal development but was otherwise unspecified; steam power, synthetic fuel plants, or slurry lines were possibilities. People in the small town of Buffalo, Wyoming, saw their way of life threatened by overwhelming numbers of miners and construction workers; surrounding ranchers saw the last unappropriated water gobbled up for a new development that also threatened parts of their rangeland. Their representative in the legislature was successful in securing passage of a bill that slapped a one-year moratorium on the approval of applications to use more than 6,000 acre-feet per year of groundwater for industrial purposes and called for a study of underground water use.[27] This became combined with another bill that extended to groundwater the long-standing prohibition against the appropriation, storage, or diversion of stream water for use outside the state without prior approval of the legislature,[28] and another section that specifically prohibited the use of surface or groundwater as a medium of transportation of mineral, chemical, or other products to another state.[29] In the same statute, however, the legislature gave its approval in advance to the appropriation by Energy Transportation Systems Incorporated of 20,000 acre-feet of groundwater for use in a slurry pipeline to transport coal to a large steam electric plant in Little Rock, Arkansas.[30]

In the following year, Montana was faced with the same problem. Knowing that prohibitions on export might run into constitutional challenge as invalid restraints on interstate commerce,[31] the Montana legislature tried another tack, adding the following language to their statutory definition of beneficial use: "A use of water for slurry to export coal from Montana is not a beneficial use. Slurry is a mixture of water and insoluble matter."[32] Since water can only be appropriated for beneficial use, this blunt instrument approach means that in Montana *no* appropriation for slurry for export can be made.

South Dakota was more subtle. Its legislature required the Water Rights Commission to submit all applications to appropriate more than 10,000 acre-feet per year to the legislature for approval, and denied powers of eminent domain to any common carrier that had not obtained such prior approval.[33]

Sales and transfers of water rights have been subject to politicization for a long time. The people of Wyoming have long thought unseemly the sight of appropriators bartering water and enriching themselves with the state's property. In 1909 they attempted to tie the water everlastingly to the land by the "no change statute," a much-criticized law that seemed to run counter to economic sense. It laid down the rule that water rights could not be detached from the land, place, or purpose for which they were acquired without loss of priority.[34] Recognizing, however, that cities and the Union Pacific Railroad could not take their place at the foot of the priority list on overappropriated streams, the original statute allowed water to be condemned to supply preferred domestic and transportation purposes. Over the years the legislature made many other exceptions, each time yielding to practical needs and economic pressures, almost like a court or administrative agency reacting to particular problems that needed solutions.[35] First it freed supplemental stored water from the operation of the statute, then it allowed transfers if irrigated land became seeped, salted, or flooded by a Bureau of Reclamation dam. Then water was allowed for new demands: steam power plants, development of a large iron ore deposit, highway construction, fish hatcheries and public fishing areas. In 1973 the legislature adopted a statute that at first was thought to replace this "Swiss cheese law" whose exceptions had swallowed the rule, but then it was the courts and the administrators who put on the brakes in coal-related cases and took a narrow and restricted view of the new statute, severely limiting the transferability of water to the coal industry.[36]

Montana had always allowed the sale and transfer of water rights, but in one of the state's first reactions to the "coal rush" her legislature placed a restriction on an appropriator of more than fifteen cubic feet per second, prohibiting the change of the purpose and use of such a right from agricultural use to industrial use.[37] This avoids large transfers to the coal interests, but it could apparently be circumvented by aggregating a number of small ones.

South Dakota adopted transfer restrictions even before Wyoming did, and provided in its 1907 water code that all water use for irrigation should remain appurtenant to the land, to be severed only if it became impracticable to use the water beneficially or economically for irrigation.[38] Perhaps because South Dakota lies closer to the arid-humid boundary, this remained unchallenged until 1978, and then the only exception added by the legislature would allow the transfer or lease of water only for municipal water supply,[39] an exception that had been built into the 1909 Wyoming law. However, as in Wyoming, the statutory rigidity had no application to rights vested prior to the date of the statute, and this left the older and most desirable rights available for sale.[40]

To the extent that resistance to transfer of water rights has been increased or revised by the coal boom, it appears to be inspired not so much by anticoal resentment as by proirrigation sentiment. The people seem unwilling to switch from "irrigation law" to "energy law." Their attitude seems to be that the farmer and rancher should not have to sacrifice their water: "Let the coal companies find their own water, not take ours."

Politics and Policies

How do such political decisions measure up to the traditional policy standard of the "public interest"? It may seem anomalous to ask, for who is better equipped to declare the public interest of a state than the legislature of that state? Yet if we turn to the specifics of the public interest as worked out in the water cases, we can ask whether these political decisions meet the cost-benefit test, whether they produce the greatest net benefits from the use of the resource. We may lack data for an exact answer, but we may be able to make an educated guess.

We have seen that water administrators might find that the public interest requires the denial of a proposed project where a better future use of the water is foreseeable. Was that the case in regard to the Texas Eastern proposal? Actually the governor ducked the decision because, he said, he did not know what need the state would have for the water. But the state has not yet had any need of the Little Bighorn's water, and no appropriation of it has ever been made. Given the very expensive means of diversion (pumps, pipeline, and offstream reservoir), it seems unlikely that agricultural users could pay for the project. Although the corporation would have gotten the lion's share of the firm supply, the state would have some agricultural water at very little cost, while now without the project it gets nothing, Texas Eastern gets nothing, and no coal is developed. Although the sincerity of the governor's doubts as to consequences of his desire for more information are not questioned, he did put a little political claptrap into his major question: "Is it in the best interests of the state of Wyoming to export its precious water resources to Texas?"[41] And yet now all the water, both the Wyoming share and the Texas share, leaves the state, exported to Montana by gravity via the bed of the Little Bighorn River, and it is likely to continue to go that way for a very long time.

We noted that the public interest also requires consideration of alternatives. One very possible alternative to the Texas Eastern slurry pipeline can be foreseen. The water could be used within the state for a coal-fired steam power plant or for a synthetic fuel plant, either of which would have a much more devastating effect on Wyoming's environment and its people's life-style than the pipeline, and either of which would prevent Wyoming's cities and farms from using the water just as effectively as if it had been shipped to Texas. Yet were the TR 12 Corporation now to turn to such a project, the state would have no political handle since the permit has already been issued.

As for the institutional question, if the state engineer had had the question of the public interest before him and there had been no necessity of seeking legislative approval for the export, would he have issued the permit for the slurry pipeline and combined state use? It seems clear he would have, since the statute giving Texas Eastern approval to take the water out of the state (conditioned on the governor signing a contract) recites that it was enacted upon the advice of the state engineer.[42]

Problems of this nature might arise also in South Dakota. The compilers of the South Dakota statute books note that after the legislature took over control of all large appropriations, the 1977 and 1978 sessions of the legislature passed resolutions approving fourteen permits for the appropriation of more than 10,000 acre-feet per year. Four of these have gone to individuals, three to cities, and the rest to irrigation projects.[43] Fine. But when will the legislature refuse its approval? What good project will be rejected because it brings up some old conflict, pits one area of the state against another, or offends the labor unions? What unsound project may be approved because of log rolling or pork barrel politics?[44] To move to Montana, what good, environmentally sound projects for use of Montana coal have been foregone because its absolutist laws barred all, the good and the bad? How much good growth and better use of water has been blocked by Wyoming's and South Dakota's antagonisms to sale and transfer of water rights?

We may also ask whether the political arena is a good mechanism for giving us the right answers. One great difference between a decision made by an administrative agency and one made by a legislature or elected chief executive lies in the type of institutional constraints upon the decision maker. The agency is bound by law to apply statutory standards, while the legislature or governor is not. The agency must act on substantial evidence;[45] the others may react to political pressures.

Another difference between administrative and political decisions lies in the relative inflexibility of the legislative process. Decisions in individual cases would seem very difficult under absolutist statutes like Montana's that foreclose all pipelines, all large transfers. While a company with what it feels is a very good proposal could nevertheless go to the legislature and ask for repeal or amendment of the law, surely this is a more difficult process than asking for legislative approval under a prior law that prescribes that procedure. And the latter is infinitely more difficult than the more or less routine application for administrative approval of a permit or transfer.

Still another difficulty the legislature may face is the handling of complicated technical facts. When the Wyoming legislature gave its approval to the use of groundwater for the ESTI pipeline, it inserted some very specific physical and engineering requirements regarding the depth to which the wells were to be drilled and the manner of their construction as conditions in the permits,[46] matters that would be very difficult to correct if found inconsistent with physical facts and matters that would be far better left to administrative expertise.

State or Federal Decisions?

Let me make it clear that I do not deny to the legislatures and elected leaders of the states the right and the duty to fix policy, to order priorities, to make the ultimate determination of what is in the public interest. They may legitimately control development of mineral and water resources, prefer one type of development over another, choose to foster full employment for the state's labor force, try to preserve a traditional way of life and a congenial environment. My objection is to the attempts to reach these objectives by the misuse of water law, by distorting water law into a land use regulating tool.

I have a warning for the politicizers, the people who seek to use water law to prevent coal development in order to preserve the great open spaces and the clear air of the big sky and in order to avoid population growth—the flooding of towns with construction workers and miners, who will compete for the deer, the antelope, and the trout. My warning is, don't bust the monkey-wrench. An old friend of mine, a great law teacher now retired, used to illustrate his functional approach to law by saying that the law was like a box of tools. In the study of prior decisions, law students and law professors are prone to criticize judges for bad logic or poor choice of doctrine, even though the right result may have been reached. The old dean would point out, however, that the judge had a job to do, that he had to drive a nail, and if he picked up the monkey-wrench instead of the hammer, what difference did it make? The nail got driven. There are, however, some dangers. You may jimmy the monkey-wrench so that it won't work very well when you want to tighten a nut.

The states have been very jealous of their water laws and very resentful of federal encroachment into this area. Yet when they deny water to a coal slurry pipeline they may be inviting exactly the federal intervention they fear. There is a real danger that the Congress will simply override their laws, that the federal government will supersede state water law with federal project law. I do not think that Congress will do what the states fear most and enact a national water law that would supplant the state's prior appropriation system. I think it highly unlikely that even the energy crisis could prevail over the united and concentrated opposition that the western states could mount against that threat. What is likely, however, is a federal project that would solve the pipeline company's problem by supplying water to it with complete disregard for state water law, state water policy, state coal development policy, and state land use plans.

We have seen that a state's legislators may, in determining the state's "public interest," make a decision that in spite of slurry pipeline's favorable cost-benefit ratio, in spite of the fact that using 20,000 acre-feet of water to move 250 million tons of coal would produce far more wealth than its use to grow more hay for cattle or crops for food—they still do not want the coal development, and they still want to keep their water within the state. They have therefore taken these decisions out of the hands of administrative agencies, and they do not want a bureaucrat to tell them that the public interest is economic efficiency and nothing else. But far away in Washington there are bureaucrats who take a broader view, who see a real need for coal in Houston, Texas, and in the Midwest, and who believe that slurry pipelines offer coal transportation on a better and cheaper basis than do the railroads. Rumors have come to me of recent statements by two highly placed federal officials in the Department of the Interior and the Department of Energy that if the states do not take the lead the federal government will step in. For instance, the federal government might solve Texas Eastern's problem in one of two ways. Wyoming has unappropriated water in the "big" Bighorn River, stored behind the federal government's Yellowtail Dam, which is located in Montana but backs water up far into Wyoming. This river is separated from the coal fields by the Big Horn Mountains, but one possible federal project is a water pipeline from Hardin, Montana, around the northern end of the Big Horns back into Wyoming near Gillette. If Congress authorized this project, the United States could take a part of Wyoming's share of the water stored in Yellowtail, bring it back into Wyoming and sell it to coal slurry companies without Wyoming's by-your-leave.[47] A possibly better pipeline project could take water from Oahe Reservoir in South Dakota and pump it into Wyoming, there to be used to transport coal to any desired destination. Another possibility is that Congress will pass a slurry pipeline right-of-way bill. A federally authorized utility would undoubtedly have the power to condemn not only the land for the pipeline but also the water to make it work.[48] I think there is no way that a state can deny to a federal instrumentality the water needed to accomplish the federal purpose.[49]

Another warning I have is that the use or misuse of water to control coal development may not work. The monkey-wrench may not drive the nail at all. The states' attempts to block slurry pipelines may fail, even without federal intervention, because such state laws may be unconstitutional.

The Constitution of the United States gives Congress the power to regulate commerce among the several states,[50] and state laws that unduly burden interstate commerce are not allowed to stand. It is beyond question that a state could not prohibit the export of the coal—states have tried this with natural gas and failed. West Virginia once had a law that tried to give its citizens a preference in the purchase and use of gas, but the Supreme Court struck the statute down.[51] Oklahoma tried to do it by indirection, by denying the power of eminent domain to pipelines that took "its" gas away. In the Supreme Court the state argued that it might reserve its resources for its own citizens. Said the Court: "The results of the contention repel its acceptance. If the states have such power, a singular situation might result. Pennsylvania might keep its coal, the Northwest its timber, the mining states their minerals. And why may not the products of the field be brought within the principle?"[52] Is water different? In 1908, the Supreme Court ruled that New Jersey might prevent the Hudson County Water Company from impairing the state's resources by exporting and selling New Jersey's fresh water to New York City,[53] but a more recent case has cast doubt upon the value of this as a precedent. When the City of Altus, Oklahoma, bought the groundwater rights under a Texas farm, the Texas legislature immediately passed a law prohibiting the withdrawal of Texas groundwater for transportation out of the state without the authority and approval of the Texas legislature. A lower federal court held this to be a burden on interstate commerce, governed by the natural gas cases rather than the New Jersey water case.[54]

The Supreme Court affirmed without written opinion, leaving the matter somewhat hazy. It could possibly be argued that since the states claim ownership of water and they can prefer one use over another within the state, similar public regulation of interstate use might sustain the statutes.[55] The United States, however, is a great nation in large part because it has had free trade over such a large, rich, and diversified area without tariffs, embargoes, or restrictions. I think it clear that a state could not keep its coal for the sole use of its citizens. I don't think it can keep its water, and I am sure that it cannot keep its coal by denying water for coal transportation.

South Dakota adds to its statute a loss of the power of eminent domain, so that a slurry pipeline might be blocked by landowners, but this is the tactic held unconstitutional in the West Virginia natural gas case. Montana's cute trick—that use of water for coal slurry export is not a beneficial use—would still allow slurry for intrastate transportation and if the Supreme Court of the United States were to find the Wyoming statute unconstitutional, I doubt that the Montana statute would fare any better. So we may find that the ultimate decisions on slurry pipelines come not from the legislatures and governors of the states, but from the federal courts.[56]

If these statutes are struck down the states have little to fall back on. In a confrontation that pits a state public interest against a national energy policy, the state is bound to come out second best. On the other hand, a real effort at planning for coal development, avoiding conflicts, easing the transition into an industrial age, and ameliorating the impact on people and the environment could find a responsive federal ear. The national government may have supreme powers, but it seldom fails to take into account the urgent needs, the earnest plans, and the sincere desires of the states and the local people.

The Need for Integrated Policies

The burden of this paper has been that the high plains states have been using water law to implement a coal development policy with some danger to both the law and the policy. The real questions addressed by the legislators are not concerned with water use but with the social and environmental effects of the new coal age. Do the people want coal mines, coal towns, slurry pipelines, steam power plants, power lines, gasification, and synthetic fuel plants? I think they fear them. The people are afraid they cannot keep their rural, semipioneer life-style, their Marlboro Country environment. Because water is necessary to all forms of coal development, they have seized upon water law as a means of control, the method of preventing undesirable effects.

My message is that water law is a poor tool with which to do this job. Water law and water policy are not enough, they will not prevent the undesired effects, they cannot effectively control and guide development. The need is for growth controls, boom town control, rural zoning, and land use planning. The desire is to save the streams, the aquifers, and the clean air for the wide open spaces and the big sky. What is needed is effective and certain mine land reclamation measures, aid to impacted towns, plant-siting laws and procedures that can insure the minimum of disruption, the mitigation of harmful effects, and the repair of spillover dangers. Most of all, the states need an overall policy: one integrated policy for energy, land use, and water. A restrictive, obstructive water policy alone will not do the job. Effective tools must be forged to implement the integrated policy. The states need to find more direct and better ways to deal with coal development.[57]

If we were to take the politics out of water law, would that mean that we take the politics out of coal development? I hope not; I think not. The policy must be political, it must reflect the wishes of the housewives, workers, business men and women, farmers, ranchers, and all the people who make up the population of the state. It must of course be a part of a national policy.

When water is needed to transport or utilize coal, water policy and water law must be consistent with the coal development policy. I suggest that when decisions have been made for coal plants and pipelines, power plants and synfuel plants—with all the land use, environmental, and social safeguards taken into account—that a good water policy would be one that would give a framework for decision making that looked something like this:

1. When unappropriated water is sought by the private sector for coal-related use, state administrative controls should insure that the appropriation will be in the public interest by employing cost-benefit analysis, environmental protections, and consideration of alternatives; and
2. When the coal industry needs water that is already being put to use, the industry should find a willing seller and buy the water right at a negotiated price, subject to administrative controls to prevent harmful spillovers and externalities that affect persons not privy to the transaction.

This is the water law we used to have, and it is the policy we should return to.

Notes

1. Wyo. Stat. Sec. 41-3-115.
2. Wyo. Stat. Sec. 41-2-301.
3. Press release, State of Wyoming, Governor's Office, May 18, 1979. For a fuller account, see Myers, "Texas Pipe Dream," *Wyoming News*, vol. 4, no. 5 (July 1979), p. 29.
4. Recognition of priority of right is also widespread throughout the world. See Trelease, "New Water Legislation, Drafting for Development, Efficient Allocation and Environmental Protection," 12 *Land & Water L. Rev.* 385 (1977).
5. Irwin v. Phillips, 5 Cal. 140 (1855).
6. Trelease, "The Concept of Beneficial Use in the Law of Surface

Streams," 12 *Wyo. L. J.* 1 (1957).

7. Coffin v. Left Hand Ditch Co., 6 Colo. 443 (1882); Willey v. Decker, 11 Wyo. 496, 73 P. 210 (1903).

8. Wyo. Const. Art. 8, Sec. 1 (1889).

9. Wyo. Stat. Sec. 41-4-501.

10. Wyo. Const. Art. 8, Sec. 3 (1889); Wyo. Stat. Sec. 41-4-503.

11. Young & Norton v. Hinderlider, 13 N.M. 666, 110 P. 1045 (1910).

12. Big Horn Power Co. v. State, 23 Wyo. 271, 148 P. 1110 (1915); in re Martha Lake Water Co., 152 Wash. 53, 277 P. 382 (1929).

13. Tanner v. Bacon, 103 Utah 494, 136 P.2d 957 (1943).

14. Alaska Stat. Sec. 46.5.080; Wash. Rev. Code Sec. 90.54.020(2).

15. See Wyo. Stat. 41-2-107 to 41-2-110; Trelease, "Recommendations for Water Resources Planning and Administration, A Report to the State of Alaska," 16, 18 (1977).

16. United Plainsmen Association v. North Dakota State Water Conservation Board, 247 N.W.2d 457 (N.D. 1976).

17. See Cache La Poudre Water User's Association v. Glacier View Meadows, 550 P.2d 288 (Colo. 1976).

18. Mont. Code Secs. 85-2-301 to 85-2-310.

19. See Idaho Department of Parks v. Idaho Department of Water Administration, 96 Idaho 440, 530 P.2d 924 (1974), opinion of McQuade, J.

20. Trelease, supra n.6.

21. 1 Hutchins, Water Rights Law in the Nineteen Western States 633 (1971).

22. Trelease, "The Model Water Code, the Wise Administration, and the Goddam Bureaucrat," 14 *Nat. Resources J.* (1974).

23. 1 Hutchins, supra, note 21, 631.

24. Ibid., 641–644.

25. Trelease, "The Changing Water Market for Energy Production," 5 *J. Contemp. L.* 85 (1978).

26. 1 Hutchins, supra, note 21, 389–396.

27. Wyo. Sess. L. 1974 Ch. 25 Sec. 3. No new legislation resulted from this study, and the moratorium expired.

28. Wyo. Stat. Sec. 41-3-105.

29. Wyo. Stat. Sec. 41-3-115(b).

30. Wyo. Stat. Sec. 41-3-115(d).

31. See text infra at note.

32. Mont. Rev. Code Sec. 85-2-102(2).

33. S. D. Comp. L. Sec. 46-5-20.1.

34. Wyo. Sess. L. 1909 Ch. 68 Sec. 1.

35. Trelease & Lee, "Priority & Progress—Case Studies in the Transfer of Water Rights," 1 *Land & Water L. Rev.* 1 (1966), and Trelease, "Trans-

fer of Water Rights, Errata and Addenda,'' 2 *Land & Water L. Rev.* 321 (1967).

36. Basin Electric Power Coop. v. State Board of Control, 578 P.2d 557 (Wyo. 1978); Trelease, supra n.25.

37. Mont. Code Sec. 85-2-402(3).

38. S.D. Comp. L. Sec. 46-5-34.

39. S.D. Comp. L. Sec. 46-5-34.1.

40. Hughes v. Lincoln Land Co., 27 F. Supp. 972 (D. Wyo. 1939); Jewett v. Redwater Irrigating Association, 88 S.D. 390, 220 N.W. 2d 834 (1974).

41. Supra n.3.

42. Wyo. Stat. Sec. 41-2-301(a).

43. S.D. Comp. Laws, Vol. 13, 1978 Pocket Supp., p. 123.

44. Some Wyoming legislators reportedly voted for the ETSI slurry pipeline because Niobara County, site of the proposed installation, needed an increase in its tax base.

45. Bank of America v. State Water Resources Control Board, 42 Cal. App.3d 198, 116 Cal. Rptr. 770 (1974).

46. Wyo. Stat. Sec. 41-3-115(d).

47. Although Yellowtail Dam is a U.S. Bureau of Reclamation project and Section 8 of the Reclamation Act requires conformity to state laws, California v. United States, 438 U.S. 645 (1978) indicates that this does not apply when state law is directly inconsistent with congressional directives.

48. As an aside, there is the possibility that a federal project could be welcomed as a very satisfactory solution to the problem. A water problem, a water shortage, exists when demand exceeds supply. Water law for the most part operates on the demand side of the scale. Typically it puts limits on demand, it tailors rights to fit the supply, it parcels out rights to unappropriated water, it chooses among competitors for water by limiting withdrawals from a deficient supply to the prior appropriators, it reallocates water by allowing the substitution of one user for another if the call on the water resource remains the same. Water projects, on the other hand, are directed at the supply side, they augment the supply, store water for use when needed or bring it from an area of surplus to the place of need. Where the opposition to water for coal is inspired by the fear that irrigation water will be taken off the land and applied to coal uses, a federal project could eliminate the problem and supply the needed water without disruption of existing water rights, state water law or local patterns of water use.

49. Solicitor's Opinion no. M-36914, U.S. Department of the Interior (June 25, 1979). Trelease, "Federal-State Relations in Water Law" (National

Water Commission Legal Study No. 5).

50. U.S. Const. Art. III, Sec. 8.

51. Pennsylvania v. West Virginia, 262 U.S. 553 (1923).

52. West v. Kansas Gas Co., 221 U.S. 229 (1910).

53. Hudson County Water Co. v. McCarter, 209 U.S. 349 (1908).

54. Altus v. Carr, 255 F. Supp. 828 (1966), Aff'd per curiam, 385 U.S. 35 (1966).

55. " 'It's Our Water'—Can Wyoming Constitutionally Prevent the Exportation of State Waters?" 10 *Land & Water L. Rev.* 119 (1975).

56. The courts are decision-making bodies and may have much to say about these cases in other ways. For instance the quantity of water in the Little Bighorn available for coal development in Wyoming will depend upon a division of that river between Wyoming and Montana, a judicial decision interpreting the Yellowstone River Compact or doctrine of equitable apportionment, and upon a quantification of the reserved rights of the Crow Indian Nation, a purely judicial function.

57. The states do not lack for planning authority, e.g., state water plans, Mont. Code Sec. 85-1-203, S.D. Comp. L. Sec. 46-17A-101, Wyo. Stat. Sec. 41-2-106; land use planning, Wyo. Stat. Sec. 9-19-101; economic planning, S.D. Comp. L. 11-1-101, Wyo. Stat. Sec. 9-3-301; plant siting, Wyo. Stat. 35-12-101; community impact, Mont. Code Secs. 90-6-101, 90-6-201. These have few sanctions and offer few opportunities for negative decisions. They seem to have no relation to these water use restrictions.

Commentary

A. Allan Schmid

When I hear the question, "How do we change water institutions for better decision making?" I always add the phrase, "better for whom?" Institutions can make a difference for whose preferences count. Thus, we can't say that one decision-making system is better, more efficient, or more equitable (as opposed to equal) without first asking whose interests we want to serve. I have selected several questions from Trelease's paper for comment. First, where should policy be made? This includes legislature, courts, or administrative agency as well as the level of government. Second, should the institutional vehicle be tied to water law or to other laws relating to land use planning? And third, can benefit-cost analysis be a guide to public decision making?

Let us first consider what branch of government we should use. Trelease makes a case for using administrative agencies. Compared with the legislatures, agencies have to apply statutory standards, are more flexible, and have the complicated technical expertise. This all sounds good, but let's ask, good for whom? Where do those statutory standards come from? That puts us back to the assertedly incompetent, emotional legislatures again, since they are the source of these standards, both those of substance as well as administrative procedure. The existence of any substantive legislative guidelines in the enabling legislation is in fact uneven and often provides only the useless slogan that decisions are to be taken in the public interest. Theodore Lowi in his book, *The End of Liberalism,* demonstrates the paucity of statutory criteria for administrative agencies. In some areas the legislature holds tightly to its control of policy, and in others it is happy to escape the political heat by throwing the ball to the agencies whose decisions they can sympathetically lament with an outraged constituent without doing anything about them.

One person's frustration with inflexibility is another's protection against unwanted change. The point is that the cost of change is part of the ability of different groups to pursue their interests. The same point can be made about technical information. Information is power. The ability to withhold, dramatize, and subsidize the learning of others is part of the assets of parties to influence public policy. It is true that if the legislature gets too detailed in matters involving technical design, they may make some stupid mistakes that benefit no one. On the other hand, there is no clear demarcation between policy making and administration. The person in charge of details can affect performance, especially if it is hard for others to monitor and understand until it is manifest and too late for change. By necessity the expert knows a great deal about a few things. But, the big questions in public policy are matters of relative priorities and this by necessity requires a generalist. There is a lot of presumed value judgment of whose interests should count masquerading as technical expertise.

In any case, each branch of government differs in the ease of access by different groups. Some can get standing before a court that would receive very little hearing before a legislative committee. It is not just a matter of flexibility, standards, and expertise—it is a matter of access. While there are important access differences between branches of government, there can be as much difference within as between depending on the detailed rules and procedures of each. For example, how does an administrative agency get public input? Does it hold public meetings (where), have a citizen advisory committee (how selected), utilize opinion surveys, or prepare detailed plans of a single alternative (or document several alternatives)?[1] What is the agency's jurisdiction; is it single function or a consolidated department of natural resources?[2] All of these details add up to give more ability for some groups to participate than others.

Much the same thing can be said about level of government. Some groups count for more if the decision is made at the local level, while others are more effective at the state or national level. Trelease recommends a larger role for zoning controls. While some states have expanded their role in zoning, it is historically a local matter. There is a strong ideology supporting continuation of this local role and to advocate the zoning tool is to advocate the local level of government. In the case of the impact of coal development that spreads to a large area, local land use controls may shut out many who would like to participate in the decision.

All of the above discussion of branch, level, and jurisdiction of government can be conceptualized as boundary issues that affect who can make their demands effective by affecting the cost of participation, who is in the minority, and the formation of winning coalitions. Boundaries are just a special sort of fence, and we know that fences are meant to keep selected people out (or others from getting away).

Trelease's major argument is that water law is the wrong tool (wrench) for the job of allocating resources to coal development. He prefers "growth controls, boom town control, rural zoning, and land use planning." What experience have we had that suggests the ability of these institutions to prevent major land use changes desired by profit-making firms? The experience in other coal regions is not encouraging. But the experience is perhaps hard to interpret since the performance of an institutional structure (as opposed to alternative structures) is hard to trace to the institution itself versus the depth of political support of its objectives. In the case of coastal zone management, we are now seeing some experiments with an enlarged state role in zoning. But this is after there is precious little undeveloped shoreline left. California law began with a large state level (commission) presence but subsequent legislative modifications have returned much of the power to the local units.[3]

The role of zoning in shaping the pattern of urbanization is a mixed bag. My impression is that nonavailability of sewers and public water supply have done more to affect the direction of land development than has zoning.

Trelease puts a great deal of faith in benefit cost analysis to guide us to resource allocations in the public interest. This is why he seems to accept coal development and slurry shipment. He suggests that if the coal companies can find a willing seller, there should be a transaction. This would be subject to administrative control to prevent harmful spillover. But, the issue is, harmful to whom? Who gets to decide? The question is not just to find a willing buyer and willing seller, but to decide just what it is that anyone has to sell. Law that decides property rights is an antecedent to exchange. You can't sell what you don't have. Benefit-cost analysis follows from the givens of the laws of property rather than being a guide to institutional choice.[4]

Instead of the environmental protection agencies fighting for amelioration in the face of coal development favored by benefit-cost analysis, what if the people (or neighbors) were granted property rights in the environment that the coal developers had to purchase just like they now have to purchase the mineral rights? The issue is who has to buy out whom. Do the people affected have a real right, which they can voluntarily sell or not, or is it only a nominal right to be mostly given away by a regulatory agency bowing to the exigencies of benefit-cost analysis? What would the benefit-cost analysis of coal slurry look like if the coal developer had to buy out the newly declared owners of Marlboro Country? I repeat: there are as many outcomes of benefit-cost analysis as there are different distributions of the antecedent property rights that the analysis implicitly adopts and often hides.

Trelease makes a good point when he suggests that outright prohibition via water law is heavy handed. If you think that some developments, in some places, and with some designs are O.K., then you want a more judgmental process. But the basic objective is up for debate. Indeed, if we want to preserve Marlboro Country, it may be impossible to maintain just a few exceptions. I think the oil situation is instructive. If we want to substantially reduce our dependence on foreign suppliers, then strict import quotas and gas rationing may be the only surefire institutions. Other more marginal changes (even a doubling and tripling of price) have not done much.

Trelease's point about "don't bust the monkey wrench" is also well taken. Those who want coal development may turn to federal water projects where state interests may not be dominant. Even if the president and Congress refuse to preempt state water law, it is possible that the federal courts may overturn state attempts to control growth via laws regulating a necessary input like water. Trelease does not argue that land law would be immune from similar review. While some local attempts to control the volume of land development via absolute growth limits have been allowed to stand,[5] other attempts to control land use have run afoul of the interpretation of the commerce clause of the U.S. Constitution.[6]

Trelease's message to the states is that the power of coal developers is dominant via their access to higher levels of government. Preservation of Marlboro Country is impossible, only amelioration via land use controls can be envisioned. Trelease is probably right. Any time there is a conflict between the opportunity of large profits by a few corporations and small environmental losses by many people scattered over the landscape, the smart money must go with the concentrated interests. So while part of the paper is about choice between land use planning and restrictive water laws, the choice is empty if you prefer preservation to the amelioration of development. The relevant institutional choices lie elsewhere. They are not matters of resources law but of fundamental rules for making rules that might change access to government. It is not easy to find political rules to offset the power of concentrated interests, but rules for financing elections might be a start.

How to change the development philosophy of the unrepresentative courts is a different matter. But, if majority public opinion actually changes, the courts often respond. If the same philosophy exhibited by the voters of Colorado in rejecting the winter Olympics begins to grow and the congressional representatives of western states do not get automatic applause every time they announce a new federal water project, it may be possible to envision preservation.

It is difficult to distinguish whether a given performance emanates from widespread agreement with that performance or if present institutions are barriers to the expression of a demand for change. Is there a problem in finding institutions to transmit a widespread demand for a new concept of the good life or is it that we retain our fascination for what Boulding has called the cowboy economy with emphasis on material throughput?

While it uses the same simile, the cowboy economy and preservation of Marlboro Country are not the same thing.

Notes

1. For a review of the literature on some of these issues, see Joseph DiMento, "Citizen Environmental Litigation and the Administrative Process," *Duke Law Journal,* no. 2, 1977, pp. 409–448.

2. For a review of these organizational issues, see Schmid, *Federal Decision-Making for Water Resource Development,* Springfield, Virginia National Technical Information Center, PB 211 441, 1971.

3. Lenard Grote, "Coastal Conservation and Development: Balancing Local and Statewide Interests," *Public Affairs Report, University of California Institute of Governmental Studies,* vol. 19, no. 1, February 1978.

4. For development of this theme see my *Property, Power and Public Chocie* (New York: Praeger, 1978).

5. For a discussion, see Michelle J. White, "Self-Interest in the Suburbs: The Trend Toward No-Growth Zoning," *Policy Analysis,* Spring 1978.

6. In addition to the cases Trelease cites, a notable example is the recent Supreme Court ruling against New Jersey in its attempt to avoid the use of its resources for the disposal of solid waste from New York City.

12
The Benefit-Cost Dilemma

Daniel W. Bromley

Previous speakers have discussed the water resource situation from several perspectives. We have heard about the expected conflicts over water use, we have heard about water quality and quantity issues, and we have heard from a distinguished legal scholar about the institutional environment of water allocation in the West. It is my task to turn your attention to the evaluation process wherein changes in the status quo would be considered. I come with a message quite unlikely to gladden your heart. To be blunt, I come to remind you of the conceptual and empirical difficulties inherent in a benefit-cost analysis. This is not a tirade against agency benefit-cost practices—though I will take a friendly jab from time to time. Rather it is a reminder to economists and politicians that one of our favorite analytic devices is not only theoretically weak, but operationally deficient in several important respects.

Before proceeding it would seem helpful to clarify some terminology. The term benefit-cost analysis is often applied to both a *process* and a decision *criterion.* One can easily advocate a benefit-cost *approach,* while remaining mindful of serious problems in the theory from which such an approach derives. The term "analysis" when added to "benefit-cost" connotes rigor and sophistication that, in many cases, is without justification.

Finally, the benefit-cost criterion is usually taken to mean the condition that present-valued benefits exceed present-valued costs.

Hence, while I am pessimistic about benefit-cost analysis in the conventional sense of that phrase, do not assume that I am critical of a benefit-cost approach. For who can be opposed to well-intended attempts to ascertain the implications of given public actions?

To anticipate somewhat, I will argue that conventional benefit-cost analysis is quite ill-suited to the resolution of coming conflicts over increasingly scarce water resources in the West. To accomplish this I will first outline the historical setting that gave birth and sustenance to traditional benefit-cost analysis. I will then turn to a brief prognosis of how the future will differ from the past. Next, I will present the conceptual and empirical problems from whence my concern and pessimism arise. Following that I will summarize the type of evaluational approach that is best suited to the conditions that we can expect to prevail.

The Historical Setting

To appreciate the several ways in which the future will differ from the past—and therefore to anticipate the ways in which benefit-cost analysis must adapt—it will be helpful to remind ourselves of the political and economic conditions that existed between the late 1930s and the early 1960s.

We must remember that this period followed by scarcely ninety years the great burst of expansion and building that resulted in the settlement of the vast majority of the western frontier. During this process, impatience was the byword. If local conditions were not suitable for some particular activity, people simply moved on to another place. Clearly capital was scarce compared to good sites—as was labor. It made little sense to spend time, money, and labor modifying any given site since the frontier promised many other propitious locations. However, as the frontier began to disappear, and as the better sites were occupied, successive waves of newcomers were left with less and less happy prospects. As settlement doubled back on itself, it became less easy simply to move to a better place.

As this happened, people's thoughts turned from movement to modification. If an area was intermittently too swampy for farming one did not move but began to drain the swamp—an infinitely more expensive activity than merely staking out a claim in a more favorable location. If the only agricultural land remaining was too arid for crops, then thoughts turned to bringing water to the land for irrigation. If periodic flooding made life hazardous and uncomfortable, then it was time to "solve" the problem by harnessing the river. These modifications became increasingly attractive as state and federal agencies evolved to plan them, construct them, and arrange for the general public (taxpayers) to bear the vast majority of the expense. These facts significantly altered the relative cost of moving vis-à-vis modification.

Having recently read Michener's *Centennial* I am struck once again by the overwhelming entrepreneurial energies of these early settlers. A landed aristocracy simply had no time to develop—in spite of the diligence of English capital, Texas savvy, and frontier "justice"—for there were hundreds of Potato Brumbaughs anxious to build a ditch, string a fence, plow a field, or dig a well if it would make local conditions a little more favorable.

If there were unfavorable conditions for the establishment of a small class of land owners, then it tells us something of the nature of property rights over certain valuable resources. Water was there for the taking, and land was too, although to a lesser extent. And, once its value was recognized by the early users, then they set about to alter the legal structure to protect their newly acquired wealth. When we mention the evolution of prior appropriation water rights we often forget that early settlers simply took water that they wanted, and *then* thought of ways to protect their current use against future claimants. They appropriated resources when property rights were vague or undefined and then created property rights to legitimate what they had done.

As this process of modifying the surroundings was in its early stages, the Great Depression struck. Now, more than ever, there was a legitimate role for government capital and technical expertise. Politicians quickly learned that it was helpful to be able to deliver public works to impoverished districts. Early on these were limited to a few irrigation projects, and some flood-control structures. Benefit-cost analysis—or any facsimile of it—did not exist and these endeavors were undertaken with virtually no concern for the favorable and unfavorable impacts. Of course, the presumption was that they would allow local farmers to improve their crops—or grow them where it was previously impossible—or that it would stop the flooding each spring. But there was no systematic attempt to judge the beneficial and adverse effects to the nation.

With the Flood Control Act of 1936 there first came some language to the effect that projects could be considered worthwhile if the benefits exceeded the costs. But of course there was no legislative guidance given on what was to be a benefit and what was to be a cost. In a sense, it was an early precursor to the approach taken in the National Environmental Policy Act of 1969. As you know, this act requires an environmental impact statement for every "major" federal action that will have a "significant" impact upon the natural environment. The parallels continue. Just as we were (and still are) unsure exactly how to measure the full range of possible environmental impacts, early economists were not well equipped to provide immediate and expert advice on what was a benefit, what was a cost, and how they might be measured. Indeed, it took over twenty years for the first comprehensive treatise on benefit-cost analysis to emerge.[1]

Hence, benefit-cost analysis was a creature of the political process; the result of politicians demanding something that no one yet knew how to deliver. Benefit-cost analysis is, therefore, the result of a search for economic answers to political choices. The tortured political history of benefit-cost practices in the United States is ample evidence of this fact.[2] The benefit-cost analyst—as well as the benefit-cost approach—has always been malleable to the wishes of those currently holding positions of power.

These two situations taken together—an exuberance for modifying one's immediate surroundings, and the fluid nature of the evaluation method for such activities—render it impossible to speak of benefit-cost analysis. There were as many different benefit-cost analyses as there were projects and analysts; the only constant seems to be the use of a ratio of benefits to costs to determine the presumed soundness of any particular proposal. And this raises the important distinction between the benefit-cost *approach* and the benefit-cost *criterion.*

The criterion has remained the same; a project must have a ratio of benefits to costs in excess of unity to merit further consideration. A high ratio was not sufficient to insure success, but a ratio less than unity was sufficient to insure oblivion. But it is the approach that has differed. While the discount rate has received most of the attention, analysts were playing a multitude of tricks with assumptions about flood frequencies, flood rating curves, crop yields, normal prices, demands for electricity, recreation use, and the like. There is (and was) infinite scope for maneuvering and the finely tuned imagination of the agency benefit-cost analyst was nourished on the challenge of meeting the one constant—a ratio in excess of unity—for those projects that had the requisite political support.

While academic economists complained of such practices, agencies and politicians blithely continued on their way. It is true that BCA was useful in separating the clearly inferior projects from those that were more reasonable, but its primary role has been one of legitimating political decisions. In a mood of expansion and invincibility it was easy to rationalize this; a young rich nation can afford to rush ahead. It was not so critical that the optimum optimorum be found. It was enough to avoid the minima. We can be rather confident that the process of carrying out a benefit-cost study—even if badly performed—was helpful in avoiding the most serious mistakes.

But if this was the past, what of the future? Are the same imperatives there to harness nature? Is it still considered smart to use every drop of water as envisioned by Potato Brumbaugh? Are the same things still scarce?

The Future

If the past can be characterized by enthusiastic growth, resource abundance, political opportunism, and the absence of active interest groups, the future will be characterized by economic stability if not contraction, resource scarcity, political caution and inertia, and a multitude of active special interests. The problems for benefit-cost analysis in this new setting are several.

The life-cycle of national development is traditionally one of early reliance upon extractive resources and agriculture, eventual transition to more industrial activity, and then a gradual shift to the tertiary sector (services). While the West will remain oriented toward extractive resources and agriculture, it will nonetheless become the center of myriad service activities as well; the climate virtually assures that. With this transition will come some changes that may look like economic decline. The extractive industries will become less important. Land will be converted from agriculture to suburbs. But the overwhelming impression will be one of moderation, of slowing down; the boom days of the 1940s and 1950s are probably past.

Instead of a period in which we are preoccupied with "putting natural resources to work" in the traditional sense, we are entering a period in which those resources will be used but not consumed. The modification of our environment to suit the whims of a few farmers, ranchers, or miners is a thing of the past.

Related to this is the issue of resource scarcity. The early period under discussion was one of apparent abundance of natural resources merely waiting to be utilized. Whether timber, land, minerals, or water, the abundance of natural wealth was rarely in doubt; the problem was simply one of controlling those resources and getting rich. Without going into detailed analysis of relative scarcities now vis-à-vis the past, it is safe to say that the sheer demands placed upon those resources now by a large number of potential users renders them scarce. It is an axiom of economics that as items become more scarce and valuable we will observe greater attention being devoted to their definition, their ownership, and their use. Surely the interest in water, land, air, and scenery attest to their perceived scarcity.

The third major difference we will observe in the future is that of a transition from political opportunism based upon exploiting resources to political opportunism based upon protecting them; the current governor of California is perhaps the archetypical opportunist in this regard. The platitudes and cliches will still abound, but the message will be one of "save" rather than utilize and consume. We are being told—correctly I believe—that the future of the United States is to be found in cautious consideration of our environment in contrast to earlier presumptions that our salvation lay with our ability to conquer nature. The more important contrast for our purposes is, however, the difference in policy formulation. Early on there were few vested interests in the status quo—ignoring of course, as we always have done, the interests of Native Americans. Who was there to object when Potato Brumbaugh utilized irrigation water that otherwise would flow into Wyoming, or Arizona, or California? Who was to object—except some illegal cattle ranchers—when the homesteaders arrived? What interest group was there to protest the mutilation of streams and forests in the search for gold? And this brings us to the fourth significant fact that distinguishes the past from the future.

In the early days there was no politically represented interest group able to mobilize opposition in the face of a threat from some resource user (or abuser). This of course is not to say that hundreds of thousands of individuals were not seriously hurt by the helter-skelter rush to "tame the West." Ranchers had trails bisected by farms and fences; others had previously used water taken from them at will; still others saw resources that they thought were theirs appropriated by someone else. In part this is a result of the ill-defined property arrangements that existed over such resources. In a sense they were open-access resources to be used by whoever was there first, or who had the strength to protect their interests whether or not they were first in time.

From a sense of open access we have now moved to one of common property resources in the correct use of that term.[3] That is, common property connotes a situation of coequal ownership—each member of the polity possesses some property (claim) in the resource. Under open access no one has any property since no one has a secure claim over the benefit stream arising from the resource. Under common property every one has property since all have some claim to the benefits. The national forests are a prime example of common property resources; all of us are coequal owners of them in the sense that we may use them whenever we please. The fact that we may not cut down a tree at our leisure is no more relevant for the property right than is the fact that I may not sell petrol in my driveway. We face a variety of covenants on the use of what we call our "property," and the fact that I cannot cut a tree in the national forest is simply proof of the fact that all of us are coequal owners; your trees are protected from my chainsaw, my scenic canyon is protected from your desire to search for gold there. One form of our individual liberty is protected by a restriction on other liberties. Such is the nature of civilization as distinct from anarchy and chaos.

Hence we may safely characterize the future as a period of careful attention to one's interest in the status quo. If the past can be characterized by an impatient desire to change things in order that we might be made better off, the future may be characterized by the desire to do very little to the natural environment in order that we not make ourselves worse off. But this conservatism has a less romantic side. Part of doing very little is also accepting the status quo use of resources. The future will surely be a period of intense fighting to protect what one already has, whether it is the farmers of the Texas Panhandle or the loggers of the northern California redwood forests. If the groundwater gives out then that is someone else's problem, as long as it will last another twenty-five years. If the redwoods are gone, so what? City people can always look at douglas fir; they won't know the difference anyway. If we send salty water to Mexico, so what? If my wheatfield replaces a breeding ground for some type of wildlife, what do I care? There are more down the road.

In short there is now a vested interest—and usually an active interest group—aligned on both sides of almost any resource issue. The limited opposition of the past has been altered to an almost pervasive opposition to any change in the status quo. And, against that is an equally determined group of interests seeking change. We are indeed in an era of "one issue politics," but the poor politicians are constantly forced to tally the votes for each of the multitude of issues they are supposed to confront. It was infinitely easier to be a politician in the old days.

Benefit-Cost Analysis: The Problems We Face

In view of the foregoing, what implications might we draw with respect to the role of benefit-cost analysis? What are the most serious conceptual and empirical problems? What modifications are called for? In what follows I will draw your attention to two rather serious conceptual problems in benefit-cost analysis; problems that logically follow from its foundation in welfare economics. Then I will turn to a discussion of some important problems in performing benefit-cost studies; while there are some conceptual aspects here, the major issues will be empirical in nature.

There are two compelling conceptual weaknesses in benefit-cost analysis that ought to receive more attention than they have. The first one pertains to the meaning of a surplus of benefits over costs. This is not the familiar criterion problem where the argument is whether one should use net present values or a ratio of benefits to costs. The problem is much more serious than that and concerns the validity, for policy purposes, of those things called net benefits.

Simply put, the entire logic of BCA rests upon the concept of the Kaldor-Hicks compensation test. That is, if there is an economic surplus created by the contemplated change that *would* be sufficient to compensate those who oppose the change (or would otherwise be made worse off by it) and still leave some excess for those who favor the change (or those who would be made better off by it), then the change is considered economically efficient. Compensation is not required, and obviously never occurs; it is sufficient to know that compensation *could* take place and leave both groups—gainers and losers—better off than if the change did not occur. The existence of net benefits for a contemplated action—or a benefit-cost ratio in excess of unity—attests to such a surplus. This is so because on the cost side of the ledger we supposedly enter all of the debits incurred.

The logic has a certain beguiling aspect to it. If each project undertaken makes us better off then how can we lose? The problem arises when we ask who it is that is made worse off by the change, and who gains? A benefit-cost study of large-scale agricultural mechanization could no doubt show substantial positive benefits—as long as we assumed that all of those displaced were able to find gainful employment elsewhere. But as long as the compensation test is potential rather than actual we are playing games with ourselves. As long as we assume that the losers of any change will be able to adjust, and as long as we assume that the new surplus accrues to the nation rather than to a few fortunate gainers able to reap situational rents, then benefit-cost analysis as ordinarily practiced is merely a legitimating device for making a few better off and many others worse off. This is compounded by the realization that it is the already advantaged–economically and politically–who are able to mobilize government in their behalf. BCA is often the lubricant of politically sanctioned greed.

Applied welfare economics–from which BCA derives–is silent on the matter of costs and benefits received by individuals of vastly different initial income positions; a $10 income loss is considered the same to a $40-per-week migrant as it is to the owner of 800 acres of strawberries. The average citizen knows better, but we somehow avoid confronting this in our analysis.[4] Given this problem, the application of benefit-cost analysis is quite consistent with making the rich richer and the poor poorer. The rich are unlikely to protest, and few listen to the poor.

The second major conceptual problem is only rarely mentioned by economists. Any configuration of prices, production possibilities, demand curves, and supply curves rests upon a technical and institutional foundation that defines what is a resource, indicates who owns what, and defines the accumulated technology (tools and knowledge) that allows the transformation of inputs into outputs. In more technical language the production possibility frontier, the utility possibility frontier, and the grand utility frontier are all uniquely defined by the current distribution of income, by the current ownership of capital and natural resources, and by the current structure of prices.

Governmental programs to dam rivers, dredge channels, and deliver irrigation water to farmers alters the very structure of resource endowments and prices that define the basis upon which we evaluate that change. We use an efficiency analysis to evaluate basic changes in economic structure–the import of which is to alter economic advantage among competing interests. It might be argued that any one project is marginal vis-à-vis the entire economy. The counter argument is that we have just experienced forty years of rather significant public works projects. Any one project may have been marginal; in the aggregate the impacts are clearly nonmarginal.

Each time a benefit-cost study is carried out we are forced to assume away certain things. The difficulty of this practice should be obvious when conducted on a large scale. When the private sector conducts a benefit-cost study of some contemplated change it is quite reasonable to assume away those things beyond the domain (and/or control) of the firm. But for BCA performed for public-sector activities we cannot be so cavalier. Yet the conceptual and computational requirements dictate that many things be excluded.

The basic problem, however, is that an efficiency calculus is being employed to judge the desirability of public sector activities that change the distribution of economic and political advantage. In an era of scarcity and confrontation this fact will assume greater significance.

A third problem concerns the correct computation of project costs. In the conventional wisdom of benefit-cost analysis it is always the benefit measurement that causes problems, while the cost side is considered rather straightforward. But this is far from the truth. Consider the following example. Assume that in any given budget period there are n possible projects that might be undertaken: $X_1, X_2, \ldots, X_n$. If we assume that the public-sector budget is derived from the number of attractive looking projects, then the correct decision rule is to keep authorizing projects until the benefits of the last project are just equal to the costs of that last project; such costs being given by the social value foregone by having those funds spent in the public sector rather than in the private sector. We might express this as:

The last project accepted: $B(X_i) = B(X_o)$

where: $B(X_i)$ = the benefits of the marginal project

$B(X_o)$ = the benefits to society of leaving the costs of project X_i in the private sector (the null project)

Here there is no effective budget constraint; the constraint on the public sector is simply the number of projects it can generate that are more attractive than the investment opportunities in the private sector. Labor and capital used in the two sectors would be costed out in a similar fashion, and we search for the optimal mix of investments between the two competing sectors.

The actual situation is, of course, quite different from that depicted. A more realistic description would start with the recognition that the public sector budget is not determined in the manner just described.[5] Rather, the size of the budget is a predetermined political choice reflecting the combined views of the executive and legislative branches on such issues as: (1) expected federal revenues, (2) expected demands for other (non-public-works) spending, (3) anticipated needs for stabilization actions by the federal government, and (4) the general role of the public sector in a market economy. Once the general level of public-works spending has been decided—and along with that some general guidelines concerning the types of public projects to be performed—then project selection consistent with those guidelines may proceed.

But in this formulation the cost of any given project is different from the previous description. Here, the social cost of a certain project is not its drain on funds from the private sector or, rather, it is not the social benefits foregone by diverting those funds from the private sector. Now, a given project's costs are the benefits foregone by not building some other project with public funds. This would be expressed as:

The last project accepted: $B(X_i) \geqslant B(X_{i+1})$ with the public works budget exhausted

Instead of a search for the marginal project in terms of private-sector funds diverted, the search here is for the best mix of projects up to the point that the previously determined budget is fully utilized.

A problem that flows immediately from the above discussion is related to the issue of the appropriate discount rate. Of all the literature on the discount rate for public actions, I have yet to see a discussion of the distinction between public investments and public rule changes. We are all familiar with the usual arguments that when the public sector undertakes an investment the benefits and costs should be converted to present values by applying a discount rate. Some economists advocate the use of a rate reflecting the private opportunity cost of capital. Others prefer the social opportunity cost of funds diverted from the private sector; the difference here is that the former reflects the costs borne by the private sector to acquire funds, while the latter reflects the social benefits given up when funds are taken away from the private sector. Yet another rate that is often advocated is that at which the public sector must borrow funds; this would tend to approach the interest rate on long term government bonds. And, there is often some sympathy for using a discount rate that reflects "society's willingness to trade present for future consumption." This might be a rate that would be determined by a number of avenues, including direct survey techniques.

There is a further refinement in the above debate that recognized that we might wish to use one rate for the cost side of projects and another for the benefit side. The logic here is to discount projects costs at a rate that reflects the higher cost of diverting funds from the private sector but to discount project benefits at a lower rate that reflects society's rate of time preference for the consumption of those beneficial aspects. Here there are also advocates of one rate for certain types of project outputs, and another rate for others. An example might be a fairly low rate for recreational outputs that the private sector would be unlikely to provide and a higher rate for those outputs where there is a reasonable expectation of a private substitute in the absence of the public alternative.

However, in all of the debate over interest rates you will not find any reference to the public sector as a rule maker. There are three types of rule making activities of the public sector along a continuum from: (1) rules to facilitate individual action toward socially desired norms, (2) rules to induce individual action to be more consistent with social preferences and priorities, and (3) rules to force individual action into socially preferred directions. Although the expenditure of public funds may accompany the promulgation of each of these, it is also possible that each may arise without any public expenditures at all.

What are some examples of these three types of rules? Facilitative rules would be found when the natural instincts of atomistic agents were consistent with social objectives yet there were some existing institutional arrangements—probably carry-overs from an earlier time when the current problem did not exist—that impede individuals from acting quickly on their instincts. A good example today would be local zoning ordinances that establish legal rights to sunlight so that people will thus be encouraged to invest in roof-top solar collectors free from the threat of shade trees. Here government is simply facilitating the self-interested wish to lower private energy costs; not incidentally this also serves important social objectives as well.

Rules to induce behavior are found where individual tendencies are not as strong as previously, yet action would be taken with some minimal help from the public sector. Investment tax credits for the installation of pollution control equipment would be an example of rules that induce certain behavior.

Finally, rules to enforce behavior can be found in the pollution-control area, in minimum gas-mileage performance for cars, motorcycle helmet laws, and so on. The rationale here is that those in a position to decide on their own will make antisocial decisions in the absence of the rules.

Now, the conceptual issue is one of how to evaluate such rule changes? This question is not an idle one, since I believe that the majority of the adjustments in water use in the West will be rule based rather than investment based. What are some of the differences? In investment analysis we assume that scarce capital is being diverted from productive uses in the private sector and hence we want to make certain that the nation is not deprived of an advantageous investment for the sake of a poor one. A rationale for discounting benefits is that one could always put the capital in the bank and over the project life be able to earn interest at the prevailing market rate. Thus, one must compare the present value of the project with the present value of the future earnings in some alternative.

But what happens in the case of public rule changes? First of all no funds are being diverted from the private sector to the public sector. Second there is no presumption of a return on the investment in which one might at least hope for some indirect benefits arising from some previously underutilized resources. And, there is no "project life" after which the benefits cease to exist. Finally, in public rule changes we do not select from a large number of projects in order to achieve some bundle of net benefits constrained by a public sector budget.

In rule changes we are instead dealing with institutional bottlenecks rather than technological bottlenecks; what I call institutional lag. When new scarcities arise—new problematic situations—the existing set of incentives and sanctions no longer coincide with new priorities. We are not trying to innovate in the sense of new technologies to solve a problem. We are, instead, fine tuning the existing system better to reflect new scarcities. This process has been referred to as involution.[6] But there is no "project life" to rule changes—unless a tax-credit program will be phased out in five years. There is no front-end capital cost requiring funds that might be spent elsewhere.

What discount rate should be used? What does it mean to talk of the present value of the benefits when two years from now something else will have changed requiring yet another rule change? We are not constructing a dam to stand for thirty-five years, we are dealing with a problem that is most troublesome today in a manner that we hope will help, but there are no implications that next year we will not have to do something else. Because of this the calculation of present-valued benefits from public rule changes via a discount rate is insufficient for a decision criterion, and it is inappropriate conceptually. I will return to this in a subsequent discussion.

The next problem we must confront is that of attaching values to both inputs and outputs of public actions to deal with new scarcities in water use. In earlier times, while this was a problem, it had less of an impact on analysis than it will in the future. As indicated earlier, the history of benefit-cost analysis is one of exuberance, of a rather slack economy, of an activist public sector, and of poorly-articulated interests in the status quo. Under these conditions, the expenditure of $x for a project was said to be justified if one could find only \$(x + 1) of benefits, appropriately discounted. In a sense, those advocating a project were not required to search for *all* of the possible benefits from a change, only enough to insure that they exceeded—by a discrete margin—the project costs. And of course they showed unmatched zeal and ingenuity in this search. But it was, nonetheless, an incomplete search; they were not forced to go as far afield in search of benefits as they would have had the opposition been more contentious.

And this is precisely the message of the future. The day of easy authorization for public actions is past, and the pressure is on the calculation of both benefits and costs. As both sides to any issue press their case, the claims and counter claims for benefits and costs will probably make an erstwhile analyst for the Corps of Engineers appear as a paragon of restraint and propriety. I do not trust either side in the coming conflicts and—more discouraging—I am not confident that economic science is sufficiently developed to allow those of us who claim dispassion to separate fact from fancy.

Related to this, and yet a serious problem in its own right, is the disjointedness in time of the realization of benefits and costs for different public actions. That is, certain proposed actions will result in obvious benefits now but costs that may not become apparent until the passage of a considerable length of time. Or, some actions will entail obvious costs now but not result in benefits for, say, twenty years. Under these circumstances it will be very difficult to perform sound benefit-cost analysis.

Another serious problem in performing benefit-cost analysis in the future will arise in the specification of the proper accounting stance. The accounting stance is the geographic scope over which benefits and costs are defined and compared. In early times where benefit-cost analysis was primarily employed in project evaluation it was rather easy to demarcate a project region or an area of major influence from the planned investment; an irrigation project would benefit a portion of one state, or hydroelectric power would be available for a multistate area. In such instances the political forces were rather clearly identified, and the regions of immediate benefit could at least be surmised.

In the new setting—where public rule making will dominate—it is not so obvious how one will demarcate regions. The gains and losses will be distributed throughout subareas of the West, and the analyst—not to mention the politician—will be hard pressed to make sense out of the myriad effects. This will not only compound the analytical task, but it will prove troublesome for the political process.

The final problem I wish to discuss is that of the proper criterion for decisions about individual actions. We have already discussed, if only briefly, the matter of net present valued benefits versus a benefit-cost ratio. In light of the foregoing discussion it should be clear that I am not optimistic about our ability to perform conceptually and empirically sound benefit-cost analyses for the type of changes which will occur in the West. If reallocation of current water use is to be the predominant means for facing the future with scarce water then what criterion for such reallocations ought we to employ? For a public body to compute net present values for all possible reallocations is a difficult—if not impossible—task.

The majority of transfers will be privately arranged, and will occur where the gainers (those obtaining the water) can compensate the losers (those giving up water) and still retain a surplus. This is the compensation test again, except that now it is *actual* rather than merely *potential.* But there are at least two problems with such privately arranged transfers.

The first problem is that we may often find drastically different income positions as between those who wish to buy water rights and those who now have them. This difference in income may translate into vast differences in power and information. If those now in possession of water rights have imperfect information about the value of water in alternative uses then one of the important assumptions for trades to benefit both parties is violated. In addition, if the difference in income and information of the two parties is pronounced, then one party will possess far greater power in the bargaining process; again one important assumption of mutually beneficial trades is violated.

The second problem relates to the costs and benefits that are to be computed by the negotiating parties. The way in which water is allocated among competing uses holds important social and economic implications beyond the immediate users. Not only do income and employment multipliers differ among uses, but the structural stability of the western economy over the long run is also at stake. A reallocation of water from agriculture to the production of energy from either coal or oil shale represents a shift in water from one use that is renewable on a yearly basis to a use that is based upon a finite quantity of a depletable resource. Once the coal and oil are extracted water will no longer be needed in those uses. But if the agricultural infrastructure has disappeared in the meantime the switch back to agriculture may be more difficult.

To summarize this discussion about the problems with benefit-cost analysis, let us briefly consider a current issue of some importance in the West—the reserved water rights of Native Americans. As you know, the Supreme Court has held that their water rights encompass sufficient water for all reservation lands that might be "practicably irrigable." When we look to benefit-cost analysis for help in this instance what do we find?

Immediately one of the assumptions of welfare theory is violated in that the basic structure of resource endowments is altered. The magnitudes of water are sufficient that this fact cannot be ignored. Secondly, an institutional change such as this is an example of the public rule changes discussed above where we may not have a "project" in the conventional sense. When the change occurs it will be of unknown duration, and the difficulties in computing present values are severe. The third difficulty is encountered when we begin to assign shadow prices to inputs and outputs. We can be assured that the type of agriculture preferred by the Native Americans would differ from the highly commercial and capital-intensive agriculture so prevalent now. If this difference is pronounced it is possible that by using conventional benefit-cost analysis the reallocation would *appear* to be "inefficient." I emphasize "appear" precisely because of the difficulties we would have in assigning shadow prices to the two disparate types of agriculture. Finally, what should be done about the appropriate accounting stance. Would one conduct analysis on the basis of an individual reservation? A state? A group of states?

Lest I leave the impression of our total inability to do anything, allow me to emphasize that certain economic analyses can surely be carried out. We can obviously ascertain the specific lands that can be "practicably" irrigated. This would take the form of farm-level budget studies, with some publicly provided irrigation infrastructure. But, this analysis would be at the farm or "project" level and would merely be concerned with the suitability of specific land for irrigation.

It is, of course, unlikely that all reservation land that is "practicably irrigable" will receive water under the Winters Doctrine. But neither will that amount be determined by benefit-cost analysis in the conventional sense. The decision will be reached by political and judicial means, with economics being employed to assist in the search for a reasonable compromise. But we cannot forget that this particular reallocation—as with the majority of reallocations—is a political one.

The basic dilemma we face is that we urgently need a thorough decision analysis *approach* that will lead us to make the correct decision about water use in the future. Unfortunately the correct decision is unknown and unknowable. Economists have an occupational predisposition for clear-cut answers to problems. I have elsewhere referred to this as the deterministic approach (Bromley, 1976). I have also argued that policy formulation is not deterministic in the pure sense of that word, but is rather a dialectical process. By dialectical I mean a process in which a solution only emerges as the result of the forces and counterforces brought to bear on a problematic situation.

The prime difficulty with the dialectical process is that we have no template against which to judge the outcome. What results from such a process bears no burden for being right or correct—it is all we have. Economists—and not a few politicians—are uneasy with this approach, preferring instead a yardstick against which to judge each alternative. The competitive market and a benefit-cost ratio in excess of unity provide this yardstick for the economist as well as for the politician. Unfortunately, the former rarely reveal to the latter the serious flaws in the yardstick. When faced with agnosticism most economists still prefer false gods.

But the process of contending with a water-short future in

the West is the quintessential dialectical problem. It would be relatively easy to calculate income created by sector per acre-foot of water and then to compute the least harmful ways in which to reallocate water. This is social cost effectiveness and our objective would be to reallocate water so as to precipitate the least economic hardship in the aggregate. Of course other things will enter the calculations.

We are, above all else, a nation of interest groups ever alert for opportunities to enhance our comparative position. The analogue of this is that we also are attentive to efforts by others to gain at our expense. Our nation grew on the nourishment of socially sanctioned—and channeled—greed.

Given the conceptual and empirical problems with benefit-cost analysis, it is expecting too much to hope for deterministic answers to the complex water allocation problems we face. But if we are confident enough of the democratic process, the dialectical approach need not be feared.

In the following section I will outline what would be involved.

Is There Hope?

The history of federal water policy is one of immense taxpayer subsidies to construct large-scale projects so that water can be given time, space, and form utility to local residents. Every taxpayer in the nation has contributed to these costs, and a few individuals have been made very rich in the process; a much larger number have benefitted to a lesser degree. Only a fool would claim to know whether or not the nation is better off than if the money had not been spent at all, or if it had been spent on other projects dealing with urban housing, mass transit, human nutrition, or whatever. This in spite of a benefit-cost ratio in excess of unity for every project for which analysis was carried out.

Such is the state of benefit-cost analysis. Why should we be any more confident of the future? I have outlined the reasons why I am pessimistic about a deterministic benefit-cost analysis that is conceptually and empirically sound. I stand by my pessimism.

But I am not so pessimistic about an approach to water policy in the future that is liberated from the apparent rigor and precision of traditional benefit-cost analysis. Such an approach would require—first of all—that the water addiction of westerners be broken. Bricks in toilets is tokenism when every suburban homeowner feels deprived without a year-round lawn. Once the presumed God-given right to water is abandoned, we can get down to business. But to continue to focus attention on only the supply side is folly.

Given the public sector's predominant role in creating the current problem it is only fitting that it remain active during the painful transition ahead. The place to start would be to develop an honest long-range planning capability within, say, the U.S. Water Resources Council to guide the West through the hazards ahead. We must avoid water reallocations that render useless capital investments now, only to find we need them again once the coal and shale oil have given out.

Along with this there could be increased technical advice given on water-saving techniques in agriculture, industry, and in homes. States could enact coordinated tax incentives to encourage water saving. There could be a variety of events in which water resource issues would be discussed. There could be stepped-up efforts to recycle water. Units selling water (cities, irrigation districts) might institute a small surcharge on water to finance research, demonstration projects, and the like. Finally, the federal government could undertake a brokerage function to facilitate consensual bargains over water rights transfers; this would also involve monitoring pending transfers for abuse of the weak by the powerful.

In all of this there would need to be an implicit benefit-cost awareness. We can assume that transfers of water rights would involve some private benefit-cost calculation. It would be the public sector's responsibility to assure that these private interests coincide with the public interest.

The basic dilemma of benefit-cost analysis is that it gives the impression of rigor and precision when in fact the truth is largely otherwise. It has taken us forty years to realize this; some still remain unconvinced. The coming problems in western water resources will require an evaluative approach that admits many things ignored in traditional benefit-cost studies, and that takes a more honest account of those effects that have always been considered. The states and the federal government will be required to work in close harmony. I see no reason why the nation's taxpayers should object to increased funding for such activity. After forty years of public works projects the required expenses for what I have outlined above will seem nominal indeed.

Notes

1. This is Eckstein's *Water-Resource Development.*
2. See Bromley (1976) and Dorfman (1976).
3. For a more detailed discussion see Ciriacy-Wantrup and Bishop (1975).
4. There are a few exceptions: Infanger and Butcher (1974) and Freeman (1967).
5. For an elaboration of this, see Steiner (1969) and Bromley (1976).
6. See Geertz (1963).

References

Bromley, Daniel W. "Economics and Public Decisions: Roles of the State and Issues in Economic Valuation." *Journal of Economic Issues,* 10: 811–838, December 1976.

Ciriacy-Wantrup, S. V. and Bishop, Richard C. "Common Property as a Concept in Natural Resources Policy." *Natural Resources Journal,* 15(4):713–727, October 1975.

Dorfman, Robert. "Forty Years of Cost-Benefit Analysis" (Cambridge: Harvard Institute of Economic Research, Discussion Paper No. 498, August 1976).

Eckstein, Otto. *Water-Resource Development* (Cambridge: Harvard University Press, 1958).

Freeman, A. Myrick III. "Six Federal Reclamation Projects and the Distribution of Income." *Water Resources Research,* 3:319–332, 1967.

Geertz, Clifford. *Agricultural Involution* (Berkeley: University of California Press, 1963).

Infanger, Craig L. and Btucher, Water R. "Individual Income Redistribution and Publicly Provided Irrigation: The Columbia Basin Project." *American Journal of Agricultural Economics,* 56(4):805–811, November 1974.

Steiner, Peter O. *Public Expenditure Budgeting* (Washington, D.C.: The Brookings Institution, 1969).

Commentary

Herbert W. Grubb

In his paper, "The Cost-Benefit Dilemma," Professor Bromley has sketched a trace of the history of settlement and economic development of the arid and semiarid western United States, and the use of public investments in water resources development in the area, including the benefit-cost analysis concepts associated therewith. He has characterized the future as one of economic stability or contraction, with resource scarcity, political caution and inertia, and special interest activism.

Dr. Bromley has identified two conceptual problems in benefit-cost analysis:

1. The meaning of a surplus of benefits over costs and to whom the benefits may accrue—that is, the income distribution arising from public investment in water resources.
2. The effect of the project being analyzed upon the project factor and project output markets in terms of prices, quantities, and distribution of economic effects.

As Dr. Bromley sees these problems, the losers are seldom if ever compensated by gainers, and the potential project(s) will have marketwide effects that are not reflected in the project evaluation data. One has to agree that both of these problems exist, at least to some extent, under present practice. Dr. Bromley points out, however, that the basic problem is "that an efficiency calculus is being used to judge the desirability of public sector activities which change the distribution of economic and political advantage." This latter point, of course, focuses the issue directly upon the questions of purpose, role, and scope of public sector, and especially federal government participation in water resources programs. I shall not join in that debate in this discussion, since to a large extent that decision has been and most likely will continue to be decided in the political arena, based on a wide range of both economic and social considerations. Instead, I shall confine my remaining discussion more toward the measurement aspects, if you will, of the methods of benefit-cost analyses of federal water projects. I do not feel that the analytic techniques of benefit-cost analyses can make the decision of "what ought to be" in regard to public versus private sector investment in water resources, any more than such analyses can perform this function for public transportation, public education, or public health.

Perhaps, as Professor Bromley has suggested, the "boom days of the 1940s and 1950s are probably past." However, I question this. Our population is still growing and our foreign trade is expanding. Thus, it seems to me, that the production of the resources of all areas of the nation will be as important in the future as in the past, both in relative and in absolute terms. Such production cannot be realized without adequate supplies of suitable quality water for the production processes in energy, manufacturing, agriculture, and the service industries; i.e., water is a factor of production. However, this factor of production is not available at the time and place it is now and will be needed in the future in order to produce and use other fixed location resources. *Therefore, the problem remains that of decisions pertaining to public and private sector investment schedules to accomplish the desired level and appropriate regional distribution of water resource services.* If the national economy fails to provide for maintenance and growth of the water supply and related sectors, through both storage and transportation of water, a critical factor of production will be unavailable, barring sufficient technological advancement to substitute for it. As a result, use of complementary existing and potential land, labor, capital, and mineral resources will be reduced or precluded altogether. Economic opportunity will be limited to an extent, resources that are freed should decline in price and become available for other purposes, and product prices should rise, other things equal, because supplies will have been reduced in a relative if not an absolute sense. This eventuality, too, has its distributional effects upon producers and consumers, and in the views of many is an undesirable condition.

I am in substantial agreement with Professor Bromley that the present microeconomic theory of the firm, business analytic methods and data, as used in individual project benefit-cost analyses, is a poor tool when applied to public sector water resources investment decisions. It suffers a number of weaknesses in that it requires aggregation of large numbers of estimates of individual water user income accounts, which for large area projects are little more than first approximations because neither the method nor the data satisfactorily take into account the ultimate effects of the project upon the price variables of the factors involved. The method is also poor from the standpoint that it requires massive quantities of data, much of which is not available and the remainder of which is extremely costly in both time and money to obtain. In addition, present benefit-cost methods are too unwieldly to be easily understood by either the taxpaying consumer or the public policymaker. Present federal constraints upon the methods require that income effects in sectors and establishments, except those of the direct water user, be ignored on the assumption that the sectors indirectly affected have equivalent opportunities that can and will be exercised or are unimportant elsewhere in the economy. Likewise, no weight, except that inherently found in the price data used in the analyses, is given to consumer surplus derived from larger supplies and a wider range of commodities in the marketplace.

Dr. Bromley discusses the range of topics with respect to the interest rate to be used in computing the present worth of future benefits and costs. However, he fails to clearly relate the private versus public interest in long-range aspects of the benefits stream insofar as the interest or discount rate is concerned. At today's interest rates, the planning horizon or payout period for projects (water or other investments), must be quite short, ten to fourteen years at the most. It takes longer to plan and construct a modest size reservoir.

Dr. Bromley suggests that the public sector might accomplish desired objectives through rules and rule making without public expenditure. From an academic standpoint, this sounds good—

less costly to taxpayers. And if the taxpayers decide to do it this way, then we have no conceptual problems. However, there may be problems of transition to such a system, which to an extent existed prior to federal involvement in water projects. But that was during predevelopment. Maybe now that development has, shall we say, advanced, the private sector may proceed at the desired rate and at the desired locations to produce additional water resources services. The problem is to find the right rules, the right incentives.

Dr. Bromley reviews the problem of reallocation of water and points out that shifts in water use among sectors in the West hold important social and economic implications beyond the immediate users. He recognizes that income and employment multipliers differ among users (agriculture vs. energy, for example) and that structural stability of the western economy (and I would add the national economy) over the long run is at stake. Having recognized this important factor, I wonder why the author did not proceed to show how economic structural relationships could be used to derive gross estimates of water demand, individual sector distribution of water demand and the potential production, waste load, employment, income, and tax base effects of reallocation of existing supplies and of new supply. Admittedly, such analyses suffer data problems akin to those mentioned earlier (much of the same data would be used), and they use average as opposed to marginal relationships, but in my opinion, economic structural analyses provide quite useful information that is more easily understood by the general public and the public policymaker. Such analyses are being done. The estimates show water resource needs in relation to other sectors. Once such estimates are obtained, then the necessary supplies can be obtained at the least cost, and the original estimates can be used as guides in allocating costs among all beneficiaries–direct as well as indirect water users.

13
Better Use of Water Management Tools

George E. Radosevich

Is this paper an original attempt to explicate the western states water law and to tell how to improve the legal tools we have at our disposal? No. There is nothing original about what I have written. I am merely trying to be a loyal carpenter to western water users and administrators and the antiwestern water law dogmatists alike, hammering away at the nails of our system of water allocation and administration at spaced intervals of time, hoping that something beneficial and constructive will evolve. Some of the nails (the principles of our water laws) may have been square when the West was being settled, but as with all important tools in constant use, most states went from square to round nails. Now we are finding a great need for the staple and special nail fitted to the local gun and the eastern power hammer.

For all this rhetoric, I wish to make a few simple but fundamental points at the outset. First, as Voltaire said, "Originality is nothing but judicious imitation. The most original writers borrowed one from another." George Eliot went on to say that "One couldn't carry on life comfortably without a little blindness to the fact that everything has been said better than we can put it ourselves." This I say with respect to scholars of water law who have examined and expounded on the many facets of the law and from whom I have borrowed ideas. Second, the system of water law that exists in the West was not a grand conspiracy against the eastern elite and governing powers, but rather a system fraught with subsystems that evolved out of implantation, and trial, error, and acceptance under a wide range of geoclimatic conditions and subject to a host of well- and not so well-intentioned political interventions from exogenous observers. Third, due to this "system of subsystems" of water laws, generations of people have established a livelihood and economy, the survival of which largely depends upon the foundations and predictability of this system. Fourth, during the past fifteen years many individuals in government and politicians have exhibited an uncanny failure to understand the purpose and basics of the how, why, and when of western water law. Fifth, the system has been evolving over time, susceptible to improvements to meet the challenges of changing conditions and often directing the changes in some systematic and socially acceptable direction.

The title of this paper is rather broad in its application to water management. For those with an engineering background, the range of tools extends from the shovel to the sophisticated computer with a host of options and modifications for the different geoclimatic conditions encountered under a wide variety of uses. The economist, likewise, can immediately focus upon economic theories, the use of water pricing, etc. Sociologists and anthropologists have been examining with great interest local institutions and cultural patterns and the role and influence that they can exert to improve resource use. The water management tools I will discuss are the legal institutions affecting water use. These range from the concepts, rights, duties, and procedures of the law to the organizational structures of both the administration and user of the resource.

Law itself is a very powerful tool, and we in the United States are intimately receptive to legal controls in spite of our international claim of freedom and independence. Bernard Schwartz wrote in the introduction of his book, *The Law in America* (1974):

> The true American contribution to human progress has not been in technology, economics, or culture; it has been the development of the notion of law as its check upon power. American society has been dominated by law as has no other society in history. Struggles over power that in other countries have called forth regiments of troops in this country call forth battalions of lawyers. . . . Our rights and obligations . . . are fixed by the law and, if need be, determined by the Courts and ultimately by the highest Courts of the states and

> nation. . . . In this sense, we are all consumers of the law, intimately by the Courts and ultimately by the highest Courts of the states and nation. . . . In this sense, we are all consumers of the law, intimately affected in all the details of our lives by the quality of the product consumed.

In the past few decades, we have seen the power of law, both in the sense of curtailing social wrongs at high levels in which it was difficult to determine on which side there were greater numbers of battalions of lawyers and in authorizing and providing for the mechanism of natural and human resources development, the likes of which few countries have ever experienced. One area that has received considerable legislative and judicial attention is control of our water resources.

Water Law As the Foundation of Water Management

In early U.S. history, water, like air and open space, was considered a common or free good. Initially, there was unrestricted use due to the minimal demands on existing supplies. In the eastern part of the United States, natural precipitation negated the needs for major surface diversions. The common law concept of riparian rights that existed in England was recognized by the courts in most all of the eastern states.

The situation in the West was somewhat different due to the lower annual rainfall and the need to supplement the natural precipitation with diversions from streams, lakes, or man-made reservoirs. Initially, there was enough water to meet the needs of all the settlers; but as the uses increased, conflicts began to develop along the river systems as simultaneous uses depleted the flow at particular times of the year. Typical battles ensued between miners, farmers, and other users until finally at various places around the country people began to recognize the need to develop some order and consistency regarding the use and management of this resource. In social terms, there was a willingness for each to give up a little so that all could have more; in economic terms, there was a willingness to internalize the cost of the externalities created through the use of this common resource. In legal terms, the pen proved to be mightier than the gun or shovel. What emerged was the desire on the part of users to develop a set of rules and standards to govern the orderly use of a valuable resource, utilizing the most socially acceptable tool to implement their objectives. Some of what resulted was borrowed from the many countries represented by the immigrants to the area. The rest evolved from the natural conditions, types of uses, and creative capability of the users.

The result is a federated system of water law in the United States in keeping with our constitutional philosophy of separate state and federal powers. The federal government holds title to public lands in all western states, and many of those lands are withdrawn from entry or reserved for specific purposes—for example, Indian reservations, parks, national forests and monuments, and oil shale reserves. On these lands, the federal government maintains that sufficient water was also reserved from allocation under state laws to carry out the purposes of the reservation. This federal water law is popularly called the Federal Reservation Doctrine. The federal government also exercises certain control, such as interstate commerce, navigation, and other proprietary interests over water. Within the last two decades it has preempted control over water quality.

At the state level, each state was entitled to adopt its own system of water law over waters rising within its jurisdiction but not to conflict with federal laws. As local customs developed and states were formed, each state adopted its own particular system of water law. Consequently, there are significant variations for quantity control of surface and ground waters among the states. State water quality control laws are more uniform, however, and follow the pattern set by federal legislation.

The evolution of state water quantity laws was simple and direct. These laws are a consequence of geoclimatic conditions, source of supply, and need and reflect the varying states of technology that existed at the time that pressure was exerted on the resource. Surface waters developed into two basic philosophies. In the humid eastern half of the country and along the West Coast, the riparian doctrine was adopted. The more arid western half of the country was faced with diversions and return flows and costs involved in constructing new water delivery and application systems. The doctrine of prior appropriation emerged as the basic western water law. Because some states have both humid and arid conditions and varying demands placed upon the resource, they adopted a mixed riparian/prior appropriation system.

Groundwater legislation occurred much later in the growth of the western states due in part to the lack of knowledge of subsurface supplies and in part to adequate surface supplies. The basic principles of use and control often follow the surface doctrines, but again, each state adopted and modified the law to fit its particular needs. Four different systems of groundwater control can be identified.

To fully appreciate the western attitude toward water law, one must accept that without water, the arid West would have a limited productive capability, at least from the agricultural point of view. One must also recall that agriculture was promoted by the federal government to be the future of the West. Through the multitude of federal policies, laws, and programs, people were induced to settle with the assurance that their use of water would be protected. Private and government investments were based upon the security of a continued right to divert water under the various state laws. As such, agriculture became the major user of diverted water in the West, accounting for 90 percent of water consumptively used. Within this agricultural economy, one finds meadows flood-irrigated for cattle raising and water pumped or diverted from streams to fields producing high cash value and forage crops.

Western Water Laws

The seventeen western states have adopted one or both of the basic water quantity law doctrines found in the United States (see Table 1 for a summary of western water law). The rule adopted by every western state is the doctrine of prior appropriation, with those states on the western seaboard and from North Dakota to Texas also applying the riparian doctrine to lands adjacent to natural water bodies. There is a definite trend to eliminate the riparian doctrine as demands on surface waters increase. For all practical purposes, most of the states with both doctrines have relegated the riparian system of surface water control to an insignificant role.

Those states in the West applying the riparian doctrine follow the American Rule of Reasonable Use. Under this rule, riparian landowners can divert a reasonable amount of water with respect to all other riparians on the stream; and, under certain condi-

TABLE 1
Summary of Western Water Law

	Legal Feature													
	Water Law Doctrines 1	2	3	4	5	6	7	8	9	10	11	12	13	14
State	*Surface Water*	*Ground Water*	*Ownership*	*Evidence of Water Right*	*Basis of Allocation*	*Criteria of Allocation*	*Preference of Use (Order)*[d]	*Date of Priority*	*Appurtency*[f]	*Water Rights Registry*[g]	*Water Quality In Rights*	*Forfeiture of Rights*[h]	*Drainage Rules*	*Basin of Origin*
1–Ariz.	P.A.	R.U.[b]	Public	Permit	B.U.	B.U.	1-2-3-4-5	D.O.A.	Strict	Original	Case	5 yrs	C.E. & C.L.[j]	
2–Calif.	P.A. & R.	C.R.	People	Permit[c]	B. & R.U.	B. & R.U.	1-2–	D.O.A. post 1914	Unlimited	Current	Case + Statute	5 yrs < 1914 3 yrs > 1914	Yes	
3–Colo.	P.A.	P.A.	Public	S.W.– decree G.W.– permit	B.U.	B.U.	1-2 over 5	S.W.–1st step G.W.– D.O.A.	None	Original (computerized)	Case	–[i]	C.L. (modified)	Yes
4–Idaho	P.A.	P.A.	State	License	B.U.	1 cfs/50 a.	1-2[e]	D.O.A.	Unlimited	Current (limited)	Case	5 yrs	C.L.	
5–Kans.	P.A. & R.[a]	P.A.	People	Permit	B.U.	1 to 2 a.f./a.	1-2-5-6-3	D.O.A.			Case + Statute	3 yrs	C.L.	
6–Mont.	P.A.	P.A.	State	Permit	B.U.	1 miners in./a.	None	D.O.A.		Original (limited)	Case	–[i]	C.E.	
7–Nebr.	P.A. & R.[a]	R.U.[b]	Public	Permit	B.U.	1 cfs/70 a. or 3 a.f./a.	1-2 over 5	D.O.A.			Case	3 yrs	C.E.	Yes
8–Nev.	P.A.	P.A.	Public	Permit	B.U.	Conditions & needs	None	D.O.A.		Original	Case	5 yrs	C.L.	
9–N.Mex.	P.A.	P.A.	Public	Permit	B.U.	B.U. & good agr. practices	None	D.O.A.		Original	Case	4 yrs + 1 yr after notice	C.L.	

10–N.Dak.	P.A.	P.A.	Public	Permit	B.U.	1 cfs/80 a.	1–2 & 5–6	D.B.U.			Case	3 yrs	R.D.	
11–Okla.	P.A. & R.[a]	P.A.	–	Permit[c]	B.U.	B.U.	None	D.O.A.	Strict	Current	Case	7 yrs	R.D.	Yes
12–Oreg.	P.A. & R.[a]	P.A.	Public	Permit	B.U.	B.U.	1–2–4–	D.O.A.	Strict	Original	Case	5 yrs	C.L.	
13–S.Dak.	P.A. & R.[a]	P.A.	People	License	B.U.	1 cfs/70 a. or 3 a.f./a.	1–	D.O.A.		Original	Case	3 yrs	C.L.	
14–Tex.	P.A. & R.[a]	A.O.	State	Permit[c]	B.U.	B.U.	1–5–2–4–3–7–6	D.B.U.		Current	Case	10 yrs	C.L.	Yes
15–Utah	P.A.	P.A.	Public	Permit	B.U.	Nature of Use	1–2	D.O.A.		Current	Case	5 yrs	C.E.	
16–Wash.	P.A. & R.[a]	P.A.	Public	Permit	B.U.	Reasonably Necessary & B.U.	None	D.B.U. & D.O.A. for permits		Current (computerized)	Case	5 yrs	C.E.	
17–Wyo.	P.A.	P.A.	State	Permit	B.U.	1 cfs/70 a.	1–5	D.O.A.	Strict	Original	Case	5 yrs	Undecided	

Key: P.A. = Prior Appropriation, R. = Riparian, A.U. = Absolute Ownership, R.U. = Reasonable Use, C.R. = Corrective Rights, B.U. = Beneficial Use, B. & R.U. = Beneficial and Reasonable Use, D.O.A. = Date of Application, D.B.U. = Date of Beneficial Use, C.E. = Common Enemy, C.L. = Civil Law, R. D. = Reasonable Discharge.

[a] All new water by P.A.
[b] Lack comprehensive ground water laws.
[c] Different types. Not for 1914 rights, riparian rights, riparian rights and percolation ground water.
[d] In this column, 1 = domestic and municipal, 2 = agricultural (irrigation), 3 = power, 4 = mining, 5 = manufacturing and industrial, 6 = recreation, and 7 = navigation.
[e] In mining districts, allocation 4 comes before 2 and 5.
[f] In this column, Strict = can transfer but criteria are established; Limited = water right for specific parcel but transferable.
[g] In this column, Original = initial filing recorded; Current = user must notify agency of name, use, place, etc.—transfers unlimited.
[h] All states recognize loss by abandonment.
[i] Ten years is evidence of abandonment.
[j] In this instance C.E. = flood waters; C.L. = natural flows.

tions, nonriparians may make a reasonable use of remaining waters.

States following the riparian doctrine recognize water as a public resource, held in trust by the state for use by the people of the state. Thus, a landowner whose land borders a stream does not have an ownership right to the waters of the stream but rather only a fundamental right by virtue of his land location to a reasonable use of the water. He is protected from unreasonable uses by others that cause him harm. The riparian is essentially a co-user with all other riparians on the water source, and as between riparian uses, priority of use does not establish priority of right in times of decreased flow. Consequently, his right to use water is not a right for a fixed quantity of flow or volume but rather is a correlative right dependent largely upon the extent of development that takes place.

The riparian right exists perpetually, even without use, so long as the land remains adjacent or "riparian" to the water source. Most states prohibit selling or transferring of riparian rights, and some even limit the size of riparian land to the smallest remaining tract of the original patented holding. Because riparian rights lack precise definition and are a part of the property rights in land, no administrative system was incorporated into the doctrine. If someone complains of a misuse by his neighbor, he has to go to court to protect his right.

Recent changes in law have resulted from the inability of existing water supplies to meet expanding demands on one side and a recognition of the public interest in water resources on the other. The changes have generally been the establishment of a permit system to allocate water among users and the creation of administrative machinery to assess and control water resources through the permit system. Among the western states, modifications are strongly influenced by the simultaneous application of the prior appropriation doctrine, increased demands on surface supplies for in-basin as well as out-of-basin use stimulated in part by large-scale reclamation projects, and heavy reliance upon groundwaters in some states, i.e. California, Nebraska, Oklahoma, and Texas. In all of the dual doctrine states (except California) new claims to the use of surface waters must comply with the statutory requirements of the prior appropriation doctrine.

The doctrine of prior appropriation exists in all of the seventeen western states in some form and like most popular principles, its origin is shrouded by controversy. Some say it evolved out of the mining camps of California. Others say it was introduced by the Spanish or other early settlers of the West. Needless to say, the argument is academic, but the practice of staking mining claims during the California gold rush can at least be authenticated in U.S. history.

Evolution of this doctrine was a fortunate event for it proved as useful for agriculture as it was for mining. As mining became more competitive, many miners and newcomers to the area began farming. The doctrine protected the first settler to use water on his land. Later settlers had to respect the prior ownership of land and the amount of water that the prior settler was using. Hence the establishment of the cliché "first in time, first in right." Although there are many variations of the appropriation doctrine among the various western states, a number of key principles exist to establish commonality, if not relative uniformity. These principles are:

1. There had to be a diversion from a natural stream or body of water. This has been relaxed in most western states during the last decade to allow in-stream use for recreation and fish and wildlife protection.
2. Water must be applied to a beneficial use. Initially, this was defined in constitutions and/or statutes to be domestic, municipal, stock watering, irrigation, and certain industrial and power uses. Some state laws, like Wyoming's, reflect the economic influences of one sector over another, i.e. railroad uses were preferred to agricultural uses. In most of the western states, however, the rural representation insured agriculture a high position as a beneficial user. Beneficial use also referred to the nature of use and will be discussed later.
3. When a diversion and application of water to beneficial use was completed, a water right was created. This right entitled the holder to continued use so long as the use was beneficial.
4. Every water right acquires a priority date such that

priority of right and not equality of right is the basis for distributing water.

The doctrine of prior appropriation is based upon the allocation of water under the concept of a property-right interest in water. Simply put, this doctrine creates the right of private use of a public resource under certain conditions and for uses that have been declared to have a public interest. The right does not automatically exist by virtue of the presence of water upon, flowing through, or under land. In all western states, waters are declared to be the property of the public, people, or state, regardless of whether the state or the public (people) own the water. The state is a trustee for the proper allocation and distribution of water and the administration and implementation of state water laws.

The right so acquired has two legal characteristics. First, the right itself is a real property right. It is an exclusive right that, like other property interests, can be defined, is valuable, and can be sold, transferred, mortgaged, or bequeathed. Wyoming law states, for example, "A water right is a right to use the water of the state, when such use has been acquired by the beneficial application of water under the laws of the state relating thereto, and in conformity with the rules and regulations dependent thereon."[1]

In Colorado, the Supreme Court very early in the state's history announced a rule that can be found in the laws of other appropriation-doctrine states. The famous *Coffin* v. *Lefthand Ditch Co.*[2] was decided in 1882 and held:

> Water in the various streams thus acquires a value unknown in moister climates. Instead of being a mere incident in the soil, it rises when appropriated to the dignity of a distinct usufructory estate or right of property . . . the right to property in this country by priority of appropriation thereto, we think it is and has always been the duty of the national and state governments to protect.

The second characteristic is that it is a usufructory right and can only be exercised when water is available and can be put to beneficial use. There is no absolute ownership in the corpus of the water prior to diversion. The water is still a public resource, and if the right holder cannot put it to beneficial use, he must allow it to flow past his point of diversion to other appropriators. However, if he can use the water and he is in priority, the water diverted into his delivery system is his personal property until it returns back to the stream or escapes his control.

The water right under the appropriation doctrine consists of several elements that give value, dependability, and security to the holder (see Figure 1). The water right

- exists in a definite source of supply;
- has a definite point of diversion;
- is for a fixed and stated quantity;
- is for a specific type and place of use, which together implies the annual time of use; and
- assures the holder of at least an implied protection to the maintenance of water quality necessary to carry out the purposes for which the water was appropriated.

As previously stated, one of the key principles to the prior appropriation doctrine is the "priority of right" that is granted to user over subsequent appropriations. It is most often this priority date, coupled with the dependability of flow in a stream and location of point of diversion that gives water right its value. In most states, the priority date is the date the application for a water right is received by the state water agency.

Several systems were developed by the states to allocate water and provide evidence of water rights. The predominant approach now is the permit system. An application is filed with the appropriate state agency, who then takes the procedural steps of evaluating and determining its disposition based upon availability of unappropriated water and nonimpairment of existing rights. If approved, a permit is issued that may contain conditions of use. If denied, the applicant is entitled to judicial review of the administrative decision. The finalized water right may be called a license, certificate, or decree.

A few states have different classes of permits that greatly enhance their ability to allocate and regulate the use of water

Figure 1
The Agricultural Water Arena

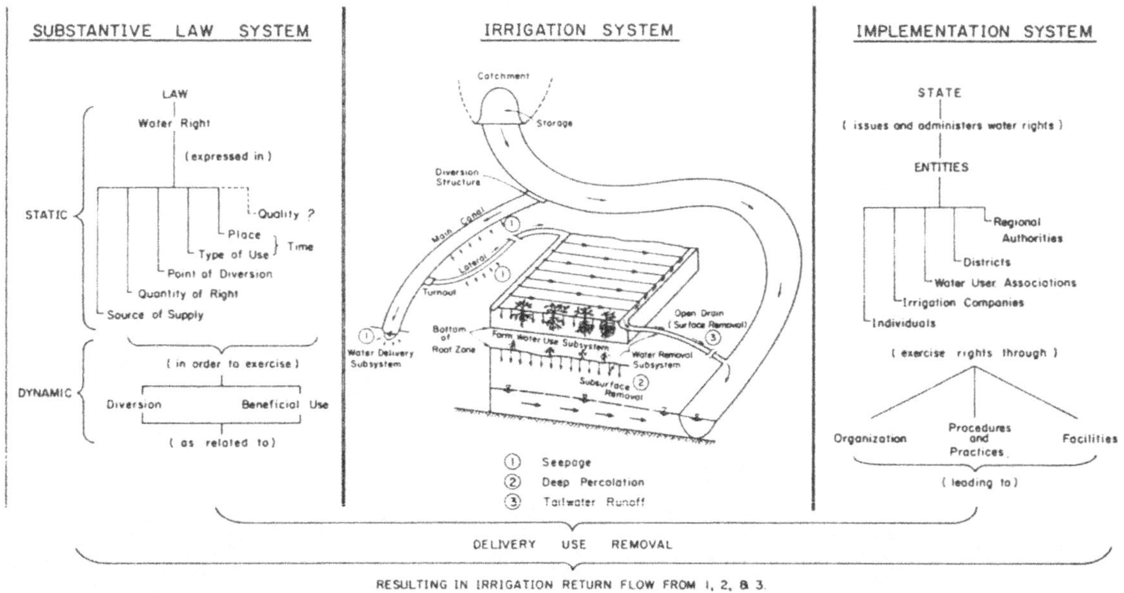

(Radosevich, 1978)

among competing interests. For example, in Texas, there are eight classes of permits:[3]

- Regular permit—a year-round perpetual right
- Seasonal permit—for a portion of the calendar year (irrigation, season, and perpetual)
- Temporary permit—for a short-lived specific use, no longer than three years
- Term permit—for a fixed number of years with an expiration date
- Contractual permit—authorizes an appropriator to contract the use of his water to another for a term
- Permit under Section 5.141—authorizes impoundment of nonnavigable stream on permittee's own property of less than 200 acre-feet and use for any specified purpose
- Storage permit—for storage of water for project
- Emergency permit—allows emergency appropriation of not more than thirty days for public health, safety, and welfare.

Oklahoma has two broad categories: permanent and nonpermanent. The former is subdivided into regular and seasonal, while the latter is divided into temporary and term.[4]

One of the frustrating problems for water administrators and planners that is often costly to water users under the current high demand for water and increased sales is the recording of water rights. The majority of states have a registry of the originally issued water rights that identifies the original appropriation, point of diversion, source of supply, amount divertable, and type and place of use. In all states, any change or transfer of place, type of use, and point of diversion must be approved by the state agency. This is primarily to protect other appropriators who may be adversely affected by the transfer if conditions of the stream and return flow are not taken into account. But few states maintain a registry of water rights that reflect current ownership. These state laws or regulations require annual notification to the agency of all ownership changes and annual water uses. In some cases, failure to provide this information is prima facie evidence of nonuse and could lead to forfeiture or abandonment of the right. The burden of notice is usually placed upon the current owner.

The cornerstone of water allocation under western law is that "beneficial use is the basis and measure of the right to use water." This is often the extent of definition found in state water laws. The concept has two aspects. In order to use water, it must be taken for a beneficial purpose. The other aspect is the use of water itself must be beneficial and carried out in a beneficial manner. Texas, for example, requires that no more water be allocated and used than that amount "economically necessary for the purpose authorized when reasonable intelligence and reasonable diligence are used in applying the water to that purpose."[5]

In addition to the requirement that water will be allocated to a user for a beneficial use, many states have adopted criteria to be followed in allocating the water to agriculture. This criteria is commonly referred to as the statutory duty of water. Little uniformity exists between states, indicating the different geoclimatic conditions found throughout the West. Idaho, Wyoming, and North Dakota allow one cfs per seventy acres, but no more than three acre-feet per acre. Montana allows one miner's inch per acre, and Kansas varies between one to two acre-feet per acre, depending upon the circumstances. Water used by irrigated agriculture may be used and reused a number of times as it goes through the diversion, application, and removal stages (irrigation return flows can occur from seepage, deep percolations, and tailwater runoff, see Figure 1, center). This dynamic process of water use and return flow gives rise to the adage that one man's waste water (return flow) is another man's water supply. Rights to continued use of return flows, should they continue to occur, can be acquired.

One other aspect of the water right that is often overlooked by those not familiar with the doctrine is that it must be exercised, otherwise it can be lost, totally or partially, through nonuse or misuse. The tool for losing the right is through abandonment or statutory forfeiture. In addition, the right may be condemned for domestic uses by municipalities or lost through adverse possession by another user. So in order to protect the right, the holder is compelled to divert his full entitlement, often without regard to possible adverse consequences to other users of junior priority or downstream location.

Laws controlling the extraction and use of groundwater have become as complex as those for surface water. As a general proposition, however, the states apply one of four doctrines: absolute ownership, reasonable use, prior appropriation, or correlative rights. The doctrine of absolute ownership had its origin in the United Kingdom. Simply stated, the doctrine holds that a landowner can withdraw any water from beneath his land without liability to his neighbors resulting from such action. In the West, only Texas has retained this rule.

Due to the extreme position of groundwater use without liability as proclaimed under the absolute ownership doctrine, many states began modifying the law into what has become known as the American Rule of Reasonable Use. This change is synonymous to the modifications in the surface riparian doctrine. The rule states that since the rights of adjacent landowners are similar and their enjoyment in the use of groundwaters is dependent upon the action of the overlying landowners, each landowner is restricted to a reasonable exercise of his own water rights and reasonable use of water on his own property in view of the similar rights of others. Nebraska applies the reasonable use doctrine, but also allows out-of-basin diversions for municipal use if no damage is done to overlying landowners in the area where the water is extracted. Considerable attention is now directed to the very rapid increase in Nebraska's groundwater use and the problems this may cause to the interstate aquifers common to the high plains states.

The doctrine of correlative rights in groundwater originated in California and is a further refinement of the reasonable use concept. Several states originally adopted this doctrine, then changed to another rule. The doctrine holds that among landowners with lands overlying an underground water supply, each landowner can make a reasonable use of that supply so long as the source is sufficient. But when the supply becomes insufficient due to the drought or draw down effect, each landowner is entitled to water in proportion to the percent of his land overlying the underground waters in relation to all other lands so situated. The net effect is to provide flexibility of groundwater use in an effort to maximize the resources, while providing equitable allocation when shortages occur.

Most of the western states found little reason to adopt a different system of law for surface waters and groundwaters. As a consequence, the theory of the prior appropriation doctrine was applied to both surface and groundwater. This does not imply, however, that surface water law was simultaneously extended to groundwater. In fact, several states initially enacted laws to control groundwaters as late as the mid-1950s and 1960s. Kansas applied the absolute ownership doctrine until 1944, then adopted the prior appropriation doctrine. South Dakota and North Dakota have no detailed groundwater laws but merely apply the surface water principles to groundwater use.

The doctrine of prior appropriation provides that groundwater is subject to appropriation for beneficial use providing the intended user complies with the statutory requirements, e.g. wellspring requirements, pumping rates, etc. The administrative official must determine if unappropriated groundwater exists and what adverse effects would occur from approving the application.

In most states, the law allows the state water official to classify the area as a critical or designated groundwater basin upon a determination that a particular groundwater basin or particular aquifer needs close management due to rapid depletion. When this occurs, the users are placed under administrative control for the protection of the aquifer and vested rights.

Western Water Administration

Under the system of government that exists in the United States, laws enacted by legislative bodies and constitutional declarations are to be implemented by the executive branch. Through time, a strong system of administrative and regulatory agencies within this branch has evolved to actually carry the mandates. These agencies have become known as the fourth branch of government due to the vast power and influence gained during the last century. They have authority under most organic (enabling legislation) acts to promulgate rules and regulations that serve to guide the agency personnel in performing their duties and inform the public of procedures and programs to be followed in dealing with the agency. These regulations often fill out the policy directives and general approaches contained in the law. In addition, some state legislatures have passed administrative procedures acts that define the basic conduct to be followed by all state agencies. These agency tools of operation can be very effective in water management.

In the area of water resources, there are three basic functions delegated to agency activities in the western states. They are (1) water quantity control, (2) planning and development of water resources utilization, and (3) water quality control.

Water administration began to evolve in the western United States simultaneously with the legislative enactments creating property rights in the use of water and declaring that it was the states' duty to insure that waters will be allocated and distributed according to the rights so established. This early structuring of government agencies for water control effectively began with water quantity activities as a result of the increased growth of the West in the last half of the 1800s. This growth was stimulated by federal land settlement schemes and the emergence at the turn of the century of a national reclamation program. Water pollution control also became a state agency activity in the late 1800s but initially only as pollution caused diseases. This was one of the activities of the State Public Health Department.

In 1879, Colorado was the first state to create a water rights administration agency, followed by Wyoming in 1890. From the very outset, the distinction between the Colorado and Wyoming approaches has influenced the subsequent organizational patterns of the other western states. Colorado's model has remained virtually unchanged over the years. Allocation of water and adjudication of water rights was the function of courts, while distribution of water and administration of water quantity control laws for exercise and protection of water rights was the duty of the state engineer.

The difficulty of having these four major duties divided between the judiciary and executive branches led Wyoming to adopt an approach in which all four duties were combined into an entity of the executive branch. Wyoming's approach is also unique and has not been duplicated in any other state, but it has served as the pattern for most of the remaining states. The Office of State Engineer was created (a territorial engineer existed prior to statehood), and the state of Wyoming was divided into four divisions consistent with the hydrologic boundaries of the four major river basins. In each division is appointed a superintendent engineer who is responsible for distribution of water in the division. The state engineer is responsible for administration of the water laws. He, plus the four division superintendents, comprise the State Board of Control, which in a quasi-judicial capacity allocates water and adjudicates water rights. Parties adversely affected by their action have the right to judicial review. The state engineer and his four superintendents are appointed by the governor. All four major water quantity duties–(1) allocation, (2) distribution of water, (3) adjudication of water rights according to the allocation made, and (4) administration of water law–were combined into essentially one agency, the Office of State Engineer. It placed the responsibility of making policy and water management decisions into the hands of those most closely associated with water distribution and administration of the law, rules, and regulations adopted by the board.

As reported by Clark (p. 103):

> Nebraska followed the Wyoming system closely in 1895. Variations were adopted by Idaho and Utah in 1903; by Nevada, New Mexico, Utah, North Dakota, South Dakota, and Oklahoma in 1905; by Oregon in 1909; by Texas in 1913; by California in 1914; by Kansas and Washington in 1917; and by Arizona in 1919.

Only in 1971 has Montana adopted an administrative structure in charge of water allocation, distribution of water, administration of water rights, and initiation of adjudication proceedings. Following a trend that began appearing in the 1950s, a Department of Natural Resources and Conservation was created with the Water Resources Division in charge of water matters. The reorganization that took place in 1971-72, however, still lacked the ability to effectively administer water rights under the recording system followed by the state. The water rights were recorded in the district courts with no central control over either allocation or planning of future use. Consequently, in 1972 a constitutional amendment was adopted, which states: "The legislature shall provide for the administration, control, and regulation of water rights and shall establish a system of centralized records, in addition to the present system of local records."[6] Following the constitutional amendment, the department was granted the additional powers by legislative enactment.

Colorado is thus the only state in the West in which administrative control over acquisition of surface waters does not exist. In Colorado, the courts, who grant surface water rights, had no real guidance or assistance in establishing priorities until the 1969 Water Rights Determination and Administration Act was passed. This act created special "water courts," one in each of the seven water divisions, to grant surface water rights and hear other water matters.

In addition to the four duties above mentioned, some of the more specific tasks performed by state water quantity agencies include:

- gathering data on water availability and use and unappropriated supplies;
- conducting studies and investigations on extent and potential of ground and surface water development;
- receiving, examining, and granting or denying applications for water rights, changes in place and type of use, point of diversion, or nature of use;
- maintaining registry of water rights;
- licensing of well-drillers;
- reviewing and approving or rejecting formation of irrigation districts;
- providing technical advice;
- carrying out and enforcing rules and regulations adopted by the agency, the policy board, or the commission of the agency;
- inspecting dams and measuring equipment;
- preparing state water plans and basin studies;
- organizing the state into divisions and/or districts;

- appointing division and/or district officers and water masters;
- regulating of groundwater withdrawals; and
- allocating and controlling the development, use, and conservation of geothermal resources.

In many states, the director of the water agency must be a registered engineer (i.e., Nevada and Wyoming). Normally, he has a central office staff and a field staff, including local water masters or commissioners, to assist in the implementation of the law and agency duties.

One particularly interesting feature in Nevada that serves as a tool to insure that the law and resources management is carried out is the power granted the state engineer and his assistants to arrest any person violating the water laws.[7] The arrested person is turned over to the sheriff or other police officer, and a written complaint is filed by the arresting water official. It is a particularly frustrating experience for water officials to know of violations of the water law (i.e., wasteful or nonbeneficial use practices, stealing water, etc.) and also to know that by the time a complaint is served by the sheriff's office, the violations will have ceased. Often, procedural rules require notice to the violator before any enforcement actions can be taken. A recent change in Colorado law took away the power similar to that granted in Nevada and for practical purposes has hamstrung local enforcement.

In a number of states (i.e., California, Colorado, Texas, and Utah), planning and development of water resources is carried out by an agency independent of the "water rights" office. In others (i.e., Montana, Washington, and Wyoming), this activity is one of the tasks of the central agency.

This function generally carries with it several specific tasks. Among the most important are

- the preparation of state, basin, and local water plans;
- the planning, development, construction, and operation or supervision of water projects;
- the acquisition of water rights for water projects and contracting out the use of water;

- the administration of financial programs for improvement of water delivery and use.

The latter task provides an important tool in improving water management practices of the users. A number of states have incentive programs that provide low- or no-interest loan and grant programs (i.e., Colorado, New Mexico, Utah, and Wyoming). But the present programs often limit the use of funds only to irrigation districts or other public entities for improvement of storage and delivery systems as they relate to improved efficiency in water quantity use. Water quality improvement is normally not one of the objectives of these state programs.

The present status of state agencies charged with water rights administration and planning and development is set out in Table 2.

Since the late 1950s, most states have reorganized the water quality control agencies along the pattern required under federal legislation to comply with federal law (California has done this since 1949). Where in the past water pollution control was one activity of the Public Health Service, under the current reorganizations, it has become one of the major activities being carried out by a state agency. In some cases, the function is still within a Department of Health (i.e., Arizona, Colorado, North Dakota, Utah), whereas in other states it is within the Department of Environmental Quality (i.e., Oregon and Wyoming) or Ecology (Washington), the Environmental Improvement Agency (New Mexico), or directly under the Water Quality Board (Texas). In all cases, a water quality control commission, board, or council is the policy and rule-making body, while the department, service, or bureau of water quality is responsible for implementing the laws, rules, and standards.

Some of the more important tasks of the water quality control agency include

- developing and maintaining comprehensive and effective programs for prevention, control, and abatement of water pollution and protection of water quality;
- classifying water streams and bodies of water;

TABLE 2
State Water Administration, Planning and Development Agencies

State	*Water Rights Administration*	*Planning and Development*
1. Arizona	Chief Division of Water Rights State Land Department	State Water Engineer Arizona Water Commission
2. California	Chairman State Water Resources Control Board The Resources Agency	Director Department of Water Resources The Resources Agency
3. Colorado	State Engineer Division of Water Resources Department of Natural Resources	Director Colorado Water Conservation Board Department of Natural Resources
4. Idaho	Director Department of Water Resources Operations Division	Planning Division Department of Water Resources
5. Kansas	Chief Engineer Division of Water Resources Kansas State Board of Agriculture	Chairman Water Resources Board
6. Montana	Administrator Water Resources Division Engineering Bureau Department of Natural Resources & Conservation	Resources and Planning Bureau Water Resources Division Department of Natural Resources and Conservation
7. Nebraska	Director Department of Water Resources	Chairman Natural Resources Commission
8. Nevada	State Engineer Division of Water Resources	Special Projects Aid Planning Section Division of Water Resources

	(Engineering Section) Department of Conservation & Natural Resources	Department of Conservation and Natural Resources
9. New Mexico	State Engineer State Engineers Office	State Engineer State Engineers Office
10. North Dakota	State Engineer State Water Commission (Legal Services Division)	Division of Planning State Engineer State Water Commission
11. Oklahoma	Director Water Resources Board	Director Water Resources Board
12. Oregon	Director Water Resources Department (Water Rights Division)	Policy and Planning Division Water Resources Department
13. South Dakota	Director Division of Water Rights Department of Natural Resources Development	Director Division of Resource Management Department of Natural Resources Development
14. Texas	Chairman Texas Water Rights Commission	Chairman Texas Water Development Board
15. Utah	State Engineer Division of Water Rights Department of Natural Resources	Director Division of Water Resources Department of Natural Resources
16. Washington	Water Resources Management Division (Water Resources Management Section) Office of Water Programs Department of Ecology	Water Resources Policy Development Section Water Resources Management Division Office of Water Programs Department of Ecology
17. Wyoming	State Engineer and Board of Control State Engineers Office and Board of Control	Wyoming Water Planning Program State Engineers Office and Water Planning Section Department of Economics, Planning and Development

- promulgating water quality standards, effluent limitation standards, and control regulations;
- carrying out a permit program for pollutant discharges;
- reviewing and granting permission and funding for location, design, construction, and operation of sewage treatment facilities;
- authorizing and monitoring underground injection of pollutants;
- serving as hearing board or officer in resolving matters of enforcement of the pollution laws;
- ordering the cessation or abatement of discharges;
- receiving and allocating funds or grants and loans made available by federal and state governments; and
- carrying out investigations to determine the nature and source of pollutant discharges.

When the original water quantity and quality agencies were created, there was little need, if ever the thought occurred, to focus also upon water planning and development as a state agency function. The two initial agencies of concern were the Public Health Service and the Office of State Engineer.

Figure 2 illustrates the range of organizational arrangements that evolved and exist today, beginning with the Type 1 (Basic) agencies described above. Since 1970, most of the state agencies have been reorganized some number of times. But the basic schemes can be seen in Figure 2 as variations of Type 2 (Independent) and Type 3 (Integrated). The trend is definitely toward the Type 3 structure with contemporary objectives often reflected in the title (i.e., emphasis on the environment or emphasis on the resources). A shift has occurred away from the use of the title "Office of State Engineer" or its equivalent to the more nonpersonal and comprehensive title "Department" or "Division of Water Resources."

Keeping in mind that the emphasis of this paper is on water management tools, the present organizational schemes found in the western states can be classed as Independent (Type 2) or Integrated (Type 3) agencies—that is, classified relative to the performance of the three basic functions of water quantity, quality control, and planning and development. From 1972 to

Figure 2
Types and Evolution of Water Administration Agencies by Three Major Functions

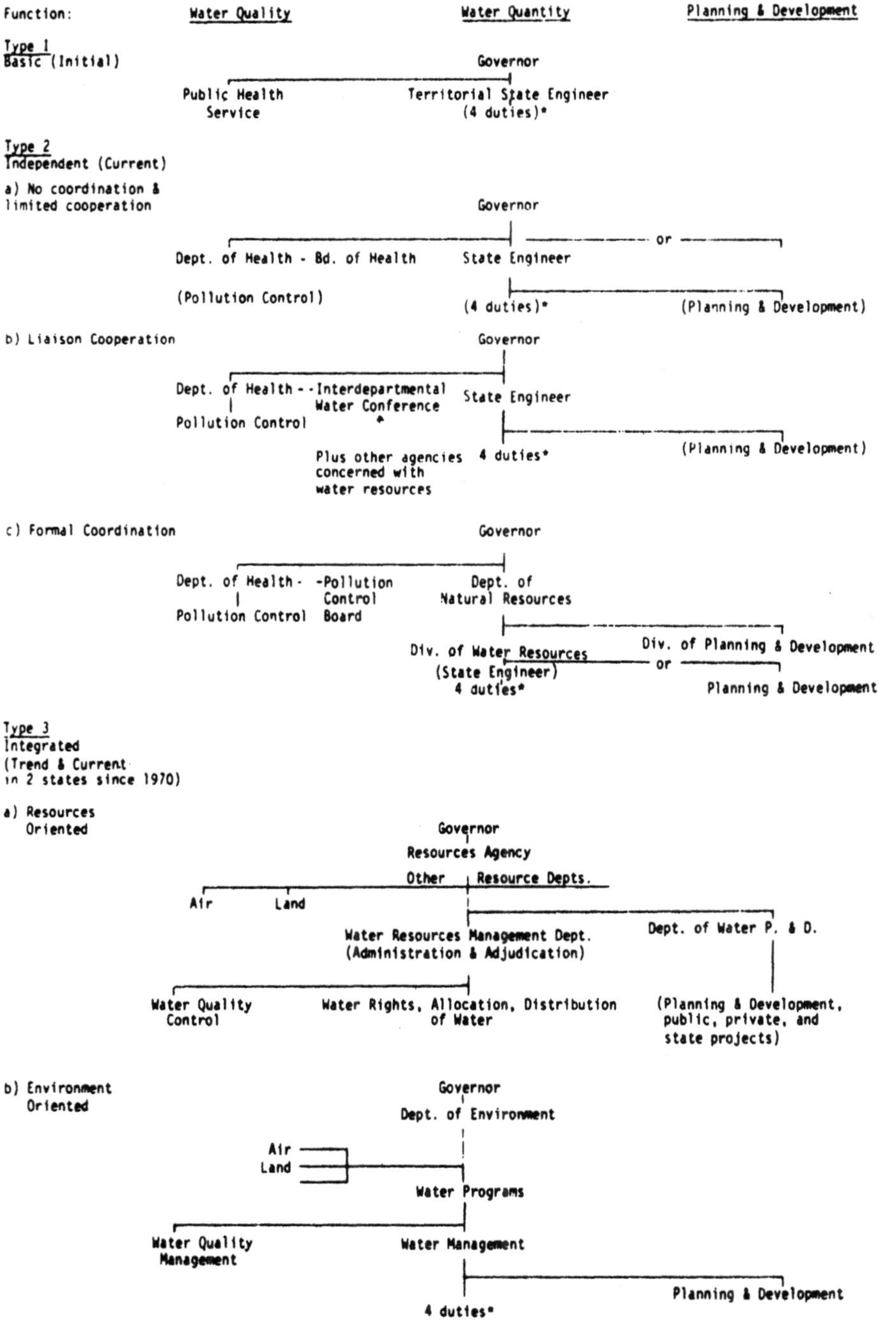

*4 duties = allocation of water, adjudication of water rights, distribution of water, administration of water laws.

(Radosevich and Skogerboe, 1977)

1977, a great deal of concern was on agency capability to implement an effective irrigation return flow, quality control program. Unfortunately, this concern was often premised upon a belief that farmers were culprits, injecting pollutants into water courses. In fact, any successful program in water quality control from irrigated agriculture should, by necessity, recognize the inseparable interdependence of the allocation of water, granting a water right, the exercise of the right through diversion, and the application of water–along with the other agricultural inputs such as chemicals–and land use practices that result in return flows (discharges) of a lesser quality.

In the Type 2 (Independent) class, the dominant features are (1) separate agencies for water quantity and quality control, (2) the planning and development carried out, and (3) the existence of a policy and rule-making body in or over either the water quantity or quality agency. These three features do exist to some degree in every western state.

It is also important to explore the degree that agencies interact. The Type 2 arrangement can be subclassified into (a) no coordination and limited cooperation, (b) liaison cooperation, and (c) formal cooperation. In the Type 2(a) organizational structure, the three functions are often performed in a vacuum. The agencies carry out their duties independent of possible impact upon the subject jurisdiction of their sister agencies. In the Type 2(b) structure, which is the current Wyoming arrangement, the agencies act independently of one another, but there exists a mechanism for all agencies dealing with water matters to get together once a month and discuss activities and areas of concern. This scheme is called the Interdepartmental Water Conference. The Type 2(c) organizational structure reflects the majority of state arrangements. Independence of water quantity and quality agencies exists, and in some cases–such as Utah–the planning and development is also independent of the water rights agency. But there is established a water quality control or policy board (Kansas, Oklahoma, Oregon, and Texas), commission (New Mexico), or council (Arizona) whose membership includes representatives from at least the two agencies with jurisdiction over water quantity and quality control.

In 1978 there were only two states that integrated the

administration of water quantity and quality law. These two states have actually reorganized to integrate all resource control (California) or the major resources activities as they affect the environment (Washington) under one supervising agency with subdivisions or departments responsible for planning and development. Type 3(b) reflects the environmental importance of the early 1970s. All three basic functions are under an office of the supervisory agency.

As previously stated, there is a definite trend toward the integrated agency approach. Several states have been contemplating reorganization for a number of years. Hutchins's statement about past changes is clearly applicable today: "They resulted from various causes. Some are changes in name only. Others stemmed from the frequently evidenced impulse to reorganize state agencies in order to meet changing and developing public needs not always confined to water resource problems" (Clark, p. 108).

In addition to the organizational structures of state government for water administration, there also evolved in the West organizations representing the interests of water users. Most of these organizations were originally oriented to the use of water by irrigated agriculture. Within irrigation systems, organizational structures emerged over a time ranging from the informal collaboration of a few individuals in the construction and maintenance of a common barrier ditch to formal irrigation companies and districts to multipurpose conservation and conservancy districts. In many instances, a great variety and multitude of irrigation companies within a given system interact in complex ways to distribute water, providing intricate patterns of optional interorganizational arrangements for improved efficiency in water delivery and management. Although it is beyond the scope of this paper to delve into the peculiarity of each organizational variation, it must be pointed out that these organizations are extremely important tools for water management. Conversely, in some instances, they serve to constrain more effective use of water under changing conditions and needs due to the adherence to tradition.

The more common and important irrigation organizations are the mutual irrigation company, the irrigation district, and the conservancy, conservation, or water management district. The mutual irrigation company may be incorporated under state law and generally is a private, nonprofit, single-purpose organization, owned by the water users as shareholders to divert and deliver water from the source of supply, often to temporary storage, to the shareholder's headgate. Occasionally, a group of companies sharing a common point of diversion or storage will federate into a water users' association to gain economies of scale while still retaining their separate identity.

Irrigation, conservancy, conservation and other forms of water management districts are quasi-public or public organizations with taxing and assessing powers. They are organized under specific state law requiring the consent of a certain percentage of affected users. The irrigation district is a single purpose entity originally created to facilitate implementation of the 1902 Federal Reclamation Act. The other super districts generally are multipurpose structures, covering the whole or part of a hydrologic basin. Some water management districts confine their activities to surface or ground waters, others to conjunctive use of these waters. A few states, such as Nebraska, have authorized the formation of multiresource management districts. Nebraska designates them as Natural Resource Districts.

Improving the Use of Our Legal Tools

I have stated in many previous papers and presentations that the greatest constraint on more effective use of water in the West is the water right. I stand by that assertion if the thesis is economic effectiveness; but if the thesis is or includes social stability and equity, the result is that the water right is still the fundamental and most effective tool for water management in the West. This right, being a real property right with a value and constitutional protection, affords those owners who wish to capitalize on its value to sell and convey varying state law requirements or enable those who wish to remain in their chosen occupation to have the security of water availability under the particular right.

Aside from the water right, several other tools were previously mentioned. Concepts or doctrines that are significant are

- criteria for allocation (beneficial use and/or reasonable use),
- place and type of use,
- duty of water,
- criteria for use and reallocation of use (beneficial use, priority of right, nonuse leading to forfeiture abandonment, fixed location and transferability of use), and
- rights of downstream users (to return flows, maintenance of level of flows, conditions of upstream/downstream transfers).

The organizations, both governmental and nongovernmental, are important tools to implement a policy of water management. Their effectiveness is enhanced through use of rule and regulation making powers. Tools for interstate and international water management include the compact and treaty. Finally, the courts and procedural processes are essential tools if used properly.

Anyone who is familiar with water law and its operation will quickly admit that there are numerous constraints to improved water use through the exercise of the water right. Nontransferability and the practice of "use it or lose it" are most often cited. However, a number of other concerns have been expressed by policy makers, water administrators, and water users that need to be identified. The improvement in any one or more of the legal tools may have a corresponding adverse impact upon others involved with the resource use. A list of concerns or issues includes:

1. Water allocation and reallocation, namely, competition by and between expanding and current uses, such as demands by growing cities, new uses, and the resurgent water right acquisition for speculative gain.
2. Water quality control and conditions, namely, the control impact upon development and use and the interdependency of water quantity use and resulting quality consequences.
3. Surface and groundwater usage, namely, priority of right, impacts of pumping on tributary surface flows,

and methods for conjunctive management.

4. Certain groundwater appropriations and uses, namely, the tapping of deep aquifers for coal slurry pipeline and other energy uses and water right speculation.
5. Instream flow maintenance for aquatic life and habitat and recreation or aesthetic purposes.
6. Federal reservation doctrine limits and impacts.
7. Interstate stream administration, namely, quality and quantity impacts from changing use conditions and energy development needs.
8. In general, federal involvement and intervention in western water use and administration, directly through operation of laws and programs and indirectly through the maze of federal rules and regulations surreptitiously affecting water use and causing financial drains and time for response and protection against such regulations.

all these concerns have spatial and temporal dimensions interlaced with the complexities of differing physical and political boundaries.

How then can we improve our use of the legal management tools? I suggest three major areas of improvement: water right status in use, water law administration, and integrated resources management.

Water Right Improvements

To systematically improve the water management through use of legal tools, changes in state laws must include efforts to

- achieve uniformity within state laws and administration;
- achieve workable uniformity in the laws between states;
- develop criteria for efficiency in water allocation and use according to key principles of beneficial use, waste, and duty of water, and apply this criteria to all uses, private and public;
- recognize and promote the public trust of water agencies and the public duty in the user for use of these public resources;
- specifically incorporate the element of water quality in water rights;

- shift to a term permit or periodic evaluation of effective water use for all new and transferred water rights;
- authorize the state agency in charge with water law implementation or planning and development of waters to appropriate in the name of the state all of the remaining waters and permit the use of these waters under contract water rights; and
- authorize a state water agency or create a new agency or division with hydrologic basin offices to operate a water brokerage.

Some of these conceptual alterations need explanation. The concept of beneficial use is constantly cited in referring to western water law. It is a nebulous concept that defines the measure and limit of a water right. The concept must be conceived and directed not only to the type of uses for purposes of allocating water but also to the nature of the use by each particular user. It must also be viewed with respect to the user's responsibility to other downstream users and the public interest. The concept should be reoriented in most states to encourage the most advanced technologically feasible management program with respect to the type of use. In addition, by adding the element of water quality specifically as a component in a water right, the beneficial use concept can be oriented to improve these practices by analyzing the consequence of the use. In effect, what beneficial use would attempt to accomplish is arriving at the best management practices.

Most states in the West grant perpetual water rights so long as the individual continues to abide by the use conditions. Unfortunately, few western states periodically review the use practices of this valuable property right. A few states have adopted term permits and periodic valuations. This concept should be adopted by all western states. A term of ten years or a term based upon the amortized period of the investment for which the water rights will be used should be considered. More favorable from the point of view of being able to manage the resource in the future would be the authorization of the state to appropriate all remaining and appropriated water in the name of the state and to adopt "contract water rights" as a means for allocating the use of this resource. Contract water rights would still enable the user to apply for any appropriated water with the advantage that the contract would be for a specific term, provide specific standards of use with respect to the type of use and the ability of the user to employ the most effective means, provide for penalties in the breach of contract or misuse of the resource, and place the burden of effective water use on the user in such a way that the cost of administration will be partly covered by the contract beneficiary. In such a manner, the economic concepts of water pricing can be implemented through the administrative system and can set the standards for private water pricing practices.

Finally, it is recommended that the state be authorized to create a water brokerage system. The operation of the water brokerage system will be discussed below, but the theory behind it is that at present, many water right holders will divert the entire amount that they are entitled to in order to preserve the integrity of their full allocation. This is done regardless of whether a beneficial use of the water is actually being made because the water right holders know that it is administratively impossible to police every water user under the present system of administration in most states. Thus, by creating a water brokerage system, an incentive would be provided the user who may only need half his allocation to offer the balance to a more effective user and receive compensation for his own thriftiness.

Water Law Administration Improvements

Most state agencies find themselves overcommitted with obligations and duties and understaffed. Their operation is often geared to the allocation and distribution of water and handling the more serious water problems. Several improvements to water administration can be made:

- The adoption of a water registry system requiring the water right owner to report annually on the nature, extent, and place of use of the water and requiring water right purchasers to inform the state of any transfer of ownership. Failure to comply with registry requirements would be prima facie evidence of intent to forfeit or abandon the right.

- The authorization of the state agency to issue orders of the compliance, immediately effective, but reviewable by a water or district court.
- The encouragement of the creation of basin or subbasin water management districts to resolve complex water right problems and water deliveries. Such a district may employ the practice of reallocating water among the district's users according to need in order to insure that all users have a usable quantity and quality available.
- The creation of a new agency or the authorization of an existing state agency to operate a water brokerage system at the basin or subbasin level.

Several of the structural alternatives suggested are already in operation in a few states. In some states, irrigation districts are used to circumvent constraints imposed by transfer restrictions. In Colorado, ditch companies operate to rent and transfer water within their system in order to avoid the cumbersome organizational impediments and thus effectively serve to manage their water allocation by taking advantage of location of reservoirs and user requirements.

The problem is that these practices are on a limited scale in the West. A means is needed of allocating or reallocating water within a basin or subbasin that takes into consideration the needs of the water users within the system, the state water development plan, and the basin, interstate and international impact. An entity responsible to the public is suggested to operate as a market center for the exchange, rental, or sale of water rights. This brokerage system would encourage water users to divert only that amount of water necessary for their operation without fear of losing the unused decreed quantity and lease or rent the balance to other users, taking into account carriage losses and adverse impact on other water users in the system. Hence, there would be an economic incentive to implement the most efficient water management practices.

An entity created at the basin or subbasin level with responsibility to the central state water office would list all available water for rent, lease, exchange, or sale. The location of available waters will determine the impact upon other vested rights, but the responsibility for delivery and protection of such other rights would rest upon either the water right holder or water acquirer. Uniform prices of units of water could be established or the available water could be transacted to the highest bidder. A percentage of the transaction price would be retained for operation and maintenance of the brokerage system.

Integrated Resources Management

The majority of states treat each resource independently for administrative purposes. As a consequence, conflicts occur between state agencies where the resources are interdependent. For example, land allocation or rezoning may have a significant impact upon watershed management or existing water rights. Often, a particular activity requiring many different resources as factors of input can have adverse consequences, such as the location of industrial plants upstream or upwind from cities and certain agricultural activities that would affect water quality.

Because agriculture is still one of the largest water users in the West, particular attention is directed to it. Since 1972, when the Federal Water Pollution Control Act was adopted, there has been an extensive effort to improve quality of return flows from irrigated agriculture. Several of my colleagues and I have conducted research on this topic for a number of years. As a consequence of that research, we are recommending that states adopt a program of influent control for irrigated agriculture, which includes out-flow analysis with criteria to determine the degree of improvement relative to needs and opportunity costs. The influent control approach is based upon the assumption that improved water management plus improved agricultural practices will significantly contribute to improved water quality. The approach consists of nine specific components:

1. Designate areas for irrigation return flow quality management and designate the responsible area entity.
2. Develop standards and criteria for beneficial use in designated areas.
3. Introduce incentives to use water more efficiently.
4. Include the element of water quality in new, transferred, and changed water rights.

Figure 3

The Goal, Problem and Solution to Irrigation Return Flow Quality Control

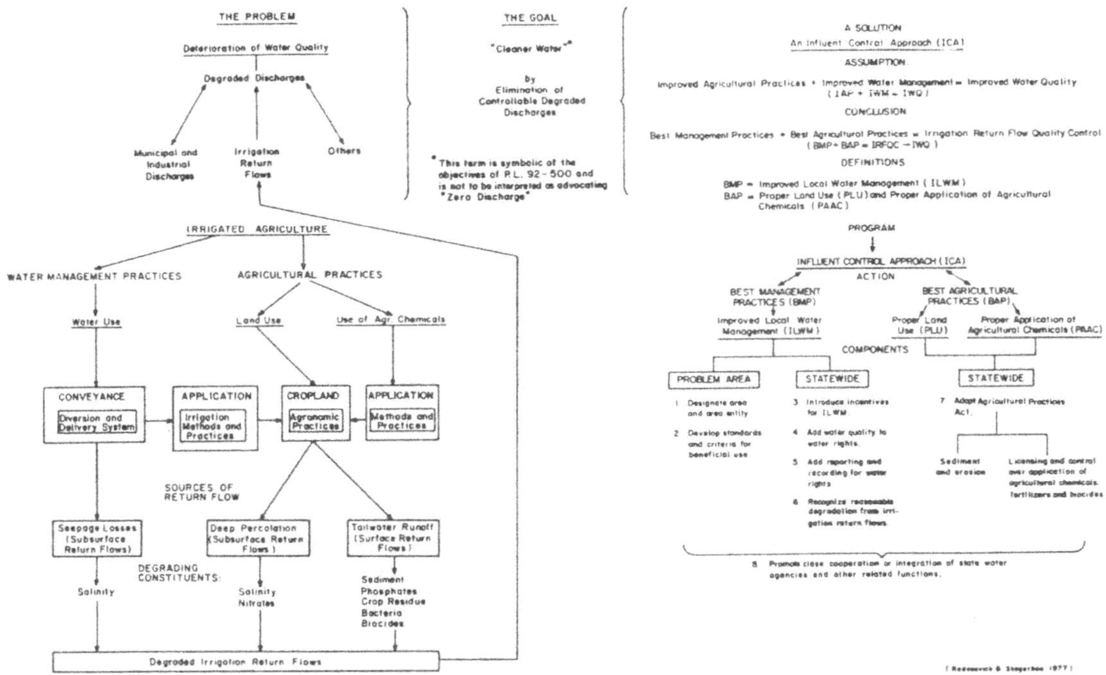

5. Adopt and enforce a reporting and recording system for water rights.
6. Recognize reasonable degradation from agricultural water use.
7. Adopt an agricultural practices act to control sediment and erosion.
8. License and control the application of agricultural chemicals, such as fertilizers and biocides.
9. Promote close cooperation or integration of state water agencies or related functions.

Figure 3 illustrates the goal, problem, and proposed solution to the irrigation return flow quality control.

Conclusion

It has not been the thesis of this paper that legal tools for water management in the past have not been effectively used. To the contrary, many states have adopted efficient and effective programs. The difficulty in making better use of our management tools is that changing needs and conditions outdate past practices. As a consequence, it is my conclusion that the most important tool that we have is our ability to employ common sense and equity in meeting the dynamic challenges for water. To be successful will require patience, humility, understanding, and willingness to internalize externalities and accept trade-offs. Before we can improve our legal management tools, all parties must understand the conditions or problems and be willing to accept change.

Notes

1. W.S.A. Sec. 41-20.
2. 6 Colo. 443 (1882).
3. T.W.R.C. Rule 129.02.05.001-.008.
4. O.W.R.B. Rule 350.
5. T.C.A. Sec. 5.002.
6. Montana Constitutution Art. IX, Sec. 3.
7. N.R.S. Sec. 533.475.

References

Clark, R. E. *Water and Water Rights* (Indianapolis, Indiana: Allen Smith, 1967).

Radosevich, George E. "Western Water Laws and Irrigation Return Flows," EPA Rep. 600/2-78-180 (August 1978).

Radosevich, George E. and Gaylord V. Skogerboe, "Achieving Irrigation Return Flow Quality Control Through Improved Legal Systems," EPA Rep. 600/2-78-184 (December 1978).

Schwartz, Bernard. *The Law in America* (New York: American Heritage, 1974).

Commentary

M. M. Kelso

The description by George Radosevich of western water management tools and his recommendations for their improvement and better use are all quite appropriate. I find no fault with any of them. Hence, I will elaborate on his discussion by running it through a different mind, using a different set of analytical ideas and a different vocabulary. By so doing, I hope that understanding of the issues and the rationale for their resolution will be enhanced.

Earlier papers in this symposium, notably those by Trelease and Bromley, discussed the need for and the desirable content of broad policy reforms surrounding water in the West. For my presentation, I will assume that broad policy decisions covering water, whatever they are, have been made; I will discuss, as does Radosevich, the water management tools available to realize established policy and how they may be made more effective toward realization of that policy.

It is instructive to begin this discussion by recalling that "management tools" related to *land* resources in this country are predominantly in the hands of the land's private owners and users, whereas those related to *water* resources are predominantly held by the public in spite of the strongly held preference for private ownership and management of resources. The federal government held all property rights in land outside the thirteen original states and Texas (and in Texas the *state* public, the government, held them). Both publics (the federal and that of Texas) alienated land management rights to private owners as broadly and as rapidly as possible.

But the ownership of water was never alienated to individual owners though the federal public alienated the management rights to water to the several states (with certain exceptions such as reserved rights and interstate commerce). The states, in turn, have never alienated ownership rights to water to private and individual users but have allotted use rights to water users. True, these allotments of use rights were mostly for perpetual terms (if certain conditions of use were adhered to), but the public always held a reserved interest and allotting and transferring these rights and the water they covered has been generally a public administrative act rather than an impersonal market bargaining act.

Why this difference between property rights in land and water? Land as a resource unit is more clearly definable, more constant, more certain in content and location; water is transient in flows that are variable both in nature and when created by man. Even stored quantities of water are more variable in quantity and quality in nature and as the result of the actions of man than is land.

The publics have recognized these "peculiarities" of water relative to property and have retained public ownership, granting only use-privileges to individuals. When a private owner of land grants use-privileges to another, it is called a landlord-tenant relation. Even when a public land owner grants use-privileges to private users (as between federal public lands and graziers), it is easily, though not universally, recognizable as also a landlord-tenant relationship.

But the relation between the public owner and the individual user of water has never been recognized to be tenancy between a public landlord (or should one say "waterlord") and a private (or individual) user. It's high time we did because we know a considerable amount about what an efficient and equitable system the landlord-tenant relationship is. If we applied this knowledge to property relations between public owner and individual user of water, we could make more rapid progress toward improved use of water management tools. In fact, the central issue in such a quest is improved performance of the public as a landlord. During a recent discussion concerning federal government-private grazier use of public grazing lands, a friend in Montana said, "It's time that the federal government behaved in its management of public grazing lands in the same way it's urged for decades that private landlords should behave toward their tenants." It is the same with regard to water except that we first have to recognize that the problem is a landlord-tenant problem. All of Radosevich's recommendations for better use of water management tools can be cast in terms of improved (public) landlord-individual (user) tenant relationships and in improved performance of the public as a landlord. Let us turn, then, to a brief review of some of the elements of an improved landlord-tenant relationship in the management and use of water.

First, the landlord (the public) should and would have the right to protect his asset (water) against unreasonable damage (waste, degradation, or loss) by its users.

- He would define "minimal good management" (which Radosevich points out is the real meaning of "beneficial use") with regard to the use of his water by his tenants.
- He would set maximum limits on permitted degrees of depletion and degradation of his water.
- He would establish the rules and machinery to prevent, mediate, or adjudicate any adverse effects on some of his water user tenants stemming from actions by others of his tenants, at least insofar as these adverse effects are transmitted through his water.

Secondly, the individual water user must have security of tenure in whatever quantity and quality of water his tenancy contract (his "water right") specifies. Security of tenure in relation to water does not mean certainty as to quantity and quality of water received at every point in time because water is so intimately affected by natural fluctuations. What it does give the user (tenant) is security against unilateral, capricious acts by either the public (landlord), any other party, or the individual user himself to alter terms and conditions of his water lease contract. Such security means that if the contract is altered it will be done only with quid pro quos for damages to all affected parties determined by negotiation (bargaining) or in a court (reasonable compensation)—except insofar as the police power of government to protect the public health, safety, morals, and welfare may be legislatively invoked.

Tenure security also requires that the term (length in time) of the water lease contract (the water "right") must be of sufficient minimum length as to make it possible for the tenant user to make reasonable use of the water conveyed, to realize reasonable return from its use, and to exhaust to a reasonable degree any long-run fixed investments he must make for efficient management and use of the water over the term of his right.

If the term of the water user's tenure is less than perpetual (as it should be in the interest of equity and fairness and long-run security on the part of the landlord, the public), the existing tenant-user should always have first right of refusal to any extension of the water lease contract upon its expiration. This should be subject to any changes that may be made in the terms of the lease contract at that time by the public landlord unless he (the tenant user) is evicted for unreasonable violation of terms of his lease (water right). If the extended lease contract (water right) is transferred to a different tenant, the new tenant should be required to reimburse the prior tenant for any remaining unexhausted (undepreciated) value of immovable investments he made that were necessary for the efficient use of the water. The public landlord may serve as referee as to the reasonable remaining value of such transferred investments.

Security of tenure for both landlord and tenant requires that there be no open end or undefined or indefinite terms in the contractual relationship as to the length of the arrangement or as to the quantity and quality of water covered (except insofar as they are nature-related). In other words, it must be clearly defined and specified who has what right to do what to whom relative to what water and what defenses.

Third, concern for security of tenure above all other considerations will convert security into a strait jacket—a trap—in which change is impossible to the detriment of the public landlord or the tenant user or both. What may have been efficient and equitable can become inefficient and inequitable for all. The system of water property relations (water rights) must provide means to secure flexibility in the use of the water (and related resources), in the location and in the conditions of its use, and in the identity of its user. Traditionally, our water management tools have emphasized security of tenure and have down-played flexibility. A considerable degree of inefficiency and inequity has resulted. The best way to break through this rigidity will be for the public landlord to establish or further the establishment of a market for water lease rights or for water itself by offering a "brokerage" service or by "licensing" brokerage services by private, cooperative, quasi-public, or other public firms or organizations.

The public landlord must, however, due to the ubiquity of externalities stemming from water use and management practices, always retain the right to be a party to (1) every exchange transaction in water leases or water that may change the terms of the water lease contract, or (2) the manner and location of use of the water in order to minimize detrimental externalities that may arise therefrom. It is for this reason primarily that the public owner–private user (public landlord–individual user-tenant) relationship in water management has universally arisen in our society despite our preference for private ownership as well as use.

In addition, of course, further flexibility in the landlord–tenant user relationship relative to water can and may arise through the use of eminent domain and the police power by the public.

Fourth, although reference throughout this discussion is to the public acting as landlord in the water lease contract relationship, it is evident that the public as such cannot perform this function directly. It will be necessary that it establish an agency to serve as its agent to carry out its landlordship role. Such an agency will likely be a bureau of water resources management or something similar.

- Such an agency must know how much water and of what quality categories (including return flows to the system) it has for which to issue lease rights. In other words, an inventory of what it has to work with by locations is essential.
- The agency should contract out withdrawal or degradation rights for each reasonably separable tributary and aquifer to no more than the reasonably probable quantity

of water by quality classes available with reasonable certainty from year to year in each such area, which, after all, is all the water the landlord has to offer.

- The agency should be made responsible to keep the volume of authorized depletions and degradations and the volumes of available water qualities in reasonable balance for each reasonably separable tributary and aquifer.
- Short term fluctuations in quantity or quality due to natural causes should be shared proportionately by all water lessees in an affected supply area (except where previously established prior rights exist). Market-mediated transfers of rights or of water, if an exchange market as described above has been created, will provide for desirable deviations from the rigid proportionalities the above actions by the public landlord agency will generate.
- Actions to increase the supply of water to an area by storage, import, transwatershed diversion, etc. should be a public function or a licensed private function. Hereafter, lease rights to any increase in long-run supply beyond that quantity needed to fill outstanding lease contracts should be allocated to users by market sale methods with the possible exception of that portion allotted to public uses (like recreation).
- The water landlord agency must maintain a continuous and current record of who has what lease rights to what water of what quantity and quality under what restraints and obligations.
- Changes in terms of water leases made by the landlord agency other than at the time of lease expiration should be made by the agency only by negotiation (bargaining) with a quid pro quo for the tenant or the landlord agency depending on which one is harmed or benefitted by the change. The only exception to the above restraint on the landlord agency will relate to legislated police power actions.
- A water management, public landlord-private tenant user system as described above can function well with suitable efficiency and equity relative to its short run—for example, season to season—consequences. But for funda-

> mental resources like water that are necessary for a viable, on-going society, the long-run consequences of the management system are crucial and must be dealt with and resolved. The competitive market doesn't rationalize these long-run consequences at all well as demands grow relative to supplies, especially as supplies are depleted or degraded, or both.

Thus, the public as the landlord responsible for society's water for its long-run welfare has a role of increasing importance to play, a role not referred to by Radosevich among his water management tools but implied by several papers at this symposium. That role has to do with finding an answer to the question, How fast—i.e., at what annual rate—should we *use up* a nonreproducible, nonsubstitutable, depletable or degradable resource such as water? And how far ahead must such a decision look to be suitably "long-run"? Well, put it this way. The "long-run" is how far ahead the current decision-making public is willing by its decisions to designate which generation is going to be the last one to have a particular depletable-degradable supply of water available to it.

When such a decision is made by the public, then its water landlord agency should grant water right leases to no more than that annual volume of consumptive uses that will insure this life expectancy of that resource. If and when the annual depletion can be increased, rights to the increased volume should be sold to prospective users. If the depletion rate later must be reduced, the public landlord agency should buy back the curtailment by market bargaining or by eminent domain.

The point is that some *public agency* must have and must exercise *the responsibility* to determine or to recommend (to the legislature, for instance) how fast to use up *an irreplaceable, depletable-degradable resource such as water.* An important water management tool all too generally ignored is long-range planning. We've got to do much, much better in our use of this tool!

Last, the above discussion implies that the water management tools we have aren't all that they should be and that even those we have are not and have not been used as fully and effectively as they could be. But we do have sets of such tools in the several states and in the federal government and property right commitments have been made under them. The need, then, is not simply to decide to build something new but to figure out how to reform and improve what we have. That raises another set of problems because changing institutions that already exist is a different matter than building new ones to fill voids. But time and space doesn't permit getting into that problem here.

We must realize, however, that in the mundane world of practical action, this problem of transforming the existing water management system can well be a tougher and more intractable problem than agreeing on what sort of a target system will be preferable as a goal or ideal to be striven for. Interim small decisions taken to reform the existing system toward something conceived to be better will certainly turn out to be a mixture of negotiated or adjudicated quid pro quo compensation payments and uncompensated police power actions. The former will run into public and political restraints on expenditures; the latter will run into political opposition on questions of justice and issues of "taking" property without due process of law. Either of these restraints on change will be ample reason to expect sufficient conflict to keep life from becoming boring!

14 The Implications of Improved Water Allocation Policy

Kenneth E. Boulding

My introduction to water policy—baptism, I am almost tempted to say—took place a little over twenty years ago when I was on a commission of the state of California to investigate the social and economic consequences of the California Water Plan. In the course of these deliberations I came up with some verses. It is alleged that these had something to do with the fact that the legislature abolished the commission as soon as it found out what it was going to say and before it could report. I cannot refrain from quoting one of the verses now:

> Water is far from a simple commodity,
> Water's a sociological oddity,
> Water's a pasture for science to forage in,
> Water's a mark of our dubious origin,
> Water's a link with a distant futurity,
> Water's a symbol of ritual purity,
> Water is politics, water's religion,
> Water is just about anyone's pigeon,
> Water is frightening, water's endearing,
> Water's a lot more than mere engineering,
> Water is tragical, water is comical,
> Water is far from the pure economical,
> So studies of water, though free from aridity
> Are apt to produce a good deal of turbidity.[1]

On rereading these verses, they sound depressingly up-to-date after twenty-one years, though this may be just my ignorance of what has taken place in the meantime. Water is still a very peculiar commodity in that it is so affected with romantic and poetic interests that it is extremely hard to deal with rationally. I must confess that I have some doubts as to whether water allocation policy can be much improved; we may have to learn to put up with what we have and hope that the costs are not too great. However, hope springs eternal in the human breast. Perhaps a more rational attitude toward this peculiar substance is more likely to develop in an age of increasing scarcity of energy and materials. Water may well be the earliest serious limitation that we reach in many projects for human development and improvement. In some parts of the world right now water is a more severe limiting factor on development than energy or other materials.

We cannot talk about water allocation policy without putting water into the scheme of human values. The earth is a vast, structured ecosystem, consisting of populations of materials and energy, physical and biological species, and human beings and their artifacts. Every time a human being does something, the ecosystem immediately around is altered, and the whole ecosystem of the earth may be altered in a small degree. The impact of human beings on the ecosystem of the earth has been quite marked even from the early days of the human race. We almost certainly produced the extinctions of the larger mammalian species; we profoundly altered the biosphere with agriculture and forestry; we diverted rivers, made huge lakes, irrigated deserts and created them. We now seem to be in the process of changing quite drastically the composition of the atmosphere and the oceans. While it is still easy to exaggerate the human impact, there is little doubt that it gets larger all the time. It may be approaching some sort of cliff beyond which there are drastic, irreversible changes in the whole ecosystem of the globe, which are highly likely to be adverse to the niche of the human race.

In this world ecosystem, water can almost be described as the dominant "species," perhaps after the human race. It is the physical basis of all life, at least on this planet. The kind of complexity of structure that life involves seems to be able to develop out of a liquid environment in a narrow range of temperatures. Within this range water seems to be the only convenient liquid available, and we can certainly say that on earth at least no life exists in the absence of water. The amount of water has a very strong impact on determining the nature of the ecosystem, ranging from deserts to forests, grasslands, swamps, rivers, lakes, and the oceans. The variability over time of the quantity of water is also very important, as it is in intermittent streams and in the intertidal strip. The quality of water, likewise, matters—whether it is fresh or salt, polluted or clean.

The significance of water in the biological ecosystem carries over into human artifacts. It is hard to think of any human artifact or commodity that is produced in the total absence of water. Some require very large amounts, agriculture is impossible without it, so indeed are most manufacturing processes. The driest lecturer will have a glass of water on the rostrum and could not lecture without an intermittent stream of water passing through the body. I have never seen any attempt to classify commodities by the amount of water their production entailed as there have been for energy. It could certainly be done, and it might even be moderately interesting.

Once the human race has appeared on the scene, the quantity, quality, and variability of water in different ecosystems and habitats becomes in part a function of human valuations. Water is diverted from rivers for irrigation, it is transported hundreds of miles through pipes to cities, it is brought down from the air by cloud seeding, purified by distillation, salinated by irrigation. These changes are the result of human valuations. If water is redistributed or transformed by human action, it is because somebody believes that it is being transported or transformed from places, times, and conditions where it is less humanly valuable to those where it is more humanly valuable.

Who makes these valuations is a tricky question. I have argued that the impact of human valuations on the ecosystems of the world is organized through three major mechanisms, though there may be considerable overlap among them and mixtures of the three. I call these the "three P's"—prices, policemen, and preachments. Prices, of course, represent the market mechanism operating through exchange and a relative price structure. In a primitive form this is a water carrier selling water through the streets at the price that presumably pays him to do it. A vestigial private water market remains in our society in water from particular springs and spas.

From very early days, however, water has been a strong concern of the political system, and it has been organized by "policemen"–legitimated threat. Indeed, as Wittfogel argues, water may even have created Oriental despotisms or at least created a social ecological niche in which despotisms could thrive and survive. Irrigation, for instance, often begins privately, and there still is a private sector in it. In very early times, it tends to become a socialized enterprise, whether in Egypt, the Orient, the Roman Empire, or the modern world. Even in a capitalist society we never really trusted private property and the market to supply us with water, as we did, for the most part, with oil. In my California experience, I asked, Why not give water back to private enterprise and tax the daylights out of it? Water is a liquid, it is found in the ground, it runs through pipes just like oil, so why treat them differently? This suggestion was always received with amusement or horror. Why what is good for water is not good for oil and vice versa still puzzles me a bit. The almost universal socialization of the water industry certainly has some rational justification in the economies of monopoly. Two water systems in a city would be as silly as two telephone systems. But there is more to it than that, and the sacredness of water as a symbol of ritual purity exempts it in some degree from the dirty rationality of the market.

This is not to say, of course, that prices may not and should not be an extremely important element in human decisions in regard to water. There is a principle beloved of economists that states if people can pay for something, they should, and that if something, through state power, is made artificially cheap or artificially dear beyond some "natural" price that reflects the alternative costs, something goes wrong with the invisible hand and it slaps us in the face. We will fail to conserve things that are too cheap; we will use poorer substitutes for things that are too dear. In the case of water, the danger is always that it is too cheap. This seems to be the case with all sacred objects. To some people, charging for water seems almost as indecent as charging to go into church. But it always remains true that somebody has to pay for it.

My second "P," which also stands for political order and is perhaps the dominant system in the water industry, interacts strongly with "prices" because the market always rests on some kind of definition and protection of property, which is a function of the political system. We cannot have exchange unless there is property in the things exchanged. The definition of property, particularly in the case of water, is a highly tricky business, as the competing water laws of different times, different countries, and in this country different states amply testify. We now find ourselves engaged in defining on a world scale the property rights in regard to the ocean, which had previously, beyond a small segment off the coast, been common property. Now it is clear that the "tragedy of the commons" applies to the oceans, as the declining yield of fish testifies, and we have to face either property, such as the 200-mile limit or beyond, or some sort of community exploitation, which is often very difficult to do. Property in water presents many of the same problems as property in land. Without property, we get tragedies of the commons; with property, we get tragedies of absentee ownership, excessive concentrations of wealth, and divorce of ownership from control, which is both sometimes deplorable and nearly always necessary and, indeed, is what the financial system is all about. The definition of property is one of these areas where the cost-benefit analysis of institutions themselves is extremely difficult, so that it becomes a major source of world conflict, insecurity, and perhaps even catastrophe.

While the problems of the interaction between the polity and the economy sometimes seem particularly dramatic in the case of water, it remains true that the relative price structure—no matter how determined, whether by competitive markets or by government fiat—affects not only the allocation of resources among different uses or employments but also the distribution of income among persons. So intimately related, indeed, are allocation and distribution that we cannot affect one without affecting the other. In classical economics (which is still pretty good), the "natural" or "normal" relative price structure is precisely that which so distributes income among the owners of resources in different occupations that there is no incentive to move from one occupation to another. If the relative price structure diverges from this, some prices will be perceived as "high" and the occupations that produce these commodities will be perceived as unusually well rewarded, while others will be perceived as "low" and ill rewarded. If, then, there is freedom to choose the occupation and the use of the resources that one owns, including one's own body, water rights, land, buildings, machinery, or what have you, then there will tend to be a shift of resources from the ill-rewarded occupations to the better-rewarded ones. This shift in itself, however, will move the structure of relative prices back towards the "normal." This is the great mechanism of the invisible hand, and no matter how we intervene in it and distort it, it still works, however clumsily.

On the other hand, the distribution of personal well-being, which is an intermediary in the process of change of relative outputs and relative prices, may be unacceptable from a political point of view. Agricultural policy in almost all countries is a remarkable example of the power of this proposition. Because of the low income elasticity for agricultural products, for the most part technical improvement in agriculture almost always requires a shift in population and, to a lesser extent, other resources, out of agriculture into other occupations. The way the market does this is to make agricultural prices "low"; therefore, agricultural income is low relative to others, and this will drive people out of agriculture and into other occupations. If the agricultural interest is politically powerful, however, it will try to prevent this, and we get such phenomena as price supports and agricultural subsidies, corn laws, and the like.

As in many other cases of public intervention, however, the results may be very different from the objective of the policy. U.S. agriculture is a striking case in point. The diminution in uncertainty consequent upon the introduction of price supports increased the willingness of farmers to invest, to practice technical change, and to increase productivity. As a result, agricultural income, especially of poor farmers, remained depressed, and we had an enormous migration out of agriculture—some 30 million people in one generation—after 1945.

The tendency has been to try to push agricultural prices up; with water, the tendency has been to try to push the price down. Up to now, at any rate, over large parts of the temperate zone, water has almost had the status in people's minds of being a free good, like air. We should say, perhaps, a cheap good rather than a free good. It has been scarce enough to appropriate. It has had a price. It has an alternative cost in the sense that it takes resources to produce it that might be producing other things, so it has entered into the price system more than air has. Now, with increased pollution, air perhaps also is becoming a scarce good with a price. There is, however, an association of water with the feeling of its being almost a free good, so there has been a strong tendency to keep the price, even where there is one, very low. The result of this, of course, is that there has been no incentive to conserve water, and it has been used with magnificent wastefulness.

Again, to go back to my California experience, the one thing I learned in that study was the great importance of pricing in a time perspective. I argued then, and I would argue now, that if we have something that is plentiful now that is going to be more scarce later on, perhaps in a few decades, the sensible social policy is to make it expensive now. The principle here is that the social policies should try to anticipate the normal relative price structure of a generation or so ahead on the grounds that otherwise we will not be prepared to meet the scarcities that seem to be coming up. When they are actually upon us, it may be too late to do much about them. In any case, to go back to the California case, I proposed at least a 400 percent tax on water. It seemed like an admirable subject for taxation. The tax would be reasonably progressive, as the rich undoubtedly use much more than the poor, but would not be unreasonably burdensome to anyone because water purchase takes a very small proportion of income. Any sharp rise in price, however, would start a long-term movement for conservation. It is a very fundamental principle that nobody will ever conserve anything that is dirt cheap, for they would be fools to do so. The same principle applies to energy, perhaps even in a greater degree. The policy of keeping oil cheap may turn out to be far more disastrous than that of keeping water cheap. If we want people to conserve energy, just as if we want them to conserve water, it must be made expensive. Yet this is politically very difficult.

The political dilemma arises because income distribution

changes may be much more in the political consciousness than allocational changes. If we make something expensive, something that is as universally used as water, everybody perceives themselves as being made worse off by this. It is extremely hard to get elected on a political platform that involves making everybody perceive themselves as being worse off. Policies, therefore, that are extremely desirable from the point of view of allocation, especially long-run allocation, may turn out to be quite politically unacceptable in the short run. After all, politics is strongly dominated by the short run. We can hardly blame it for that, for it is in the short run that people get elected or not elected, as the case may be. It is a common criticism of the market that it overstresses the short run and that the horizons of a market system rarely go beyond the year or two of forward contracts and futures markets. Even corporate executives rarely have a longer active life than politicians, at least in the positions of power that they tend to reach in their sixties, and the principle of "après moi le déluge" is noticeable in corporations, though perhaps not as much as it is with kings and presidents.

A very important question in social policy, which certainly applies to water policy as much as it does to any other, is whether the distributional impacts from the price structures that are desirable from the point of view of allocation can be modified sufficiently to make them politically acceptable without destroying the necessary motivation for allocational change. If everybody is completely protected against all distributional impact, there is no motivation to do anything but what they are doing now, and we have to guard against this. The slowdown in technical change that we seem to be encountering in the 1970s may be partly attributable to the distributional impact of the "industrial welfare state" when it is applied, for instance, to the Chrysler Corporation, Lockheed, and other big corporations in trouble. If bankruptcy becomes a privilege of the poor, one of the main sources of legitimacy of the market and of capitalism will be eroded. Similarly in the labor market we may be developing a "new feudalism" in that labor leaders deploy their members almost like feudal serfs in the interest possibly of their own power but also in the search for protection against the income effects of allocational change.

Up to now, I must confess that the misallocation of water resources is a problem that has given me a very few sleepless nights. I have no doubt at all that there is misallocation, largely as a result of an absurd pricing system. I am sure that there is also unnecessary waste, again as a result of the pricing system. I discovered, for instance, in my California experience, that in the Los Angeles Basin water was expensive enough, even in the fifties, to develop a whole profession of water savers who went around to the farms and taught farmers how to conserve irrigation water. In the Central Valley water was absurdly cheap, thanks to the U.S. taxpayer, so no such profession existed and I have no doubt that the waste of water was enormous. A dramatic example of the power of high prices to inspire conservation was the recent drought in the Bay Area, especially in Marin County, where high price structures produced quite spectacular conservation. Even though at low prices the demand for water is inelastic, beyond a certain point the demand for water becomes extremely elastic, and, with high enough prices, we will consume a twentieth or perhaps a hundredth of what we do now. Up to now, however, water has really been such a small part of the economy that we have been able to afford mistakes and wastefulness, and it is doubtful whether these mistakes have drastically affected the health and welfare of the total society.

We may now, however, be moving into a very different era. There is some critical point as scarcity increases when it becomes cheaper in terms of real resources to conserve a gallon than it does to produce it. In some cases, we may have reached this point some time ago without realizing it. What becomes increasingly clear, both in the energy and in the materials fields, is that we are moving into an era where it is cheaper to conserve than to produce. It is probable that we have reached this position with regard to oil, though we are very slow to act on it. We will reach this position with regard to water irregularly—at different times in different places and in different circumstances—but that we will reach it (if we have not reached it already) in many instances seems highly likely. Unfortunately, our economic indicators reflect a state of mind that assumes it is always easier to produce something than to conserve it. Conservation does not get into the GNP and other indicators, and we may easily be reaching a position now where our economic indicators become very dangerously misleading.

Under these circumstances, the heterogeneity of the system also becomes much more important than it was before. It is a dangerous tendency to think of energy in terms of BTU's and water in terms of gallons. What is significant is human valuations. What humans are concerned about in the case of both energy and materials—including water—is not the aggregate but to have them when and where and in the form that we want them. An assumption of much water policy has been that a gallon is a gallon is a gallon, or maybe an acre-foot. As we begin to approach water as an important limiting factor, however, the heterogeneity of water used becomes increasingly important. When water is virtually a free good, there is no harm in flushing the toilet with drinking water. As water becomes increasingly scarce, the desirability of dual systems or even multiple systems for different uses becomes of great importance. It may be that another hundred years from now the idea of flushing a toilet with drinking water or even flushing a toilet at all may seem the height of absurdity. Like energy, water is not valuable in itself but only in the right time at the right place in the appropriate quality and use. We can see the beginning of this recognition in industrial recycling, in ever more stringent effluent restrictions or even taxes, and in using various grades of water for irrigation. However, as far as I know, the principle is very rarely applied to domestic use. There is a whole field of study here that needs much more support and further work.

The third mode of coordination of human values, "preachments," is the moral order, an extraordinarily subtle and complex process in society whereby human valuations are learned and changed. Economists have rarely been willing to go beyond the level of abstraction at which human valuations are simply assumed. A realistic examination, however, of the dynamics of society has to face the fact that human values change. They may have a genetic base in part, but this is relatively small and consists of certain very general prejudices and directions. Almost the whole structure of human valuations is learned from birth on, if not before. The processes by which valuations are learned are very mysterious. Part of the process is one of association (the old-fashioned psychological term in which learned valuations are associated with genetic ones). This is perhaps why the culture of the parents is so easily transmitted to the children, though perhaps less easily today than it used to be. There are also very complex processes of feedback from valuations into experience and back again. There are two opposing principles at work here. One I have called the "sour grapes principle"–if you can't get what you want, you decide not to want it, that it is not valuable after all. The other is the "perserverance principle"–that if at first you do not succeed, you try, try again. The balance between these two principles opens up a possibility of occasional, very dramatic reversals of valuations (for instance, in conversion experiences–religious or political–or even in falling in love).

It might be thought that water is so commonplace and plentiful as to be exempt from these kinds of considerations, which would be a very dangerous assumption. The value a thirsty person puts on water undoubtedly has a genetic origin, but after that water becomes the object of a very complex structure of evaluations, rituals, superstitions, and attitudes. It has been the subject of sacred observances from very early times in human history. It is no doubt too Freudian to suggest that the curious difference in our attitude between water and oil rests on the fact that we get baptized with water at the beginning of our lives in Christian societies, and we only receive Extreme Unction with oil at death, but these symbols do affect our value judgments.

There is a more commonplace level at which political reactions to water policy are by no means unconnected to the peculiar place that water holds in our symbolic system. It is so holy and valuable to us as a symbol that we are apt to carry the production of it and the transportation of it far beyond the point of rational economic returns. Having to conserve it is perceived almost as an insult to the personality. As noticed earlier, there is still a strong feeling that water, like air, should be a free good. The faucet in the household is a perpetual spring of blessing, and it seems almost indecent to charge for it. There are some things where the legitimacy of the market wears thin, particularly where sacredness is involved. Water is curiously close to this boundary. This means that we almost certainly go past the point at which it is cheaper to save a gallon than to produce it. We are always in danger of over-investment in the provision of water and under-investment in its conservation.

A very interesting question is whether the general development of a conservation ethic would lead to change in these valuations. The environmental movement so far has devoted most of its energies in this regard to cleaning up pollution and expressing a demand for clean water in rivers, lakes, and oceans. There is a great legitimacy in this demand. It certainly does not derive merely from a symbol of ritual purity. Nevertheless, there is a lurking danger behind environmentalism that it can become a subtle attempt to preserve the privileges of the rich at the expense of the poor. Its distributional impacts always have to be carefully scrutinized. One way of avoiding this danger would be a shift from a more preservationist ethic to a more conservationist ethic. How this can be done in a way that will command widespread acceptance and will also have significant effects on human behavior is a tough problem.

These considerations may seem somewhat remote from the issues of water policy, but in the long pull they may be extremely significant. It is ultimately the moral order that dominates the other two, for neither politics nor exchange can survive and flourish in the absence of a legitimating moral order. Politics, indeed, tends to follow the changes in the moral order with perhaps a ten- or twenty-year lag. Prohibition, income-redistribution, civil rights, antidiscrimination, and so on all show the political order following changes in the moral order, although this does not preclude what may be very important feedback from the political order to the moral order. Legislation passed by a very few may eventually become accepted by the many. Even the economic order depends much more on legitimation than economists usually think. In fact, they usually take the legitimacy of exchange for granted. But it took a very long time to establish the legitimacy of exchange, and in many areas its legitimacy has been destroyed and is still threatened, as, for instance, in the Marxist denial of legitimacy to the capital market. Similarly, Proposition 13 represents a certain denial of legitimacy to aspects of the tax system.

In thinking about the future of water policy, therefore, especially the long-run future, the changing structure of legitimacy with regard to conservation, to price structures, to property, to regulation or to particular political structures, there is something that we cannot simply take for granted. The dynamics of legitimacy, however, even though they may eventually dominate the social system, are extremely mysterious and so far remain in the area of the highly unpredictable. My advice, therefore, is to keep a watchful lookout for changes in legitimacy and not take too many things for granted. Sometimes the things that seem to be taken for granted are quite suddenly not granted and we find ourselves in a very different, unfamiliar, and often frightening world.

Notes

1. Stanza III of Kenneth E. Boulding's "The Feather River Anthology," *Industrial Water Engineering,* 3, 12 (December 1966):32–33.

Symposium Participants

Mr. Jerry Abts
President
Lindsay Manufacturing Co.
Lindsay, Nebraska

Dr. Duane C. Acker
President
Kansas State University
Manhattan, Kansas

Mr. Ralph Adkins
CF & I Steel Corporation
Pueblo, Colorado

Mr. J. David Aiken
Assistant Professor
Department of Agricultural Economics
University of Nebraska-Lincoln
Lincoln, Nebraska

Mr. Charles A. Ames
Martin Marietta
Denver, Colorado

Dr. Raymond Anderson
Economics Department
Department of Agriculture
Colorado State University
Fort Collins, Colorado

Mr. Wayne D. Angell
President
Council Grove National Bank
Council Grove, Kansas

Mr. Cleveland Anschell
Vice President and Associate Economist
Rainier National Bank
Seattle, Washington

Ms. Christine H. Anthony
Chairman
Oklahoma City Branch
Federal Reserve Bank of Kansas City
Oklahoma City, Oklahoma

Mr. John W. Arlidge
Manager
Nevada Power Company
Las Vegas, Nevada

Ms. Sandra D. Atchison
Business Week
Denver, Colorado

Mr. James Aucoin
Lincoln Journal
Lincoln, Nebraska

Dr. Thomas G. Bahr
Director
New Mexico Water Resources Research Institute
Las Cruces, New Mexico

Dr. Maurice E. Baker
Professor
Department of Agricultural Economics
University of Nebraska
Lincoln, Nebraska

Mr. Harvey O. Banks
President
Water Resources Division
Camp Dresser and McKee, Inc.
Walnut Creek, California

Mr. Robert V. Barnes
President
Agribusiness/Transportation Group
Gifford-Hill & Company, Inc.
Dallas, Texas

Mr. William F Barratt
President
Federal Intermediate Credit Bank of Spokane
Spokane, Washington

Mr. Frank Baver
Dekalb Agresearch, Inc.
Dekalb, Illinois

Mr. Dennis Becker
Chairman
Board of Water Management
Pierre, South Dakota

Mr. Ralph Becker
Bonneville Associates
Salt Lake City, Utah

Mr. David Beeder
Omaha World Herald
Omaha, Nebraska

Mr. Sanford A. Beldon
Deputy Governor
Office of Administration
Farm Credit Administration
Washington, D.C.

Mr. Fred Bement
The Federal Land Bank of Omaha
Omaha, Nebraska

State Senator John Beno
P.O. Box 11447
Pueblo, Colorado

Mr. Wilber T. Billington
Senior Vice President
Federal Reserve Bank of Kansas City
Kansas City, Missouri

Mr. Kenneth J. Binkley
Assistant Vice President
Farm Mortgage Department
The Equitable Life Assurance Society of the U.S.
New York, New York

Dr. Dillard Bishop
Longmont, Colorado

Mr. Robert Bisson
BCI Geonetics
Grand Junction, Colorado

Mr. A. Harry Bliss
Editor
Journal of Environmental Health
Denver, Colorado

Mr. Sheldon Boone
Soil Conservation Service—USDA
Washington, D.C.

Dr. Kenneth Boulding
Professor of Economics
University of Colorado
Boulder, Colorado

Mr. Gray Breidenthal
President
Security National Bank
Kansas City, Kansas

Mr. James A. Bright
Executive Vice President
Jefferson Bank and Trust Company
Lakewood, Colorado

Dr. Daniel W. Bromley
Professor of Resource Economics
Department of Agricultural Economics
University of Wisconsin-Madison
Madison, Wisconsin

Dr. Ralph H. Brooks
Assistant Director
Division of Water Resources
Tennessee Valley Authority
Knoxville, Tennessee

Mr. Donald J. Brosz
Coordinator
Water Resource Programs
University of Wyoming
Laramie, Wyoming

Mr. Felix Buchenroth, Jr.
The Jackson State Bank
Jackson, Wyoming

Mr. Bruce Bullock
Research Manager
Farmbank Services
Denver, Colorado

Mr. John C. Bumgarner
Senior Vice President
Corporate Development & Planning
The Williams Companies
Tulsa, Oklahoma

Mr. Lyle E. Bush
Land and Water Resources Dept.
Adolph Coors
Golden, Colorado

Mr. Gene Butler
Program Officer
Four Corners Regional Commission
Albuquerque, New Mexico

Mr. A. J. Canaday
Executive Vice President
First National Bank of Omaha
Omaha, Nebraska

Mr. C. K. Cardwell
Deputy Governor
Office of Supervision
Farm Credit Administration
Washington, D.C.

Mr. Fred Caruso
Executive Director
Colorado Water Congress
Denver, Colorado

Dr. Emery N. Castle
President
Resources for the Future
Washington, D.C.

Mr. Brad Caswell
BCI Geonetics
Grand Junction, Colorado

Kip Cheroutes
U.S. Representative Pat Schroeder's Office
Denver, Colorado

Mr. George Craft
American Water Works Association
Denver, Colorado

Dr. Raymond G. Cragle
Director
Agricultural Experiment Station
University of Illinois
Urbana, Illinois

Mr. Glen Crim
Senior Vice President
Federal Intermediate Credit Banks of New Orleans
New Orleans, Louisiana

Mr. John Causten Currey
The Sun
Colorado Springs, Colorado

Mr. William Dabaghi
American Bankers Association
Washington, D.C.

Ms. Patsy Ann Danner
Federal Co-Chariman
Ozarks Regional Commission
Washington, D.C.

Mr. Thomas E. Davis
Senior Vice President
Federal Reserve Bank of Kansas City
Kansas City, Missouri

Ken Decker
Johnson Division, U.O.P., Inc.
Montrose, Colorado

Mr. Loel S. DeMuth
Denver, Colorado

Mr. J. U. Dickson
Director
Energy Research
Burlington Northern, Inc.
St. Paul, Minnesota

Mr. Daniel M. Dooley
Chief Deputy Director
California Department of Food and Agriculture
Sacramento, California

Mr. Vincent H. Dreeszen
Director
Conservation and Survey Division
University of Nebraska
Lincoln, Nebraska

Professor D. M. Drury
Chairman
Department of Economics
University of Denver
Denver, Colorado

Mr. Marvin Duncan
Assistant Vice President and Economist
Federal Reserve Bank of Kansas City
Kansas City, Missouri

Mr. M. E. Eddleman
Director
Security Bank
Billings, Montana

Mr. Bill Edelman
Denver Chamber of Commerce
Denver, Colorado

Mr. Matthew Eichler
BCI Geonetics
Grand Junction, Colorado

Mr. Leo M. Eisel
Director
United States Water Resources Council
Washington, D.C.

Willis Erwin
Regional Supply of Water and Land
Bureau of Reclamation Operations
Denver, Colorado

Mr. Bill Evans
Vice President
Oklahoma City Branch
Federal Reserve Bank of Kansas City
Oklahoma City, Oklahoma

Mr. William D. Farr
Farr Farms, Inc.
Greeley, Colorado

Mr. A. L. Feldman
President
Frontier Airlines, Inc.
Denver, Colorado

Ms. Ann Feeney
Managing Editor
Colorado Business Magazine
Denver, Colorado

Mr. Roland Fischer
Colorado River Water Conservation District
Glenwood Springs, Colorado

Mr. Jim Flanery
Omaha World Herald
Omaha, Nebraska

Mr. Robert R. Forester
Assistant Vice President
Planning and Financial Management
Mountain Bell Telephone
Denver, Colorado

Ms. Lucy Fox
Planner
Energy and Minerals Department
State of New Mexico
Santa Fe, New Mexico

Mr. B. G. Frengel
Atlantic Richfield Co.
Denver, Colorado

Mr. Joseph F. Friedkin
Commissioner
United States Section
International Boundary and Water Commission
El Paso, Texas

Mr. Gary R. Friehauf
Manager
South Platte Water District
Sterling, Colorado

Mr. Gary Fritz
Administrator
Department of Natural Resources and Conservation
Water Resources Division
Helena, Montana

Dr. B. Delworth Gardner
Director
Giannini Foundation
Berkeley, California

Mr. William S. Garnsey, III
Chairman
Garnsey-Wheeler Motor Co.
Greeley, Colorado

Mr. John Gerstle
Wright Water Engineers
Denver, Colorado

Mr. Mark W. Gillaspie
Vice President
San Marco Pipeline Co.
Houston, Texas

Mr. Steven A. Goodsell
General Solicitor
Union Pacific Railroad
Salt Lake City, Utah

Mr. H. Dean Graves
Senior Vice President
Federal Intermediate Credit Bank of Wichita
Wichita, Kansas

Mr. Eugene B. Graves
Vice President
Planning and Economics
Agrico Chemical Co.
Tulsa, Oklahoma

Mr. Tom Griswold
Water Resource Engineer
City of Aurora
Aurora, Colorado

Dr. Herbert W. Grubb
Director
Planning & Development
Texas Department of Water Resources
Austin, Texas

Mr. Roger Guffey
President
Federal Reserve Bank of Kansas City
Kansas City, Missouri

Mr. Joseph W. Haas
Assistant Administrator for Water Resources
Soil Conservation Service—USDA
Washington, D.C.

Mr. C. J. Hansen
Atlantic Richfield Co.
Denver, Colorado

Mr. Ed Harshbarger
Assistant Vice President and Economist
Federal Reserve Bank of Kansas City
Kansas City, Missouri

Mr. Larry D. Hauschen
Assistant Economist
Federal Reserve Bank of Dallas
Dallas, Texas

Mr. Bruce Heitler
President
Heitler Development, Inc.
Denver, Colorado

Mr. Keith A. Henry
President
CBA Engineering, Ltd., Consulting Engineers
Vancouver 5, B.C.

Mr. Bryon Higgins
Senior Economist
Federal Reserve Bank of Kansas City
Kansas City, Missouri

Mr. R. J. Hildreth
Farm Foundation
Oak Brook, Illinois

Mr. Glenn C. Hoaglund
Group Vice President
Engineering and Construction
Iowa Beef Processors, Inc.
Dakota City, Nebraska

Mr. Donald D. Hoffman
President
Central Bank of Denver
Denver, Colorado

Mr. D. L. Hovendick
President
Federal Intermediate Credit Bank of Omaha
Omaha, Nebraska

Mr. Dick Howard
Deputy Secretary
Department of Water & Natural Resources
Pierre, South Dakota

Dr. Charles Howe
Professor
Department of Economics
University of Colorado
Boulder, Colorado

Mr. Joe J. Huckfeldt
President
Gering National Bank & Trust Co.
Gering, Nebraska

Dr. Robert P. Huefner
Director
Institute of Government
University of Utah
Salt Lake City, Utah

Mr. George D. Irwin
Director
Economic Analysis Division
Farm Credit Administration
Washington, D.C.

Mr. Tom Jackson
U.S. Fish & Wildlife Service
Denver, Colorado

Mr. Neil G. Jaquet
Land and Water Resources Dept.
Adolph Coors
Golden, Colorado

Mr. John J. Johnson
Climax Molybdenum Co.
Golden, Colorado

Dr. Gerhard von Jonquiere
First Secretary
Agricultural Affairs
Embassy of the Federal Republic of Germany
Washington, D.C.

Mr. Chris Jouflas
Chairman of the Board
Agriculture Council of America
Washington, D.C.

Dr. Maurice M. Kelso
Professor Emeritus
University of Arizona
Tucson, Arizona

Mr. James B. Kenney, Jr.
President
Board of Water Commissioners
Denver, Colorado

Mr. Ray Kipp
San Diego Union
San Diego, California

Mr. Richard A. Kjoss
President
Security Bank
Billings, Montana

Mr. Allen V. Kneese
Senior Fellow
Resources for the Future
Washington, D.C.

Mr. Jerry Kotas
U.S. Environmental Protection Agency
Water Planning Division
Washington, D.C.

The Honorable Ken Kramer
House of Representatives
Washington, D.C.

Mr. Roger E. Krempel
City of Fort Collins
Fort Collins, Colorado

Mr. Jack Kyser
Union Pacific Railroad
Omaha, Nebraska

Ms. Ann Laing
Research Associate
Federal Reserve Bank of Kansas City
Kansas City, Missouri

Mr. Daniel F. Lawrence
Director
Utah Division of Water Resources
Salt Lake City, Utah

Mr. Gary N. Leger
Research Associate
Department of Agricultural Economics
University of Nebraska-Lincoln
Lincoln, Nebraska

Mrs. Yvonne Levy
Economist
Federal Reserve Bank of San Francisco
San Francisco, California

Mr. David Lewis
Business World
Denver, Colorado

Glen Loomis
Department of Agriculture
Washington, D.C.

Mr. Glenn Lorang
Farm Journal
Colorado Springs, Colorado

Mr. Edward D. Lotterman
Agriculture and Applied Economics
University of Minnesota
St. Paul, Minnesota

Mr. Guy R. Martin
Assistant Secretary for Land and Water Resources
U.S. Department of the Interior
Washington, D.C.

Mr. Wayne W. Martin
Senior Vice President
Denver Branch
Federal Reserve Bank of Kansas City
Denver, Colorado

Governor Scott M. Matheson
State of Utah
Salt Lake City, Utah

Ms. Judi Maxwell
Agriculture and Applied Economics
University of Minnesota
St. Paul, Minnesota

Mr. William S. May
President
Federal Land Bank of Wichita
Wichita, Kansas

Mr. Felix McDonald
Chairman
Texas Water Commission
Austin, Texas

Mr. J. William McDonald
Program Administrator for Water Resources
Colorado Department of Natural Resources
Denver, Colorado

Mr. Charles I. McGinnis
Annandale, Virginia

Mr. Donald W. Meinhold
Vice President
Farm and Ranch Mortgages
Metropolitan Life Insurance Co.
Overland Park, Kansas

Mr. Glenn H. Miller, Jr.
Vice President
Federal Reserve Bank of Kansas City
Kansas City, Missouri

Mr. W. H. Miller
Manager
Denver Water Department
Denver, Colorado

Mr. Wayne W. Miller
Eastman Kodak Company
Kodak Colorado Division
Windsor, Colorado

Mr. Harold E. Miskle
Department of Public Utilities
City of Colorado Springs
Colorado Springs, Colorado

Mr. Maurice Mitchell
President Emeritus
Center for the Study of Democratic Institutions
Santa Barbara, California

Mr. Victor B. Neet
Vice President
Mortgage Loan Division
Van Schaack & Co.
Denver, Colorado

Mr. Warren R. Neufeld
Secretary
Department of Water and Natural Resources
Pierre, South Dakota

Mr. Ronald M. North
Institute of Natural Resources
University of Georgia
Athens, Georgia

Robert Oberst
Pacific Power and Light
Portland, Oregon

Mr. Rod Olson
President
Federal Land Bank of Spokane
Spokane, Washington

Mr. Posey B. O'Neal
Senior Agricultural Investment Officer
Agricultural Investment Department
John Hancock Mutual Life Insurance Co.
Kansas City, Missouri

Mr. George Ormiston
Program Officer
Four Corners Regional Commission
Albuquerque, New Mexico

Mr. Jack Pixler
President
First National Bank of Montrose
Montrose, Colorado

Mr. Vito P. Pizzuto
Manager
Plant Engineering
Sundstrand Corporation
Denver, Colorado

Mr. Jim Porterfield
Assistant Director
Natural and Environmental Resources Division
American Farm Bureau Federation
Park Ridge, Illinois

Dr. George E. Radosevich
Attorney at Law
Insurance Exchange Building
Denver, Colorado

Robert Raschke
Western Regional Representative
National Association of Conservation Districts
Lakewood, Colorado

Mr. Frank W. Rhea
Engineering Consultants, Inc.
Englewood, Colorado

Mr. Barry K. Robinson
Vice President
Federal Reserve Bank of Kansas City
Kansas City, Missouri

Mr. Charles B. Roe, Jr.
Senior Assistant to Attorney General
Olympia, Washington

Mr. James Rogers
Federal Intermediate Credit Bank of Houston
Houston, Texas

Mr. C. R. Rose
Manager
Plant Services
Rockwell International
Rocky Flats Plant
Golden, Colorado

Mr. John Rosine
Economist
Board of Governors of the Federal Reserve System
Washington, D.C.

Mr. Harold L. Russwurm
Senior Field Representative
Lubbock, Texas

Mr. Bernard J. Ruysser
President
Commercial National Bank
Kansas City, Kansas

Mr. Theodore M. Schad
Director
Commission on Natural Resources
National Research Council
Washington, D.C.

Mr. William J. Scherle
Valmont Industries
Valley, Nebraska

Dr. A. Allan Schmid
Professor
Department of Agricultural Economics
Michigan State University
East Lansing, Michigan

Mr. Harold Schmucker
Engineer Appraiser
Federal Land Bank of Houston
Houston, Texas

Mr. Max Schnepf
Editor
Soil Conservation Society of America
Ankeny, Iowa

Mr. James M. Schurr
Vice President
Credit Administration
Federal Intermediate Credit Bank of Sacramento
Sacramento, California

Mr. Delano E. Scott
The Routt County National Bank
Steamboat Springs, Colorado

Mr. Earl W. Sears
Executive Vice President
National Cotton Council of America
Memphis, Tennessee

Mr. George William Sherk
Attorney
Department of Energy
Golden, Colorado

Mr. Harris D. Sherman
Executive Director
Department of Natural Resources
State of Colorado
Denver, Colorado

Mr. Doug Short
Tri-State Generation and Transmission Association, Inc.
Thornton, Colorado

Dr. Robert N. Shulstad
University of Arkansas
Fayetteville, Arkansas

Mr. Myron M. Sigaty
Vice President
Real Estate Investment Dept.
The Travelers Insurance Co.
Hartford, Connecticut

Verna Sigg
St. Vrain Water Conservancy District
Longmont, Colorado

Mr. Larry D. Simpson
Assistant Manager
Northern Colorado Water Conservancy District
Loveland, Colorado

Mr. Joe Sims
Special Assistant to the Board
Board of Governors of the Federal Reserve System
Washington, D.C.

Mr. Richard A. Simms
General Counsel
Natural Resources Department
State of New Mexico
Santa Fe, New Mexico

Dr. George E. Smith
Dean of Agriculture
University of Missouri
Columbia, Missouri

Mr. R. H. Snodgress
Manager
Martin Marietta
Denver, Colorado

Ms. Karen Spencer
House of Representatives
Washington, D.C.

Mr. John F. Spencer
Assistant Director
Department of Ecology
St. Martins College
Olympia, Washington

Mr. Michael R. Stansbury
Division Manager
Rocky Mount Regional Office
Denver, Colorado

Mr. John Stencel
President
Rocky Mountain Farmers Union
Denver, Colorado

Mr. William C. Story
American National Bank
Denver, Colorado

Mr. John P. Strawn
Atlantic Richfield Co.
Denver, Colorado

Dr. Harold M. Stults
Economics, Statistics, and
Cooperative Services
U.S. Department of Agriculture
Washington, D.C.

Dr. Raymond J. Supalla
Associate Professor
Department of Agricultural
Economics
University of Nebraska-Lincoln
Lincoln, Nebraska

Mr. Robert S. Swift
Minister
Embassy of Australia
Washington, D.C.

Mr. Paul Sylla
Federal Intermediate Credit
Bank of St. Paul
St. Paul, Minnesota

Marty Thorp
Los Angeles Times
Denver Bureau
Denver, Colorado

Dr. John F. Timmons
Charles F. Curtiss Distinguished
Professor
Department of Economics
Iowa State University
Ames, Iowa

Dr. Frank J. Trelease
Professor of Law
McGeorge School of Law
University of the Pacific
Sacramento, California

Mr. Frank J. Trelease, III
Vice President
Wright Water Engineers, Inc.
Cheyenne, Wyoming

Mr. Linus L. Tumbleson
Director
Argriculture Development
Burlington Northern, Inc.
St. Paul, Minnesota

Mr. Albert E. Utton
Editor
Natural Resources Journal
Albuquerque, New Mexico

Mr. Gary M. Vaughn
Vice President
Federal Land Bank of Houston
Houston, Texas

Mr. Ken Vaught
Land and Water Resources Dept.
Adolph Coors
Golden, Colorado

Mr. Elvern Varilek
Chairman
Board of Water and Natural Resources
Geddes, South Dakota

Mr. William H. Vernon
Santa Fe, New Mexico

Mr. John Waelti
Agriculture and Applied Economics
University of Minnesota
St. Paul, Minnesota

Mr. Richard Walker
President
Public Service Company of Colorado
Denver, Colorado

Mr. Gilbert White
Chairman of the Board and Professor Emeritus
Institute of Behavioral Sciences
University of Colorado
Boulder, Colorado

Mr. Cliff Whitney
Legislative Assistant to the Honorable Bob Eckhardt for the Interior Committee
House of Representatives
Washington, D.C.

Mr. Carroll H. Wilkerson
Assistant Vice President
Federal Reserve Bank of Kansas City
Kansas City, Missouri

Mrs. Jean O. Williams
Vice President
Camp Dresser and McKee, Inc.
Walnut Creek, California

Mr. Joseph H. Williams
Chariman of the Board
The Williams Companies
Tulsa, Oklahoma

Mr. William Williams
Investment Officer
Agricultural Investment Dept.
Connecticut General Life Insurance Company
Dallas, Texas

Mr. J. Mark Wilkinson
Vice President
Real Estate Investments
The Prudential Insurance Co.
Newark, New Jersey

Mr. E. R. Wyma
Plant Services Admin. Manager
IBM Corporation
Boulder, Colorado

Mr. W. H. Zwick
Vice President
Federal Land Bank of St. Paul
St. Paul, Minnesota

For Product Safety Concerns and Information please contact our EU representative GPSR@taylorandfrancis.com
Taylor & Francis Verlag GmbH, Kaufingerstraße 24, 80331 München, Germany

www.ingramcontent.com/pod-product-compliance
Ingram Content Group UK Ltd.
Pitfield, Milton Keynes, MK11 3LW, UK
UKHW021954180926
475701UK00003B/27
9780367216320